Our Times &
Our Stories

Our Times & Our Stories

The Minnesota Baptist Conference

A 150-Year Retrospective 1858–2008

By Truett M. Lawson

Published by:
Bethel University
3900 Bethel Drive
St. Paul, Minnesota 55112

First Printing: September 2014

ISBN: 978-0-9889298-2-1

Cover Design by Dave Bradley

Printed in the United States of America

Table of Contents

Preface

The Minnesota Baptist Conference, its churches and people, have shaped my life for over 50 years. In 1951, I was an eight-year-old in Olivet Baptist's Sunday school as the church started out in the Franklin Creamery on Minneapolis' north side. I was a youth pastor at Edgewater during my Bethel Seminary years in the late 60s, watching amazing lay leaders, like Warren Eastlund, support their church. I pastored in Aurora and Isanti (Elim) through1982 and returned to lead the district from 1990 to 2008 during a time of tremendous opportunity. Jill and I have retired from active ministry but enjoy being a part of two MBC church plants-Crosswinds in Stillwater and Journey North in Brainerd.

"You're the only one who can write this history!" I do not know exactly who on the 150th Anniversary Committee said those words in 2008, but I took the bait. Actually I would like to think it was Virgil Olson who with great effort had joined our sesquicentennial planning group in that year, after having also been the celebrated author of our centennial history 50 years before. Such service is evidence of God's grace in Virgil's life. It is part of the blessing of a conference with both a distinguished past and an opportune future.

I must be candid. Writing this book was one of the most difficult things I have ever done. I am an activist. I am a visual learner although I have made peace with books in print. My modest accomplishments in life have come because I am a leader and because I have been blessed with the need to dream and the energy to achieve. I am not sure any of these skills helped me move this research and writing project through its extensive reading, note taking, organizing and finally its writing and editing.

But ideas can transform us. It has happened to me in the last eight years. I simply became enamored with Philip Spener's *Pia Desideria* (1675) and the origins of our conference's Pietism. Spener represented for me the right path to a Godly life. The fact that Pietism is clearly traceable from Spener to us through the German chaplains of armies, the revivals of Swedish prisoners, the repression of civil religion and the courage of immigrant preachers, absolutely captured my heart. I read, I wrote and eventually I helped curate the American Swedish Institute's exhibit of this history. This book bears much of my thinking and writing in those years.

I know my parents, Maurice and Muriel Lawson, would be pleased with this work as they always magnified the Christ-centered spiritual life at the core of our movement. My mom in her final years would ask how the book was going. Jill Mckenna Lawson, my wife, sustained me through the self-doubt in the early research and the endless long days in the end. Jim Spickelmier was my great encourager and I wish he were here to receive my final draft. Alas, that was not to be, and it would be Carole Spickelmier who joined me in the trenches as we completed the manuscript. Carole's editorial vision for this project is imprinted on every chapter. In addition, Curt Petersen at ASI, Joel Nelson at the MBC, Dave Bradley, Woody Dahlberg, and Scott Wible were all there when I needed them.

And I want to thank John F. Anderson and Dan Carlson, representing the Minnesota conference in 2008, and also the Friends of the History Center, for their financial partnership in this project. This decade has been a golden age for the celebration of BGC history. But most of all, I want to thank the people of the Minnesota Baptist Conference who lived out this history and personified its ideals. I hope you enjoy this record of *Our Times & Our Stories*.

—Truett M. Lawson

Minnesota Baptist Conference Executive Ministers

In the early years of the MBC, leadership for the districts was provided by pastors, lay people and certain ministers appointed as state missionaries. By the 1940s, districts were hiring district secretaries, later called district executive secretaries, to provide leadership. Today this primary leadership role is titled the District Executive Minister.

Since the 1940s the following people have provided such leadership for the Minnesota Baptist Conference:

J.G. Johnson	March 1949–March 1964
S. Bruce Fleming	January 1965–November 1969
Emmett V. Johnson	December 1969–January 1979
Richard "Dick" Turnwall	March 1979–December 1984
John F. Anderson	January 1985–December 1989
Truett M. Lawson	July 1990–December 2007
Daniel H. Carlson	January 2008–

— Chapter 1 —

The Legacy to Preserve

Our official story began in 1858. A group of Swedish Baptist churches from various settlements gathered in Scandia, Minnesota, now called Waconia. It was a natural location as nine Swedes from the Scandia settlement had founded the Baptist church in this growing Carver County community in August 1855.

Scandia was also re-
garded as the epicenter of
the small group of Swedish
Baptists because of the
presence of F.O. Nilsson.
In these early formative
years, Nilsson was the pastor at Scandia but he was
the apostle for Minnesota.
He gave leadership to the
Scandia church and extend-

Members pose in front of the Scandia Baptist Church.

ed his leadership to Swedish settlements in Chisago Lakes, Wastedo, Carver, and Grove City. Nilsson's importance to the Swedish Baptist movement in Sweden, America, and finally Minnesota cannot be understated.

Nilsson went to sea at age 19. His voyage became a spiritual one as he began to consider the restlessness in his soul on his trans-ocean journeys. After receiving evangelistic challenges through the Mariner's Church in New York, Nilsson's life course would change in 1834 as he, on board ship, received the forgiveness of Christ with the words, "My Lord and my God!"

Sweden was not ready for the spiritual passion that Nilsson would unleash. With the outside financial support of an international ministry to sailors, Nilsson was free to teach and encourage Lutheran believers who hungered for biblical teaching and a challenge to live a righteous life. Many of these were gathering in home groups to support their spiritual growth. In Nilsson, these pietist Swedish believers found a champion for their cause. He was gaining rock star status, and in 1850, when Swedish officials heard that Nilsson had formed a church, officials sought to arrest him. Nilsson left Sweden, was baptized by immersion in 1847, and was later ordained by the Baptists in Germany.

The call of God to F.O. Nilsson would model the emerging theology of the Minnesota Baptist Conference. We are conversionists.

The Royal Court's Banishment of Nilsson

"The Royal Court has taken into consideration what concerns this question, and for that Frederick Olius Nilsson has freely confessed to having embraced the positions that child-baptism, not being commanded in holy Scripture, is only a human institution; that baptism therefore ought only to be administered to men arrived at a full knowledge of Christian doctrine; and then only with immersion of the whole body in water; and also that the holy communion can be received worthily only by persons of this persuasion: and for that Nilsson, having caused himself to be re-baptized at Hamburg, has in a society there founded, been received as an elder and teacher of the Baptists there in this realm;...and has caused forty-seven or forty-eight persons to receive his doctrines and form a separate congregation to the members thereof, he in the character of teacher administers baptism and holy communion...and after having been admonished by the chapter of Gothenburg, has yet persisted in disseminating these his doctrines...because therefore Nilsson has made himself guilty of the misdemeanor referred to in the code of offences of the Royal Court, in virtue of the said last command, justly condemns Nilsson for that wherein he has offended, to be banished from the kingdom." –April 26, 1850

Orthodox theology and well-written creeds are not replacements for an authentic experience with the living God, expressed in a believer baptism by immersion. This Baptist evangelical theology would anchor all of the waves of our growth during the next 150 years.

Sweden had a history of repression when it came to non-conforming religious groups. A Conventical Decree in 1726 forbad people, beyond a family, from gathering for spiritual edification unless it was authorized by the local parish. In spite of this, home meetings (conventicals) were thriving. Called the "läsare" (readers), these believers found personal spiritual devotion to be trivialized in their state church parishes. They were confronted with threats, shunning, and outright persecution by officials and neighbors, all in the name of national church unity. The church and the state in Sweden had become so entwined that any spiritual movement other than sectarian Lutheranism was treated as a non-conforming cult.

But name-calling did not diminish this pietist movement. It had strong theological foundations that had emerged in Germany in the 18th century. The pietists believed in the centrality of the Scriptures, the priesthood of the believer, high standards of morality, and the spiritual education of the heart as well as the head. What was surprising was that while other European nations were well on their way to religious freedom, Sweden in the 19th century unleashed a final, fresh wave of repression.

Returning to Sweden in 1850 to encourage the 35 members of his church, Nilsson and his followers endured a new low when a mob entered their church meeting uninvited during communion. With sticks and clubs, they beat church members and hauled Pastor Nilsson to the sheriff where he was imprisoned, tried, and exiled from Sweden. Nilsson was the only Swede to have received such severe punishment for religious activity alone.

These origins would mark the conscience of the Minnesota Baptist Conference. Issues of religious liberty and the separation of church and state would be closely guarded. In later years, these convictions would come to debate on our conference floor, as we debated federal aid to education and contemporary issues of church and state relationships.

Without a country, and under severe persecution, Nilsson pleaded his case unsuccessfully from Denmark, but another life-changing move for Nilsson was imminent. On May 5, 1853, 21 members of the Swedish Baptist Church were joined by Nilsson's family and a delegation of Danish Baptists. They sailed on the Jenny Pitts, headed for Boston, then overland through the river ways of America to the Root River valley of present day Houston, Minnesota. The Swedish group took up residence beside a tribe of 40 to 50 Dakota Sioux native people and assembled on August 18, 1853, to praise God for safely bringing them to this place. Native people often silently appeared at their door, curious or hungry after a journey or a hunt. They would receive a meal, always, and if they saw something they liked they could take it – after all, they were there first.

Nilsson, who had remained in Rock Island, Illinois, for a year with a group of Swedish Baptists, traveled to rejoin his friends in Houston. He found a discouraged group of Swedes. Fever had deteriorated their strength; a prairie fire had destroyed their hay. That winter, the worst would occur – an epidemic of cholera swept through the settlement. Four adults and a child died within four days. These beginnings were tumultuous and painful for the Swedish Baptist movement in Minnesota.

Although the Houston church did not survive its early trials, several years later it would reconstitute with new immigrant blood. It did not see much more of Nilsson until he decided, at the end of his ministry, that this Root River community was the best place to retire and be buried.

The Treaty of Traverse de Sioux encouraged the settlement of the Minnesota Territory. Nilsson staked out a claim near Clearwater Lake (now Lake Waconia) in Carver County. It was early in Minnesota's immigration history. After all, there were only 7,000 non-native residents in the Minnesota Territory in 1850. But the opportunity to own and operate a farm in Minnesota would electrify Swedes who were experiencing religious oppression in their homeland.

From 1850 to 1870, large numbers of the immigrants left Sweden to escape religious persecution. This trend would force the Swedish Rikstad, or parliament, to grant religious freedom in the 1860s. A second wave of immigration in the late 1860s and 70s was motivated more by famine and economic oppression than by religious persecution. Owning farmland in Sweden was nearly impossible for most. And after years of bad crops, Swedish young people followed the trails of their ancestors and looked to America for a fresh start. By 1890, Swedish Americans

The Personal Impact of F.O. Nilsson

When F.O. Nilsson was called before the Swedish consistory to answer charges of false doctrine, his journey profoundly affected others.

Anders Wiberg (1820-1887) was an atheist at Uppsala University. He studied the Christian faith and decided to become a Lutheran clergyman. A profound spiritual experience with Christ led him to have conversations with F.O. Nilsson. Nilsson convinced him to be baptized. Wiberg would resign his clerical position in the state church and become a key figure in the emerging Baptist/pietist theology of Sweden. He spent two three-year periods in America.

Gustaf Palmquist (1821-1887), whose own mother was läsare (a reader), watched F.O. Nilsson's courage in his trial in Stockholm. Deeply affected, he was converted and baptized. He became the founder of the first Swedish Baptist church in America on August 13, 1852, in Rock Island, Illinois.

would own 12,000,000 acres of land in the US, more than any other immigrant group.

These immigrant roots would define the Minnesota Baptist Conference in its first wave of church growth. We were a mission to Swedish-speaking people and would always define ourselves as missional rather than ecclesiastical. But interestingly in the 1970s and 80s, those roots would return to our conscience. They would motivate us to build bridges to new immigrant groups in America making us a leader among evangelicals in welcoming and equipping new immigrant populations.

In Iowa, Nilsson met a unique young pietist Lutheran fruit farmer named Andrew Peterson. In years to come, Peterson's apple grafting would be recognized for helping to establish the apple industry of Minnesota. Nilsson baptized him in Iowa shortly after his immigration. Together they explored available land in Carver County, Minnesota, where both staked claims in the community of Scandia. Peterson, an extraordinarily gifted and devout layman, contributed mightily to our movement and to Minnesota. Like many pietists, he was a diarist (Nilsson kept a diary for 10 years). He recorded his daily activities for 48 years, from the day he decided to leave Sweden until three days before his death in 1898. These diaries, with more than 48,000 entries, were discovered by the famed Swedish novelist Vilhelm Moberg in 1948, and used to form the life and character of Karl Oscar in *The Emmigrants* historical novel series. Why would someone write the details of daily life for 48 years in a diary? Pietists believed that daily work was a divine call. Peterson no doubt read the devotional works of fellow Scandinavian Hans Nelson Hauge, who advocated a strong Christian work ethic and a diligent approach to life.

Pietism in Sweden was a lay movement. Its cathedrals were the private homes where lay people gathered in forbidden meetings. Its enemies were the elite clergy whose pastoral positions did not protect them from their fleshless spiritual bones. Andrew Peterson was a prototypical layman securing his church while supporting his entrepreneurial pastor. Twenty years later, this recognition of laity would allow a woman school teacher from St. Cloud to become our first international missionary. Our history will reveal that in moments of great vision, it would be the engagement of the lay people that would catalyze the greatest conference initiatives. Accomplishments like Trout Lake Camp and Love Lift for Ukraine are examples.

Andrew Peterson built Nilsson's first log cabin home. In the summer of 1955, they would build a 20' x 26' log meeting place for their Scandia Church. But the Andrew Peterson's legacy was more than buildings. When the Hammerberg family lost their father, the Petersons supported them for two years. There was always a place in their home for a homeless traveler or tramp. This kind of benevolence marked the Swedish Baptists.

Olaus Okerson had experienced ship wreck in his 1864 immigrant journey. Converted in Sweden, he too, joined the

Andrew Peterson's orchard (as envisioned by Tom Foty).

Scandia community. As many of the men in Scandia were volunteering for the Civil War, Okerson, a man of enormous strength, and Peterson would assist fatherless families with farm work. In his diaries, Peterson describes their love gatherings which "broke down the barriers of wealth, culture and status... ."[1]

As the Baptists became known for their benevolence outside the church, they also were known for their strict discipline within the church. A member was dismissed for a questionable horse trade. Entertainments were looked at with a frown. There was a puritanical zeal for discipline, Carl Tideman, a pastor in Scandia after the turn of the century, would report.

The tension between church holiness and social compassion would re-emerge in the Minnesota Baptist Conference during the next century. American fundamentalists were rejecting social action as a "social gospel." Conference churches proudly carried their message of holy living and a separated life, but were also known for their concern for the poor and needy. With the dawn of the Civil Rights movement in the 1950s and 60s and the youth revolution in the 1960s and 70s, the conference agenda strongly embraced benevolence, then racial justice and social ministries.

The rapid growth of Swedish Baptist churches in many settlements was a scourge to Lutheran leaders who, with immigration, expected that to be Swedish meant to be Lutheran. After receiving strong resistance to the Baptist presence in Chisago Lakes, the Baptists decided to re-settle in Isanti County. This would become one of the strongest Swedish Baptist settlements in the state. In most cases Lutheran members were forbidden to attend Baptist gatherings. If they did attend, they would be denied participation in communion. A Baptist pastor would never be allowed to pray or speak in a Lutheran church. Yet the early Baptists seemed to offer a very different kind of welcome to Lutheran leaders.

This was certainly the case when the great Lutheran leader Eric Norelius, who founded Lutheran Social Services and Gustavus Adolfus College, visited the Scandia settlement. He was visiting to see if there were enough Lutherans to start a church in Scandia, but the Baptist congregation invited him to preach. Norelius records that he spoke from Zechariah 12:9-12. He notes that the church was strongly discussing the doctrine of election and mentions visiting one of the

Baptist members, a farmer named George Madson, who studied the Bible in the original Greek.[2]

Norelius' visit to Scandia demonstrated a rare spirit in church movements in the day. Here, the rigorous doctrinal discussions in the church and the serious study of the Bible as represented by Mr. Madson did not end in a sectarian exclusiveness and ecclesiastical separation. Eric Norelius was recognized in the church as the great leader he was. He was welcomed to preach. Later history would force us to examine our role in the church and the world, and in crucial moments we would rediscover our roots and emerge as an "irenic" fellowship and chart our course in that calm sea. Even in modern times, it would be this Scandia spirit that would allow us to set aside our "Baptist" church names in order to better reach the growing population of unchurched in America.

Intellectual and ecclesiastical openness has its rewards, as well as its risks. John Alexis Edgren left a career as a naval officer to pursue his pietistic Baptist passion. A brilliant thinker, artist, and theologian, Edgren edited a theological journal for the growing conference movement. In 1871, he founded a seminary to train pastors for Swedish Baptist churches. This was the beginning of Bethel University which would eventually be located in St. Paul, Minnesota. The partnership between Bethel and Minnesota churches would be profound for more than a century.

A couple of years before Edgren founded his seminary, Nilsson returned to the Root River valley and Houston, Minnesota, with his wife. He once again led the group of Baptists he had founded as a church 16 years before. America had changed after losing 600,000 souls in the Civil War. The Houston church had changed and Nilsson himself was struggling with his own faith journey. Nilsson became fascinated by the Free Thought movement in Sweden which, although Unitarian, shared his abhorrence for state religious oppression. He was reading the works of Theodore Parker, the transcendentalist preacher who questioned the infallibility of the Bible and the divinity of Christ – not to mention Darwin and German rationalists. A group of 13 left the church in protest of his free thinking. Old friends such as Anders Wiberg appealed to him. Newer acquaintances in the conference, like Olaus Okerson, condemned him. He confessed to suffering from depression and desperate unhappiness.

Many remained with him through his dark journey of doubt and were greatly encouraged by his words to a friend four days before his death: *Have had great temptations to forsake everything in religion. But the Lord is faithful and will not let us be tempted beyond our strength. With Him is grace and love. Jesus Christ is my only hope, on that Rock will I rest, who has saved me. May the Lord help me to the last.*[3]

To tell our Minnesota story without its struggles is to miss the true tension of mind and heart. We are, and always were, at risk in our fragile affirmations of faith and mind, devotion and belief, conviction and tolerance. But this is the higher road the conference has taken.

Notes

[1] Josephine Mehelich, *Andrew Peterson and the Scandia Story,* Mehelich and Ford Johnson Graphics, 1984, p. 35.

[2] Eric Norelius papers, Augustana College Archives, Rock Island, Ill.

[3] John F. Anderson, address to the Friends of the BGC History Center, August, 2006.

— Chapter 2 —

The First Wave of Extraordinary Growth

The Homestead Act and our spiritual pioneers

Marked by their persecuted founders and life-encompassing biblical convictions, the Swedish pietist believers moved into a westward-expanding America. At the start of the Civil War, there were only 18,000 Swedish-born people in the U.S. In the next century, more than 50 million Europeans would find new homes stateside. Of these, 1.3 million would be Swedes who found America to be a hopeful new land. Immigrant groups of European descent (Irish, Polish, and Italian) were populating the cities of the East and fueling the industrial revolution. But large numbers of Scandinavians and Germans ventured to the Midwest, especially Minnesota. They knew how to farm, but land ownership had not been an option in their homelands. The earliest of these immigrants were the real pioneers. Because of the intensity of persecution in Sweden, significant numbers of them began to settle in the Midwest. They organized farming communities, starting Swedish Lutheran and Baptist churches.

Immigrants congregated in the city to earn money to homestead.

In 1858, the Minnesota Conference would organize as a loosely related fellowship ("conferencia") of churches from Houston, Chisago, Carver, Scandia, Wastedo, Grove City, Isanti, and other Swedish settlements. There was an inherent bond in these early pioneers that led them to not only keep track of each other, but also to aggressively expand their beliefs and way of life to other Minnesota immigrant settlements. A surge in evangelism and church planting formed the first wave of growth in the journey of the Minnesota Baptist Conference.

Immigrant Life and the Astrachan Apple

Vilhelm Moberg credits the Andrew Peterson diaries with one of the most powerful images of immigrant life in his novels. Vilhelm Moberg's pioneer wife, Kristina, in her grief for Sweden, recalled the Astrachan apples she enjoyed there. Moberg writes: "She made a special Sweden out of her longings…a Sweden she carried with her, a land that no one had ever seen or no one would ever see." (*The Settlers*, p 390) Carl Oscar, her husband, concerned for her homesickness, planted an Astrachan (Swedish) apple tree for his wife, but though the apple tree survived each year, it was unsuccessful in bearing fruit because of the early Minnesota frost. Like Kristina, it never bloomed or bore its fruit. That is, until the end…. when Kristina warned Carl that if he wanted to have another child, it would be the death of her but that she trusted God that she must be a wife to her husband in every sense. Indeed, in the novel, the birth of the child would take Kristina's life but it would give her a deeper understanding of her life and family. As Kristina's life fails, Carl has not noticed that the Astrachan apple tree has yielded its first fruit. When he sees the apples, he joyously brings one to Kristina. Kristina bites down realizing that, like the Astrachan apple tree, she too has struggled. As her apple tree has finally born fruit, so too has her family become rooted, productive, and fruitful in this new land.

Benny Andersson, the brilliant composer (*Mama Mia*) and founder of the rock group Abba, created a musical for the theater based on the Moberg novels. Kristina (*Kristina från Duvemåla*) debuted in 1995 in Sweden and sold more theater tickets than any production in Swedish theater history.

On May 20, 1862, Abraham Lincoln signed the Homestead Act. For a decade, political groups like the Free Soil Party had been pressuring the Congress to release government lands to the people for homesteads. The government was acquiring land at an accelerating pace by a multitude of "treaties" with Native people. During the 1850s, in Minnesota, large amounts of land were "sold" to the government by tribal leaders for 7.5 cents an acre. With the Homestead Act, these lands were made available to immigrant families. A man, woman or head of household could acquire 160 acres of undeveloped land for $18 in fees with the agreement that he/she would develop the land with a home and farmable acreage. After six months of habitation, the homesteader was free to purchase the land for $1.25 an acre, but needed to retain the land for a mandatory five years.

In spite of efforts to manage this highly effective government program and help poor immigrants in the process, there were many abuses. Speculators managed to gain ownership of more than their fair share of land. There were corporations who did the same, recruiting the poor and paying their fees, in order to eventually acquire their land.

The Homestead Act would fuel Swedish immigration in the later half of the 19th century in Minnesota, as immigrants sought their quarter sections of farm land to begin life in America. These new farmsteads became settlements, often with various ethnic characteristics – Swedish, Norwegian, German, or Dutch. Their town names reflected their ethnicity. With Swedes there was Scandia, Vasa, Uppsala, and Oscar. Some of these settlements would remain Minnesota towns, but others would find their settlement names, and often their church names, disappearing in the sands of time.

Lay preachers build a church movement

Evangelization and pastoral ministry evolved from the spiritual gifts of ordinary laymen in the early stages of Minnesota church growth. God was raising up largely self-taught church leaders who provided guidance and order for newly organized churches in the settlements. Every cluster of immigrants was an opportunity for a church.

Interestingly, the Homestead Act would often provide material support for these early bi-vocational pastors. F.O. Nilsson came to Scandia (Waconia), Minnesota, and registered a claim for a farmstead. With the help of his resourceful layman, Andrew Peterson, Nilsson built a home for his family. At the end of the mandatory five years (1860), Nilsson sold the farm and returned to Sweden.

Olaus Okerson became well know in Minnesota for his itinerant preaching and aggressive church planting. He rode a pony across the state to Minnesota's Swedish settlements, preaching and organizing churches. He brought animal skins in the winter rather than borrowing from the settler's sparse beddings. But he also homesteaded land in west central Minnesota, in the Cambridge area, and in Fergus Falls. After organizing many churches in Minnesota, including Bethlehem, Fergus Falls, Stanchfield, Cokato, Grove City, and others, he moved to the Pacific Northwest, supported by the American Baptist Home Mission's Society, and started churches in Tacoma, Seattle, and Portland.

Johanna Anderson, Early Missionary to Burma

Johanna Anderson from Minnesota to Burma in 1888 (painting by Tom Foty)

In the early 19th century, Baptist missionary zeal had focused on William Carey and his work in India and then shifted to the courageous young couple Adoniram Judson and his wife Ann Hasseltine Judson who went to Burma in 1812.

In 1868, young Johanna Anderson immigrated with her family from Varmland, Sweden, to St. Cloud, Minnesota. There she received her education and became a teacher. After the death of her mother in 1888, Johanna Anderson, at the age of 32, departed for Toungoo, Burma, and became the first Swedish Baptist foreign missionary. For ten years she worked among the Karen people in a mountain village called Loikaw which was accessible only by rope ladders. In these difficult conditions, her health deteriorated rapidly and she was forced to return to the U.S. to rehabilitate. She later returned to Burma, but in 1904 she died and was buried there.

At a time in history when women were primarily preparing themselves for domestic lives, Johanna's courageous example inspired many women to consider missions in the years to come.

Transitions and the rise of urban Minnesota

In the final two decades of the 19th century, population growth and immigration would shift toward the developing towns and cities of the state. Six churches were clustered in Isanti County and six in Duluth. In 1882, immigration peaked when 64,607 Swedes came to the U.S. Most of the available homesteads were gone in the state, with only marginal land in the far north remaining. Immigrants were forced to work in emerging American industries in Chicago, Minneapolis, or St. Paul. Urban churches grew large with immigrants who were at a stopping point for their future life. Bethlehem of Minneapolis and Payne Avenue/Trinity of St. Paul were the largest churches in their cities. Bethlehem (First Swedish) averaged more than 800 worshipers each Sunday. By 1890, our Swedish Baptist churches numbered 79 congregations statewide, some barely surviving and some thriving.

World War I virtually closed the door on Swedish immigration, but the rate of immigration in Minnesota had slowed after the turn of the century. The 20th century would provide a very different challenge to our Swedish Baptist churches. Without the mission field of new immigrants, could the conference churches successfully retain their English speaking youth? Could we make the transition from Swedish to English in our church services? Could we evangelize and grow in our second home, with our second language? The answer was slow to come as we watched our numbers decline in the first half of the 20th century.

Swedish Baptist Churches in Minnesota in 1890

Albert Lea

Alexandria-First Baptist Church

Alma

Amor

Alvarado-Alvarado Baptist Church

Anoka-Elim Baptist Church

Atwater-First Baptist Church

Bigstone

Blomkest-Blomkest Baptist Church

Brainerd-Temple Baptist Church

Brunswick

Burchard

Brook Park-Quamba Baptist Church

Cambridge-First Baptist Church

Cambridge-North Isanti Baptist Church

Harris-Fish Lake Baptist Church
Cokato-First Baptist Church
Comfort
Dalbo-Dalbo Baptist Church
Deerwood
Duluth-Bethany Baptist Church
Duluth-Bethel Baptist Church
Duluth-First Baptist Church
Duluth-North Shore Baptist Church
Duluth-Temple Baptist Church
Duluth-Third Baptist Church
Evansville
Fahlum
Fergus Falls-First Baptist Church
Gibbon-Clear Lake Baptist Church
Grass Lake
Grasston-Grasston Baptist Church
Greenleaf
Grove City-First Baptist Church
Henning-First Baptist Church
Houston-Houston Baptist Church
Hutchinson-Shalom Baptist Church
Isanti-South Isanti Baptist Church
Isle-Opstead Baptist Church
Karlstad-Karlstad Baptist Church
Lake City-Calvary Baptist Church
Lake Elizabeth
Lancaster
Leenthrop
Long Lake
McIntosh
Mankato-Bethel Baptist Church
Maple Lake-Maynard Baptist Church
Mille Lacs Lake
Minneapolis-Bethlehem Baptist Church

Minneapolis-Elim Baptist Church
Oscar
Pipestone-First Baptist Church
Poppleton
Red Wing-First Baptist Church
Rock Creek-East Rock Creek Baptist Church
Rothsay-Rothsay Baptist Church
Rush City
Rush Lake
Russell
Silver Creek
Slayton-Lake Sarah Baptist Church
Soudan-Soudan Baptist Church
Spencer Brook
St. Cloud-Calvary Baptist Church
St. Francis
St. Paul-Trinity Baptist Church (Payne Ave.)
Stanchfield-Spring Vale Baptist Church
Stanchfield-Stanchfield Baptist Church
Stephen-Eagle Point Baptist Church
Thief River Falls-First Baptist Church
Upsala
Vega-Waconia-Waconia Baptist Church
Wanger
Willmar-First Baptist Church
Winona
Pickwick Baptist Church
Worthington-Indian Lake Baptist Church

The Pioneers

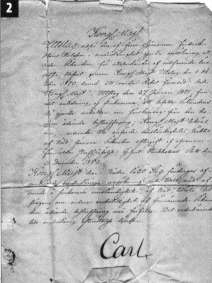

1. A converted sailor, F.O. Nilsson was tried and exiled from Sweden for his preaching.

2. On December 11, 1860, King Carl XV pardoned Nilsson with this document, now held in the archives.

3. Nilsson and his congregation arrived in the Root River valley near Houston in 1853.

4. Houston Swedish Baptist Church at the turn of the century.

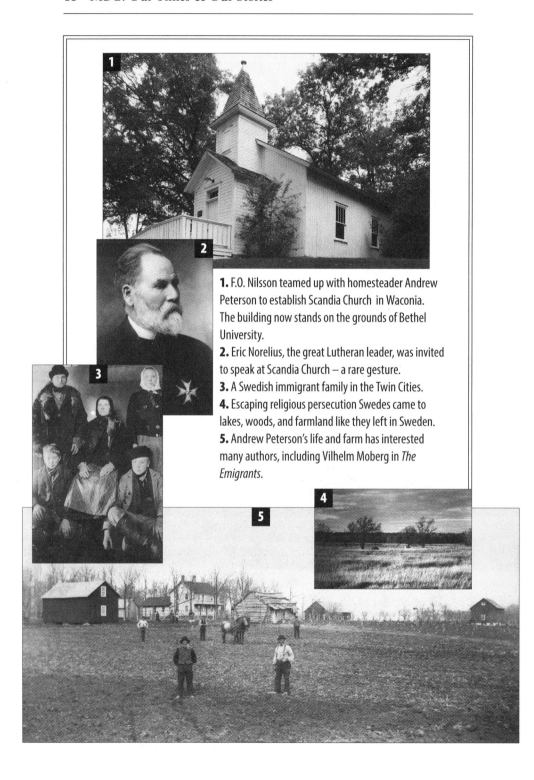

1. F.O. Nilsson teamed up with homesteader Andrew Peterson to establish Scandia Church in Waconia. The building now stands on the grounds of Bethel University.
2. Eric Norelius, the great Lutheran leader, was invited to speak at Scandia Church – a rare gesture.
3. A Swedish immigrant family in the Twin Cities.
4. Escaping religious persecution Swedes came to lakes, woods, and farmland like they left in Sweden.
5. Andrew Peterson's life and farm has interested many authors, including Vilhelm Moberg in *The Emigrants*.

1. Eric's brother, Andrew Norelius, became a Baptist leader in the churches in Isanti.
2. North Isanti Swedish Baptist Church at the turn of the century.
3. South Isanti Church formed as an early schism among the Isanti Baptists.
4. Olaus Okerson moved around the state starting churches where he homesteaded.
5. Swedish artist, Gustaf Cederstrom, depicted a baptism called "Les Baptiste."
6. In a similar scene in Argyle, Minnesota, new believers are baptized.

1. Fergus Falls church built this building after its organization in about 1882.
2. First Swedish Baptist Church in St. Paul.
3. First Swedish Baptist became Payne Avenue Baptist when it relocated, and later Trinity Baptist.
4. A Swedish Bible could be found on many pulpits in the early-twentieth century.
5. Traditional Swedish regional dress in a photo session.
6. Weekly and monthly Swedish publications of the BGC, started by Edgren in 1871.

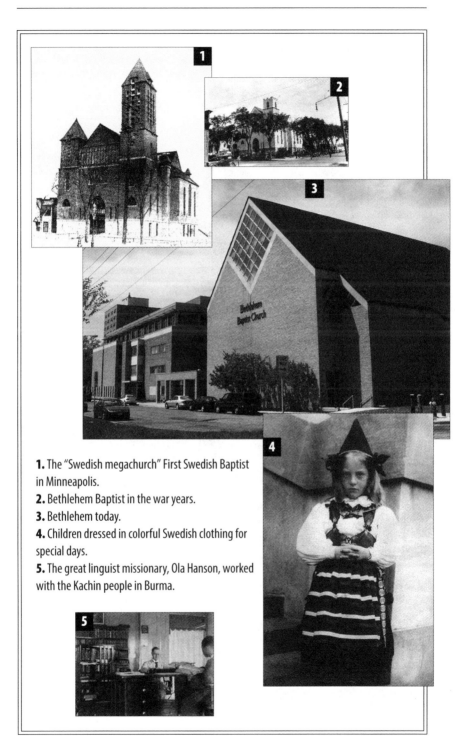

1. The "Swedish megachurch" First Swedish Baptist in Minneapolis.
2. Bethlehem Baptist in the war years.
3. Bethlehem today.
4. Children dressed in colorful Swedish clothing for special days.
5. The great linguist missionary, Ola Hanson, worked with the Kachin people in Burma.

1. Youth for Christ rallies in 400 U.S. cities sparked the great evangelical awakenings.
2. A young Billy Graham begins evangelizing the world for Christ.

3. The MBC considered the long view and purchased a point on Big Trout Lake.
4. How do you make a swamp into a ball field?
5. A WWII dredge and a lake full of sand create the ball field.

1. Building a lodge in the manner of a national park.
2. Men from across the state created a youth camp on Trout Lake.
3. Great cooks prepare to serve 100's
4. J.G. Johnson discovered the property and preached many times at its cypress wood pulpit.
5. Taking the nice ride to Big Trout Lake Bible Camp.

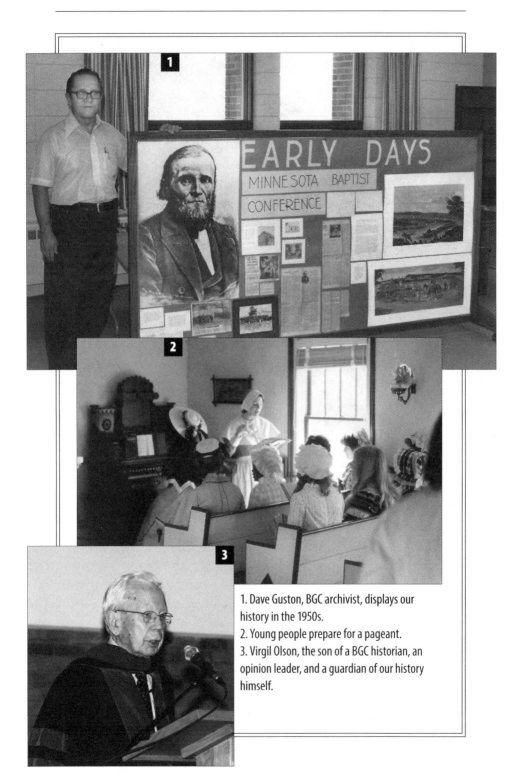

1. Dave Guston, BGC archivist, displays our history in the 1950s.
2. Young people prepare for a pageant.
3. Virgil Olson, the son of a BGC historian, an opinion leader, and a guardian of our history himself.

— Chapter 3 —

The Paralyzing Nostalgia for Swedishness

Our mission frozen in social change

The strength of the first wave of growth in the Minnesota Baptist Conference would carry us into the first decades of the new century, although the context of ministry was radically changing. The rural demographic of the Swedes in Minnesota was transitioning.

The numbers of immigrants remained high up to the end of WWI, but for several decades, the majority of immigrants were urban young men and women, not the families of the earlier decades. This new immigrant tended to come to America looking for jobs, so the industrial centers of the east were an attractive venue. There had always been a percentage of Swedish immigrants who, after staying several years in the U.S., decided to return home. But after 1890, significant numbers of younger people would return to Sweden with a nest egg and a desire to resume life there. This pattern was especially strong with young men who, after finding a bit of fortune in an industrial job, would return home to find a Swedish girl and new opportunities there. Over one fifth of the total Swedish immigrants would return immigrate.[1]

Our Swedish-speaking churches were well aware of the challenges they were facing. By the turn of the century, there was a strong population of second-generation Swedish Americans. Some remained in the church. Some were lost to English-speaking churches and some were lost to the church altogether. Although there were other Swedish cultural organizations, the church was far and away the largest center of expatriate Swedish culture. Church was a place to worship and serve the Lord, but it was also a place to celebrate Swedishness. Young people, now more American than Swedish, would journey from the city to their cultural church homes for special occasions. Once again they could enjoy church in their cultural traditions. Our identity was clearly understood to be a mission to reach Swedish-speaking people with the gospel. Our historic churches bore the mark of both our spiritual and cultural traditions.

Through the 20th century, many historic rural churches would close. With family farms and rural communities in decline, churches were profoundly affected. The youth of the church inevitably moved to the city. Rural churches found only a handful of families remaining. But best of luck to the executive minister that recommends closure or merger. Church officials often call these churches "cats." They have nine lives. Church executives have been trying to close them for generations. Word of an attempted closure would light up of the switchboards at the district office as large numbers of extended families erupted in anger sensing that they were about to lose their greatest connection to their Swedish roots.

Bethlehem's extraordinary linguists, the Hansons, in Burma.

The difficult transitions in language and culture definitely took their toll on the Minnesota churches during the decades of the 20s, 30s, and 40s. We were 333 churches nationally in 1927, but 288 in 1944. Churches began providing English speaking services in the 20s and English became the dominant language in the 40s. But we were running behind the change, instead of getting ahead of it. In many ways the conference followed the patterns of immigrant families. We saw our identity changing, but the change was so personal and painful, it could only be addressed when no more alternatives existed.

We are "hesitant, weak, and lacking in purpose"

The BGC did not remove Swedish from its conference name until 1945. *The Standard*, our official denominational publication was printed in Swedish until 1941. "The Conference is hesitant and weak and lacks a unifying purpose," J.E. Klingberg, the respected founder of the

Ola and Minnie Hanson Create a Written Language

Swedish immigrant Ola Hanson followed Christ after an accident nearly took his life. Having received his seminary training he was ordained and commissioned by Bethlehem Baptist Church in Minneapolis (then First Swedish Baptist). In 1890 he and his wife Minnie were appointed by the American Baptists to work among the Kachin people, an unruly tribe in northern Burma.

The Kachins were 100% illiterate, but they were rich in oral traditions and mythology. As Ola and Minnie learned their language they heard the Kachin stories of creation and death and, of high interest to Ola, the story about their language. The story said that each race had received a book from a meeting with God. The Chinese book was written on paper and the Burmese book was on parchment. When the Kachin leaders were journeying back to the Kachin land they became famished and ate the book, thus destroying their written language. But, the story continued, the Karens, a neighboring tribe, received a prophecy that a foreigner would return their language book. Ola Hanson determined that he would fulfill that legend.

Over the next 37 years, Ola and Minnie created a written Kachin language by collecting and recording 25,000 words, peering into the mouths of Kachin speakers to understand how their word sounds were produced. They produced an 11,000 word Kachin to English dictionary and wrote a book on Kachin culture. Ola translated the Bible and hundreds of hymns into Kachin and taught people to read and write their new written language. He became a revered spiritual leader for many Kachin believers.

In 1990 Tom Stellar, mission pastor at Bethlehem Baptist, saw a stranger in the service and introduced himself. The man, Hken Naw, had journeyed from Burma to Minnesota. He wanted to see the church of Ola Hanson. Five years later, Stellar went to Burma expecting to speak to a group of 3,000 Kachin believers. He was amazed when the crowd gathered, for 30,000 people had come to hear the man who returned to the Kachin from the church of Ola Hanson!

Klingberg Children's Home in New Britain, Conn., chided in an address to the conference in 1929.[2] C. George Ericson, editor of *The Standard*, editorialized that the "real missionary problem" was that there were no conference missionaries who wanted to go to the mission fields. The denomination supported only one missionary couple and raised partial support for two or three others. Perhaps the war affected this drought, Ericson mused, "but perhaps it is also a preference for prosperity."[3] Other ethnic denominations, such as the Danish-Norwegian conference, were also in trouble. The Danes merged with the American Baptists. This malaise that seemed to grip us would last until the mid-1940s.

The 1940s also brought world war. Many of the young conference leaders were serving their country in Europe or the South Pacific. During the 86th Annual Meeting at Central Church in St. Paul in 1944, Dean Emory Johnson stood to remind the assembly of what must have been on the minds of every delegate. "There are 4,500 of the Conference men serving in the armed services. Of these, 1,200 are from the State of Minnesota." An honor roll of Minnesota conference "boys," who had made the supreme sacrifice, was read. There was a period for silent prayer.[4]

There were also organizational and financial struggles within the Minnesota conference. A nagging operational debt kept the Trustee Board nervous about expansion. A special gifts program was put in place in 1941. The next year, with more desperation, the outstanding debt was divided between the churches in the hopes of repayment. Only a minor portion of the churches responded.

The relationship with the national conference evidenced the financial weakness in the districts. National subsides were common. Minnesota's annual meetings were an opportunity for the national leaders to show their preaching skills and report on their leadership in the conference. It was not like a visit from the Pope, but these presentations demonstrated that what was described as the "conference work," was largely that ministry that was generated from the national office.

There was a Trustee Board during the 30s and early 40s in Minnesota. We had our own name, constitution, women's work, and financial support for "mission" churches, but rarely did those ministries emerge out of specific Minnesota needs or goals. The Minnesota conference leader was called the State Missionary. If you consider that title, you understand how its meaning reflected the organizational relationship of

Minnesota to the national conference. A missionary is one who is sent to some place to represent the mission and interests of the sender. The national conference provided financial assistance to the states for this leadership position. In many ways, until World War II, the conference was one organization. Districts were state manifestations of the central organization. This was about to profoundly change.

Joining a typical district Annual Meeting in the 1940s

Annual Meetings in the 1940s illustrated these realities. Meetings were four days long. They included 15 sermons or devotionals together with many hymns and special numbers. There were more than a dozen greetings from outside organizations and nearly as many staff and field workers reports. Between these items, the business of the Minnesota conference was carried on. But until the mid-1940s, it is difficult to identify what locally proposed ministry goals or accomplishments were being put into place or celebrated.

Many guests brought fraternal greetings from their organizations. National conference leaders spoke. R.A. Arlander, the Home Missions representative, always had a part. Representatives of the Anti-saloon League, that would later become the United Temperance Movement, reported on their cause. V.L. Peterson always had a part, updating the delegates on outreaches to the Jews. Several representatives from Bethel brought greetings. Occasionally, special missionaries from within the fellowship, such as Albin Carlson's ministry in Waskish, brought a greeting. Clearly the conference was in a state of nostalgia with little excitement to pull it out.

In 1943, L.E. Peterson brought a greeting from the Baptist State Convention of the Northern (American) Baptist Churches. Rev. Peterson, who would eventually join the conference, spoke of Minnesota Swedish Baptists and the American Baptists as "comrades in a common task."[5] This moment had representational significance for the Minnesota Baptist Conference. Peterson had come out of the Danish Baptists. This group, with so many parallel tracks to the conference, had in its decline decided to be assimilated into the American Baptists. The conference had strong voices which seemed to be expecting the same destiny for our group.

Next, the American Baptist Residences for the Aged solicited the support of the conference for its homes in Winnebago, Red Wing, and

New Prague. The Trustees regularly reported conference gifts given to the ABC World Emergency Fund. In 1941, a motion had come from the floor to investigate the feasibility of helping the missionary pastors and workers of the conference to join the Ministers and Missionaries Pension Fund of the Northern (American) Baptist Convention. You can understand the interests of these pastors. The conference was in decline, its churches were struggling, and a wealthy suitor stood at the door – the American Baptists. And they were holding more than a bouquet of flowers. The M&M pension fund was a cutting-edge provision for people in ministry. It would cost something to say no to the ABC.

Maurie's Memories

After 1925, when the flow of Swedish immigration nearly ceased, the Swedish Baptist churches entered a period of risk and decline. It was increasingly difficult for the aging churches to interest their young people in the life of the church. Maurice Lawson, my father, grew up in the Franklin Street Swedish Baptist Church in Meriden, Connecticut. He loved Pastor Peterson but began to lose interest in church as he entered his teens. However all that changed when the blind Swedish evangelist, A.J. Freeman, came to the church for evangelistic services and young Maurice gave his life to Christ.

Maurice recalled his overwhelming desire to grow in Christ and to serve. But his home church seemed to be dying. People brought their Sunday school quarterlies to church rather than their Bibles! He remembered attending a prophetic conference at the Adventist church to hear more from the Bible on prophetic teaching, but it was also clear that this church movement did not represent his core doctrinal convictions.

He saved his every penny during the depression years, and in 1931 he and fellow student Clayton Bolinder hitchhiked to Bethel Academy in Minnesota to begin preparations for ministry. Maurice and a host of others formed a new generation of leaders that stayed the course during the years of decline and stepped up to the plate in 1944 to reinvigorate the conference.

When R.A. Arlander, the leader of Conference Home Missions for more than a decade, was recovering from a health crisis in 1944, he wrote his thoughts in *The Standard*. He reflects on the old days. "There was much in the lives and practices of the pioneers from which we can learn today. They certainly had zeal…they believed in the future of the denomination. Almost every state had a state missionary or field worker. Somehow we lost much of that aggressive spirit during the language transition period." But having just received a hospital visit from the head of the Evangelical Covenants, he mused that the cooperative spirit of the conference had survived separatist chants that had invited us in their camps through the years. "How well I remember the pioneers of the immigrant church of 50 years ago…they looked askance at each other. We had no fellowship with one another and any cooperative joint effort was unthinkable in those days. I thank God for the changes that have taken place in this respect."[6]

What is fascinating about Arlander's comments is that both his aspirations for the conference were about to be realized. A new energy was about to be ignited. A new sense of mission was about to be born. This would be a second wave of growth in the conference and in Minnesota. But Arlander's hopes for a conference whose values would include fellowship and cooperation would also be fulfilled. The conference was about to separate itself from some of the fundamentalist negativity that had crept into it, and launch itself into a period of unique opportunity.

A renegade group of young conference leaders

When the delegates of the national conference met at the Minnesota State Fairgrounds in June 1944, leadership was convinced that survival meant moving further under the umbrella of the American Baptists and their foreign mission society. But on June 23, a renegade group of young conference leaders brought a proposal to establish our own foreign mission board and raise support for our own missionaries. These young leaders were deeply concerned with certain policies in the ABC. Some American Baptist missionaries espoused beliefs that called into question the divinity of Christ, the virgin birth, and the authority of Scripture. The leadership of the American Baptists had adopted an "inclusive policy" and chose not to challenge the credentials of these missionaries. This and other issues led to the schism of the GARB churches in 1932 and the Conservative Baptists in 1947. Certainly the conference had sympathies with the theological concerns of these movements. But it stepped away from the GARB schism in 1932 and was doing the same with the political alignments that would form the Conservative Baptist Mission Society in 1947.

So when the conference voted on June 21, 1944, to form its own foreign missions program, it was in essence gently removing itself from the American Baptist relationship without joining its damaging politics. Eric J. Anderson, pastor of the Central Baptist Church of St. Paul, had challenged this proposed direction in an editorial in *The Standard*, June 16, 1944. He argued that we are "obligated to support missionaries under American Baptist foreign missions," and that organizing our own board was "inviting trouble" into our churches. He believed that such an action would be a "desertion of the missionaries who are members of our own churches." Additionally, we would be abandoning the "good, true, faithful, and loyal Baptists" within the American Baptist Convention. He reminded the reader that the Minnesota Convention (of the ABC) placed a Swedish Baptist representative on the State Board when scarcely any of us could speak English. Now that we had become mature, an English-speaking denomination, we are, wrongly, "considering breaking away."[7] But the train had left the station long before Anderson's appeal. And, in keeping with its manner, the conference's separation from the American Baptists was gracious.

It is impossible to overestimate the impact this decision had on Minnesota and the foreign mission advance that followed. Indeed, the BGC and the MBC had found a unifying purpose which had been lacking. Missionaries stepped forward from across the state. New goals in church planting, Sunday school, and camping emerged.

The conference had bet the farm. Such a risky venture would require a new generation of leaders. With 1,200 Minnesota conference members serving overseas in 1943, many of its young leaders were in the military. There is no question that the vote of 1944 was a generational leadership coup. The future activities and actions in the Minnesota conference would include outstanding leaders like Virgil Olson, Maurice Lawson, Bob Norstrom, Bruce Fleming, Ed Nelson, Warren Magnuson, Harold Christenson, William Tapper, Roger Goodman, Roger Youngquist, John Bergeson, Truman Halvorsen, Franklin Nelson, Alrik Bloomquist, and Harold Carlson. The door was not yet open to women in leadership on the denominational level. But these were exceptional young leaders, in step with rapidly changing America. The fields of Minnesota were white unto harvest.

The New Evangelicalism, where do we sign on?

On September 25, 1949, Billy Graham, a Baptist from North Carolina, launched his Los Angeles evangelistic crusade. This was followed by a Minneapolis crusade in 1950. Graham, from his first crusades, preached a very positive life-changing message. He also broke with the separatism of many of his conservative colleagues and cooperated with a wide theological spectrum of Christian denominations. This cooperation drove away a significant number of fundamentalist churches.

The conference had always had fundamentalist voices within its fellowship. But when fundamentalism went political, it often became doctrinaire and elitist. This was a contemptible Christian expression in the

---

Mounds Park and Midway Hospitals of St. Paul

Nels Lindahl, a member of the Payne Avenue Baptist Church in St. Paul (First Swedish Baptist), and Dr. Robert Earl had a vision for a Swedish sanitarium in St. Paul. In 1906, Mounds Park Sanitarium was erected and quickly expanded. Two additional small hospitals in the Midway and Merriam Park area were purchased in 1922, and five years later they were merged to become Midway Hospital on University Avenue. A school of nursing, later known as the Mounds-Midway School of Nursing, began just a few months after the opening of the Mounds Park Sanitarium.

MBC people were active in supporting and using these hospitals for their medical needs, and many MBC students attended the School of Nursing. In the 1970s nursing students went to Bethel to take liberal arts courses as they sought 4-year degrees. When the Mounds-Midway School of Nursing phased out its diploma program in 1983, the Bethel B.A. in Nursing began. In more recent years these hospitals have been absorbed into the Health East organization. A historical display of the work of the hospitals and the nursing school is housed in the former Midway Hospital building. (Bethel University and HealthEast websites)

mind of the conference. Without realizing it, as the conference recaptured its mission in the late 40s, it was professing the religious ideals of the New Evangelicalism. Our second wave of growth in the 1950s and early 60s was part of the new expression of evangelicalism in America. For the 20-year period from the mid-40s through the early 60s, membership in Minnesota Baptist Conference would grow by 75%, with 38 new churches started.

Trout Lake Bible Camp, the cause for change

For the Minnesota Baptist Conference, it was the vision for a state assembly grounds that would begin the confidence building process of forming and implementing a new Minnesota district structure and vision. In 1944, lay and pastoral leaders emerged who championed the vision of creating Minnesota's own youth camping facilities. A unique property on Trout Lake near Pine River was purchased, and the leaders of the conference committed to raise the $19,000 purchase price plus, and an additional $35,000, to prepare the property for use. These financial commitments would amount to more than double the total budget of the district at the time.

A profound shift was about to take place. Instead of assuming the ministries that others had created, the Minnesota district was creating a ministry that its own vision and passion had generated. Previously led by state missionaries, the Minnesota conference renamed Albert J. Bergfalk, as its executive secretary in 1943. A mission's director position was added to assist the executive secretary. The Sunday school director staff position would evolve into a Christian education director that included responsibilities for Trout Lake Camp. At the same time that national ministries were being transformed through the energy of our foreign missions surge, Minnesota was betting its future on Christian camping.

Notes

1 Swedish Immigration in North America, Augustana College, Rock Island, Illinois, augustana.edu/general-information/swenson-center-/swedish-american-immigration-history.

2 C. George Ericson, *Centenary Glimpses*, Baptist Conference Press, p. 29.

3 C. George Ericson, "Our Real Missionary Problem," *The Standard*, July 28, 1944, p. 4.

4 Minutes of the 86th Annual Meeting, 1944.

5 Minutes of the 85th Annual Meeting, 1943.

6 Ragnar A. Arlander, "Cards of Thanks," *The Standard*, November 3, 1944, p. 3.

7 Eric J. Anderson, "Throw Away the Hammar, and Buy a Horn," *The Standard*, June 16, 1944, p. 8.

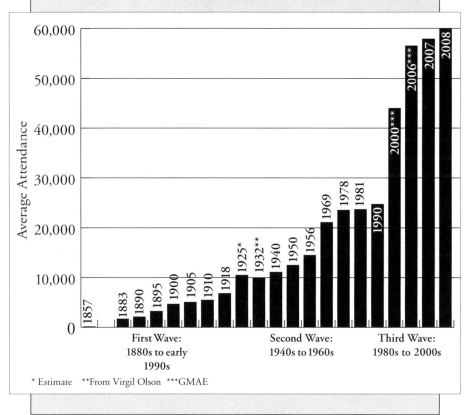

MBC Average Total Attendance
1857-2008

First Wave:
1880s to early
1990s

Second Wave:
1940s to 1960s

Third Wave:
1980s to 2000s

* Estimate   **From Virgil Olson   ***GMAE

— Chapter 4 —

Our Recent History Begins in the Fabulous 50s

Growing in a time of economic and spiritual opportunities

In 1958, the Minnesota Baptist Conference was feeling the developing momentum of the greatest ministry opportunity it had experienced since its early decades of service in the 1870s, 80s, and 90s. The conference's centennial year captured its distinguished past while it charted an exciting future.

Dwight D. Eisenhower, the great general of WWII, was elected president. Indeed, most of America was re-entering life with new energy for individual and national opportunities. But the war had brought a changing worldview. The extremes of Communism and Fascism had been witnessed first hand in the Holocaust. Refugees of communist East Germany were flooding into central Europe and the U.S.

The industrial might of a wartime America was being transformed into a prosperous, peacetime period – the Fabulous 50s. Young men returned from war with their eyes opened to issues of racial reconciliation. Women, who had assumed the many Rosie the Riveter jobs, were now joining men in the workplace. The scarcity of goods in wartime was changing into expanded commerce, new jobs, and new homes. The family farm that had been the incubator of American economic and social life was in severe decline as industrial expansion drew more and more new families to urban areas, and eventually, the suburbs.

When potato fields were bulldozed to accommodate the streets of Levittown, New York (the first experimental suburb), no one knew how profoundly the shift from rural to urban America would be. This suburban community would form the template for thousands of other similar housing communities in Minneapolis/St. Paul and every other urban area in America.

All of these changes made an impact on the Minnesota Baptist Conference. Our group was seeing generational change as an entire new corps of young leaders took its place in the conference. Church planting, which had always focused on Minnesota's towns and countryside, would soon be setting urban goals. "No one in the city should have to drive more than four miles to a conference church," leaders exclaimed.[1]

Women's changing position in society raised the possibility of emerging leadership roles for women in the conference. In a similar way, black,

Evangelicalism, the shoe that fit after WWII

After WWII, the conference could not find a good fit with either mainline churches who were moving to the theological left (including the American Baptists) or the fundamentalists with whom there were issues of identity and manners.

But it found a partner for its journey in the new post-war evangelicalism. In 1944, 75,000 Chicagoans gathered in Soldiers Field for a Youth for Christ event to remember the fallen soldiers of the war that had just ended. But they were also energized to renew the church in America and to reach the world for Christ. This happened not just in Chicago, but in 400 other cities as well, that saw similar gatherings organized by Torrey Johnson and Youth for Christ.

Evangelicalism rallied the energy of American believers with a call to the Bible, to conversion, to the atoning work of Jesus Christ and to the shared mission of Christ. Its spokesperson was the young evangelist, Billy Graham. It would build a solid theology through the statesmanship of Harold J. Ockenga and the theology of Carl F. H. Henry, John Stott and others.

Evangelist Billy Graham and the birth of evangelicalism.

white, Native, and Hispanic Americans, who were soldiers fighting side by side in war, irreversibly established a multiracial and multiethnic ideal for the nation and the conference.

But it was the expectations, hopes and dreams of the American family that would most profoundly affect the ministry plans of the conference in the 1950s. Family shows dominated the new television industry. *Father Knows Best, Ozzie and Harriet*, and *Leave It to Beaver* invited young families around their new televisions in the evening. The MBC hopped into this powerful social current as it retooled the churches in Sunday school, Christian camping, and key evangelism strategies. In order to meet these tremendous opportunities, profound changes needed to take place within the conference.

Warren Magnuson, "a sincere hope for our future"

In the May 1958 issue of *Missions in Minnesota*, Chairman of the Centennial Committee Warren Magnuson announced the upcoming year of celebration. "On May 11, 1858, Minnesota took its place among other states in the Union as the thirty-second state," he wrote. "In the fall of that year...five churches with a total of 157 members, most of whom were Scandinavian immigrants, were represented at that historic meeting on Monday, September 30, 1858."[2]

Magnuson was referring to the excitement of that first gathering of Swedish Baptist congregations in Scandia, Minnesota. He announced that a year of programming around the theme of "100 Years of Progress with God's Promises" would be "not simply an evaluation of our heritage but a sincere hope for our future as the Lord tarries in his return."

It was announced that the First Baptist Church of Cambridge would host the four-day event September 4-7, 1958. This was intended to be reflective of the strength of the early Swedish Baptist work in Isanti County. Local churches appointed committee members to promote the event. A state-level centennial committee with a dozen members worked to create activities and projects. It was during this year, under the leadership of Dave Guston and the Historical Committee, that Virgil Olson was enlisted to plan, and Florence Jacobson to research, a first draft for the centenary publication "Pioneering with God's Promises." This 80-page historical summary of the first hundred years of the Minnesota Baptist Conference was published at the end of the year.

The 100th year celebration of the Minnesota Baptist Conference will always parallel Minnesota's statehood celebrations. In 1958, the state sent a train of three rail cars around the state to 87 destinations. This *Centennial Train*, filled with historical displays, attracted more than 633,000 visitors between April and September.

Our centennial celebration – exhaustive and exhausting

The Minnesota conference also sought to inform its growing constituents about the conference's distinguished history. Plans were laid for a September celebration. The best preachers (Carl Lundquist and Eric Lindholm) would preach. But also proposed was an exhaustive and (as it proved to be) exhausting historical pageant presented on Saturday night to a church full of visitors. One has to be impressed with scope of this theatrical presentation, written by Virginia Bowers, but what most attendees remember is its length. All the highlights of our hundred-year history were covered – 30 pages of script, seven vocal numbers, four acts with a prologue and epilogue, 20 characters, a readers' chorus, narration, and slide accompaniments.

The 1958 welcome brochure included an acknowledgment of Swedish American missionaries outside the conference.

A perhaps little-noticed participant was Karin Larson, a young woman from Clear Lake Baptist Church who participated in the chorus of readers. Karin and others would play key roles in personal and financial leadership in the future ministry of the conference.

In the middle of its second wave of growth, now with 126 churches in the Minnesota conference family, the conference was feeling confident in God's provision for a bright future.

Notes

[1] Eric J. Anderson, "Throw Away the Hammar, and Buy a Horn," *The Standard*, June 16, 1944, p. 8.

[2] Warren Magnuson, *Missions in Minnesota*, Vol. XI, No. 4, May 1958, p. 2.

— Chapter 5 —

The J.G. Johnson Era (1949-1964):
"Happy" Johnson
Is Beloved Leader

A fisher of fish and men

J.G. Johnson (short for John Gottfried) began his role as executive secretary of the Minnesota conference in 1949. He was born Minnesotan, growing up in Reynolds, Minnesota, and finding Christ at the Reynolds Baptist Church. That experience not only marked the life of Johnson for Christ but it would touch his heart for the small church. To read the monthly "Jottings by J.G." is to see the heart of an evangelist and a church leader who was inseparably and passionately linked to the small and the rural church.

In his youth, Johnson was an outstanding athlete and a gung ho leader. As a high school student, he became a youth pastor and was called to be the senior pastor of a union church in Round Prairie, Minnesota, when he was only 19. He pastored six Minnesota rural churches, served as the conference evangelist for four years, and concluded a 14-year pastoral ministry at Elim in Minneapolis before the call

After strong leadership in the acquisition of camp grounds, J.G. Johnson is elected Executive Secretary.

came for him to serve the Minnesota conference as its leader and executive secretary.

In the late 40s, it was clear that Johnson had the credentials to be considered for the Minnesota position, but so did many others. He played a key leadership role in the search to find a conference camp and assembly grounds, however, which no doubt caught the eye of the search committee. The minutes of the 1945 Annual Meeting include details about plans to establish an assembly place on newly acquired property on Trout Lake. Johnson was called on to present the project. Taking the initials of the suggested name "Big Trout," Reverend Johnson pointed out that B.T. could stand for "Bergfalk's Treat" (Bergfalk was the state leader), "Better Trolling" (the fishermen's hope), "Blushing Tic-ups" (with reference to the young people) or, best of all, "Blessed Triumphs." An offering was taken and $770.72 was collected. Few could collect a better offering than J.G. Johnson. As the treasurer counted the cash, very few would have realized that Johnson's humor was a prediction of the "blessed tie-ups" that indeed would be found at Trout. Many would find their mates through camp romances.[1]

As the Minnesota conference's executive secretary, J.G Johnson was the same J.G. that people knew as a pastor. He had a ministry of evangelism and encouragement. His sweet spirit and love for Jesus was a gentle call to come to Christ. The native people called him "Happy Johnson." This pastoral calling guided the role he defined for his position. He was called to encourage the churches, especially the rural churches.

By the time of the 1958 Centennial, 20 Minnesota churches had been started, a bit more than two per year. But the district leaders were looking for more visionary leadership in their executive secretary, and Johnson was not a corporate leader. Rather than suggest an early retirement, they built new structures of management and hired new staff in areas of conference ministry needs.

Johnson presided over the conference when it was establishing itself as an American evangelical group. He was a positive force in our development.

His love for Christ kept the conference connected with its past and focused on its core identity. His reports were about his ministries to the churches. In his sensitivity to the smaller and weaker churches, he advocated for their importance even as Minnesota began to discover its new and greater opportunities in the exploding cities and the new suburban areas. Strong new leaders were emerging that would take the state conference, and our churches, in new directions.

Big Trout Lake Bible Camp – for such a time as this

From its dark days prior to WWII to its centenary year in 1958, it is clear that the Minnesota conference was thoughtfully interpreting not just the Scriptures, but also its spiritual opportunities in a changing culture. The year 1958 is regarded as the official end of the postwar baby boom, although birthrates continued to be quite high until 1964. After the war, there was a period of economic expansion that would continue into the 1970s. The GI bill provided funds for veterans to receive education, as the American workforce became more skilled. Prosperity spread to more families. Young people married young, many still in their teens. They had more children. In 1957, the average number of children per family had increased to 3.9. In the middle of this demographic explosion, there was a deep concern for the religious life of families and the spiritual opportunities of children and youth.

In 1946, when Trout Lake Camp was only a developing dream for the conference, the conference leadership prepared a 16MM movie showing the building of Trout Lake. The movie was shown to the delegates gathered at the Annual Meeting. They then turned to Pastor Carl Lindman of Pillager to speak. Rev. Lindman proceeded to ask the question "Where are the Young People?" He cited deplorable conditions among the youth in Minnesota – 266 murders, robberies, and rapes. He cited the negative influences on youth by the alcohol and the booze industry. Hollywood had its teaching tool in the movies. From the cinema, there was a slippery slope to misconduct among the youth. He cited the discouraging percentages of youth who were attending Sunday school. He closed with the parable of the king's feast and his command to "go out on the highways and the byways and bring them in." He suggested providing children with transportation to Sunday school and camp in "consecrated cars."[2]

World War II had hardly been won when the leaders of the Minnesota Baptist Conference stepped forward with a plan to create a conference assembly ground that would accommodate the gathering of the statewide membership, while at the same time provide opportunities for the evangelization and instruction of a growing number of children and young people in churches across the state. The concern for children would eclipse the original vision of an assembly place. Ed Nelson was pastor of Wheelock Parkway Chapel in St. Paul. Nelson, together with a group of area pastors, presented a resolution to the Minnesota conference Trustee Board on August 22, 1944, calling for the acquisition of a "suitable camp grounds." The matter was brought to the Annual Meeting and received unanimous consent.

Land prices were down and money was available to borrow. Conference leadership considered more than 50 possible sites ranging in cost from a few hundred dollars to $100,000. The focus of the search narrowed when the board realized that the geographical center of the state (Brainerd) would place 77% of the churches and 86% of the constituents within a 135-mile radius of that location.

In 1945, J.G. Johnson, at that time a pastor in Minneapolis, came to Temple Baptist in Brainerd for two weeks of evangelistic meetings. During the daytime hours, he and Vincent Tellgren, who was the pastor there, drove nearly 700 miles and walked countless miles looking at properties. But an accident would prove to be a fortunate misfortune. Rev. Johnson had an injury to his leg and this challenging overland trekking was aggravating the problem. He went to see Dr. Holliday in Brainerd who told him of the availability of Trout Lake Lodge, a resort and restaurant with seven or eight cabins that were in mothballs. Leaders would quickly gather at the site to examine its suitability as a camp. There was a clear excitement that this was the place God had prepared.[3]

The project of creating Big Trout Lake Camp became an overwhelming passion and a nearly impossible burden in the next decade. There were nine deteriorating buildings that came with the mile of Trout Lake shoreline – Cedar, Norway, Hemlock, Balsam, Tamarack, White Pine, Jack Pine, Spruce, and Birches. Projects were conceived and executed by volunteers. Pastors stepped up to organize the camp schedule and develop programs. Everyone suggested plans for future development, but almost everything needed to be accomplished with volunteers. The Men and Women's organization came alongside. Dr. Ewald Chalberg and the Minnesota Baptist Men (later called the Men's Brotherhood) raised significant money and provided volunteer labor for projects. The state Women's Union found projects at Trout as well. A 40-acre tract of tall pines was bought, logged out, and sawed to build the dining and recreational main building. However, as the camp grew and its management became more critical, the conference realized that permanent staff was necessary.

Building a legacy with "Chief" Lee Kingsley

In 1952, Lee Kingsley came onto the staff to be the director of Big Trout and provide assistance to the churches in Christian education. On the local church level, Sunday school was seeing a renaissance. In the late 40s, a Sunday school commission was organized under the leadership of Clifford Larson. Churches were resourced in children's Bible schools through Minnesota publications. An annual Sunday school contest encouraged churches to boost Sunday school attendance. Sunday school was becoming a key evangelistic outreach to new families who had not yet formed their religious habits after the war. In the summer, students from the Baptist Young People's Union were sent out from Bethel College to serve in rural communities, organizing daily vacation Bible schools and then Sunday schools. Each summer, a dozen of these student missionaries brought back amazing stories of God's work being accomplished. New churches were organized from many of these children's outreaches. Many of these youth would be spiritually marked by these ministries, sending some into pastoral ministry and others into full-time missionary service. The conference realized the importance of these kinds of ministries and called a full-time state missionary to work with the executive secretary. The state office became a staff of three ministry leaders – an executive secretary, a camping and Christian education director and a state missionary.

Lee Kingsley was a hands-on leader at Trout. He had grown up in the Grantsburg, Wisconsin, area and was invited to the Trade Lake Baptist Church Sunday school. As a youth, he committed his life to Christ at Wood Lake Camp and became a teacher in the Trade River Elementary School. Ministry was his dream, however. After five years of teaching, he left to finish his degree at the University of Minnesota and enter ministry training at Bethel Seminary. He became a student pastor in Dalbo, and upon graduation from seminary, joined the Minnesota staff where for 15 years he would lead Minnesota's work in camping and assist the churches in Christian education.

Lee had intelligence and a work ethic. With limited resources he was able to improve the camp experience. In later years, a story circulated about Kingsley's years at the University of Minnesota. He was on the debate team, together with Harold "Chris" Christenson. Their team became a formidable national winner. Lee had the intelligence and the discipline to research every possible nuance of the assigned topic and find the most compelling arguments. Chris had the powerful persona to eloquently deliver the points to their intimidated opposition.

As the years went on, Kingsley's many strengths were not fully appreciated by some. He was not the charismatic communicator that some would have liked to see. But Lee had extraordinary wisdom. He led the conference's Christian education emphases at a time of unusual opportunity. He build Trout Lake Camp from a "you bring the pizza, I'll bring the Coke" organization to a highly regarded model of a Christian Bible camp. And his widow's mite approach to finances gave conference families a quality camping product for a bargain fee.

Bruce Fleming would salute his work after he had completed 15 years with the Minnesota Baptist Conference. "Though he did not solicit the title, Lee is affectionately known as 'the chief' by multitudes who shared the ministry of Trout Lake Camp and other camps throughout Minnesota. No brief biographical sketch can properly convey the warmth and gratitude of our 20,000 Conference Baptist people in Minnesota. Engraved upon the hearts of many is the spiritual impact of the dedicated Christian camping ministry."[4]

One has to be impressed that camping at Trout Lake could evolve at the pace that it did. In 1952, with mostly volunteer leadership, Trout Lake was serving more than 1,200 children and youth campers in nine summer camps. The "Main Building," finished in 1949 (later called the Dining Hall), accommodated dining, recreation, and staff housing. It was designed in the manner of national park reception buildings with massive timbers and iron plates that would forever be remembered in the minds of campers. Those same campers may not have realized that they were sleeping on WWII soldier's beds. Four hundred of them were purchased as post-war surplus for 65 dollars. The dining tables too were provided by the war effort. Amazing feats were accomplished with men's work groups and volunteer workers.

Dredging sand from the lake to create an athletic field would leave the Department of Natural Resources breathless today. But when Mike Olson, Burton Barry, and some enthusiastic GIs found a $200 surplus dredge and a raft, they remedied one of the greatest limitations of the Trout property. By pumping out deep holes of sand from the lake, they transformed a swamp and created a ball field and a large open space for games and activities.

Annual men's and women's retreats rallied large numbers on the new camp grounds. In 1950, more than 300 men slept in their cars as all beds were full. Each year new cabins were built by church men's brotherhoods. But there were overwhelming burdens. The conference was taking on debt from the development of Trout. The state men's organization was responsible for raising the camp's operational budget each year. The conference was encouraging churches to place Big Trout on their church budgets and to contribute to camp by providing the pastor and gifted laypeople as program volunteers. State BYPU leaders such as Wayne Peterson were enlisted for leadership in the youth camps during the summer. Pastors with energy were recruited as program directors for the camps, which initiated a tradition that would develop for a couple decades. Pastors and associate staff would plan into their summers a week of volunteer work at camp.

These early years of development at Trout Lake would not have been completed as successfully without the leadership and administrative ability of one Jack Bergeson. In addition to pastoring his church in Isle, Bergeson was everywhere, putting together Trout Lake's summer program. He would return to the Minnesota Baptist Conference in a new role in later years. Unknown to many, he had earlier played a pivotal role in the history of Trout.

Trout Lake Camp, the soul of the conference

In the reports of the Trustee Board, genuine concern was expressed that the financial obligations of the camping program were greatly limiting other mission works of the conference. The ministries discussed included starting churches, assisting small churches, and expanding ministry to Native Americans. Although this critical situation would improve over the 1950s, it is also clear that the conference had to act wisely to maintain its financial integrity. The road the board chose in those years was to limit the staff of MBC ministries. In the late 40s, Orville Burch had been called as the state missionary, alongside executive secretary Albert J. Bergfalk. This position would disappear in the 1950s, and responsibilities for Minnesota missions and church planting would shift to executive secretary J.G. Johnson. It would not be until the 1960s that the Minnesota staff would again include a missions director.

When the conference approached its centennial year of 1958, camp fees together with church and individual contributions were feeding into a livable budget for camping. Kingsley and his family were forced to live all over the camp in the summers, so the camp board decided to remodel Cedar cabin for a director's residence. An administration building was badly needed to provide the staff a place to register campers for camp. Staff housing was a critical need, so plans were put in place for a motel type building to house staff. From his first year as director, Kingsley had built a cabin a year to the north of the Main Building. Maple, Oak, Elm cabins stretched down the shoreline, preparing the way for the "Boy's" area when the camps went coed. A new washhouse was built, but the greatest need was for a chapel.

Camp, in those days, was trying to balance its income between operational expenses and badly needed capital projects. The men's and women's organizations both provided support and came alongside Trout in voluntarism and giving. But there is little doubt that permanent staff made the program work and most of them lived very modestly on the income that camp could provide. Ann and Erik Ek contributed their most vital years in the maintenance and food service of the camp. Bob Wallberg taught boating, canoeing, and sailing and kept the beach and lake free of accidents for decades.

The chapel had iconic meaning to our Christian camp. A site was selected on the hill overlooking the central camp area. The building would look like a church with a 30-foot tall A -frame structure and a balcony. The building was not designed for winterization. And the tiny narthex permitted only single file entrance and exit.

The Trout chapel project was the designated project for the Centennial offerings in Cambridge in 1958. The next summer, a stone bell tower was built by a local stone mason. It was handsome, but it was never used for a bell. In spite of these design problems, each year 150 campers made first time commitments to Christ, including this author. More than 200 young people were considering spiritual decisions such as vocational Christian service. Rev. Lindman's dream was being fulfilled.

With the tremendous challenge of cultural change and the amazing opportunities for church growth through the evangelical movement, one could challenge the timing and demands of Trout Lake on the district overall. It was actually an extraordinary burden for the conference and might be considered, at first glance, as "the tail that wagged the dog." Although Trout indeed encumbered the Minnesota conference, it also energized the conference and expanded the vision of what it really could accomplish. It was a prototype, home-grown ministry that had no assistance or support from the national conference. This kind of agenda-setting by a district was not part of the conference model before the 1940s. The camp initiative in Minnesota would redefine the Minnesota district's relationship with the national organization. Minnesota was stepping out from under the paternal relationship with national. It was exercising its own vision for camping. This would mark its future as camping, and then other ministries, would emerge from the district organization. Trout would also leave a mark on the conference people of Minnesota for generations, to the point that one could call it the "soul" of the Minnesota conference.

Church planting from towns to cities

Historically, the conference had employed the term "missions" to refer to its efforts in starting new churches, assisting smaller churches and establishing ministries to ethnic groups, such as Native Americans. The governance of the conference was in the hands of the trustees. But the ministry initiatives came from two standing boards, elected by the conference. A Christian Education Board was responsible for church education and camping. There was also a Mission Board of elected leaders from the areas of the state. During the 1950s, when opportunity was high, and available staff was low, this board was critical to the mission and ministries of the MBC. The executive secretary, in addition to his leadership role in the conference was the staff person assigned to the Missions Board.

After 1942, the mission work in the state was promoted in the publication *Missions in Minnesota*. When J.G. Johnson assumed leadership in the conference in March 1949, he retained this venerable publication, expanded its distribution, and began writing a column in it called "Jottings by J.G.," rather humbly placed on one of the last pages.

Minnesota was entering its second wave of growth in a period of great opportunity. During the Second World War, home construction was severely hampered by the lack of materials. In New York, an extremely successful custom home builder named Levitt and Sons began buying up land on Long Island. The war ended and the military began discharging millions of soldiers. Most came home to severe housing shortages. William Levitt, the son of the builder, convinced his father to begin building small homes for returning GI's like himself. With its land in Long Island, the Levitt Company created a planned community of homes using prefabricated materials. Homes were a modest size built on a slab with an unfinished attic for expansion by the owner. As has been mentioned, this community of homes was named Levittown and would spark many such communities called "suburbs."

Recognizing the post war housing problems, the government created housing incentives in the GI bill by forming the Federal Housing Administration. FHA established lending policies to make home ownership and the American dream affordable. Levittown went from its original plan to rent homes, to its new plan to provide FHA homes for sale, and every city in America began to make plans for its own "suburbs."

In Minnesota, the first true suburb was Richfield. Richfield exploded with inexpensive new housing as in the Levittown model. Soon afterward came: Robbinsdale, Brooklyn Center, Fridley, Columbia Heights, St. Anthony, Roseville, Falcon Heights, Maplewood, Newport, South St. Paul, West St. Paul, Mendota/ Mendota Heights, Edina, St. Louis Park, and then Golden Valley.

The Minnesota Baptist Conference was not prepared to match this growth opportunity with new churches. Orville Burch, who had been Minnesota's mission director in the late 40s, wrote about the "methods of our work" in *Missions in Minnesota*. A new church work starts "with the State Missionary who has the responsibility to open new fields… with, of course, cooperation by working through already established churches. We begin visitation, in search of a local nucleus of spiritual people who are concerned for their community. In most cases, we begin with prayer services in order to gain the blessing of God on the work and bind the people together…from this point, we let the Word of God develop as it will, under the available leadership of a pastor and the guidance of God."[5]

Looking back, church planters in the 1990s would critique the methods espoused by Burch. The comments made the denominational office, and its staff, the primary church planting agency rather than the local church. When the local church senses its responsibility to reproduce, it multiplies the resources and support, as well as enlarges the opportunities. Modern church planting strategists would wince at Burch's comment that an "available" pastor would allow the work to develop. Church planters in the 90s would be assessed, placed in internships – and then and only then – called to start a church. Nonetheless, the Burch method would continue into the mid-80s.

J.G. Johnson had a heart for the small church and especially the rural small church. He loved to preach and evangelize, and there was always an invitation for him at the many smaller churches across Minnesota. And Johnson was the staff representative responsible for the Missions Board, and through it, the church planting strategies.

As the decade of the 50s progressed, it became clear to many of the Twin Cities pastors that Johnson's love for the smaller church was becoming a missed opportunity for the exploding suburbs of Minneapolis/St. Paul. This was about to change. The growth of the conference, even under Johnson, was coming from churches started in the suburbs. Between 1947 and 1949 five churches were started, and by 1958 these churches had contributed almost 2,000 attendees to the conference: Oak Hill in Columbia Heights, Calvary in Roseville, Olivet in Robbinsdale, Edgewater in south Minneapolis, and Wooddale in Richfield.

Twin Cities Extension Committee challenges the office

For some years, in the mid-50s, pastors and laymen representing the Twin Cities churches had met with the concern that the conference was missing the opportunity of starting churches in the rapidly expanding suburbs. This group, the Twin Cities Extension Committee, began to plan and finance an initiative to increase the opportunity of new church development in Minnesota's suburban areas. In the Mankato Annual Meeting, Rev. Maurice C. Lawson challenged the conference to a new vision for the cities. "A very significant aspect of our state program lies in the rapidly growing suburbs of our larger cities…new suburban cities of 100,000 people are growing up, and if we consider the rate of our developing churches, we will need 25 additional Twin Cities churches in the next 25 years just to keep up with this growth."[6]

A month later, in an article in *Missions in Minnesota,* Lloyd Nordstrom would announce that the Twin Cities Extension Committee was calling a full-time Twin Cities Extension director to carry out the vision of the group. The conference office would work with this awkward parallel effort in church planting for the next several years until finally, with the call of John (Jack) Bergeson, the Twin Cities vision would be merged with the conference leadership vision. It was this independent effort that would put the MBC back in the business of aggressive church planting.

In the 1950s, Minnesota inherited an "aid" program for weaker churches that was jointly sponsored by the national Home Missions budget and the Minnesota conference budget. Coming out of the 1940s, there were nearly 40 churches that received financial aid. Some of the assistance was being channeled to allow small churches to provide a salary for a pastor. The balance went to assist new churches to meet their start-up expenses. The number of aid churches reduced somewhat in the 50s. Leadership was becoming frustrated in these years with this expenditure. J.G. Johnson several times reported that the conference was incurring indebtedness to pay the commitments to aided churches. Warren Magnuson, in a moment of candor in his Board of Trustees report, confessed that "a consistent lack of the necessary funds makes this extremely trying."[7] Lloyd Nordstrom actually pleaded with aided churches to "endeavor to the best of their ability to reduce their aid." He went on to note that some of these churches, in spite of their aid, did not seem inclined to keep their pastor's monthly salary at the monthly minimum of $200 suggested by the budget committee.[8] The problem of creating self-sufficiency to mission-aided churches would continue in the district and national conferences well into the 1980s. No one, however frustrated, seemed to have the courage to pull the plug.

The Minnesota/Alaska mission connection

In 1958, the world missions program of the national office was reaching a peak. The conference in Minnesota was mesmerized by the expansion of the world mission efforts launched by the foreign missions department of the Baptist General Conference (BGC). Many of those pioneer missionaries were from Minnesota. Minnesota churches were a major source of support for world missions. Although Minnesota represented 25% of the constituency of the general conference, it supplied more than 35% of the revenue for world missions. But it was all pure joy. Every year, the Annual Meeting welcomed returning missionaries with affection.

Some missionaries held a special interest for Minnesota in the 50s. Albin M. and Ellen Carlson were sent by the BGC to be missionaries near Anchorage, Alaska. They had roots in Waskish, Minnesota, and

Albin was a Minnesota pastor. But there may be a story behind the Carlsons' decision to start a church near Anchorage, Alaska.

As part of the New Deal, President Franklin Roosevelt established several experimental communes, initiated by the government, and somewhat on the order of farm collectives in Russia. It was one small part of Roosevelt's large public works program during and after the depression. One of those collective projects was the Matanuska Colony in the Wasilla Valley, a bit northeast of Anchorage. Farm families were offered passage and 40 acres to join a pioneer agricultural collective, the rules of which had initially been drawn up by New Deal social engineers. Those same planners decided that the ideal candidates for this experiment were Scandinavian descendants, farming in northern Minnesota. The farmers were in terrible difficulty because of crop failures, and the depression had left them desperate. Because of their cold weather experience, they could best manage the arctic climate of Alaska. All of the early departing families were from Minnesota, mostly from the northwest. The experiment failed, as many of the families gave up on the experiment and moved elsewhere in Alaska. But because so many of them were northern Minnesota Scandinavians, there was always a link between Minnesota's northern communities and Alaska. This history was no doubt part of Albin and Ellen's choice to work as missionaries near Anchorage.

Racial prejudice and a great opportunity missed

In 1958, Minnesota's two largest non-white populations were African-Americans and Native Americans. The Latino population would increase after 1970. Minnesota was not a major destination point for black slaves migrating out of the South after the Civil War. The train seemed to stop in Chicago for them. Few black communities developed in Minnesota, in spite of the fact that Minnesota granted non-whites suffrage earlier than most states. However in the 1950s and 60s, this pattern changed radically. African Americans migrated in large numbers out of the oppressive ghettos of Chicago, settling in St. Paul and North Minneapolis.

In 1956, Pastor LeRoy Gardner formed a Bible study in his home in St. Paul. He was working as a barber and had attended Bethel College. He was the first African American to attend our school. Gardner organized a Sunday school that met in the Ober Boy's Club operated by the Union Gospel Mission in the Frogtown area of St. Paul. The Gardners were able to purchase a home for the church to meet in. In the early 60s, the church was able to buy an adjacent lot and prepare for building a more suitable church. In spite of Pastor Gardner's history with Bethel and strong Baptist conviction, the North Central Baptist Church was relatively unknown to the Minnesota conference in its early formative years.

Between 1950 and 1970, the population of African Americans in the cities increased 400%. One might assume that with an expanding population of blacks in the state, conference leadership would see an opportunity there. After all, Baptist churches among African Americans in the U.S. were legendary. However, it was not until well into the 1960s that ministry partnerships with black churches began to develop. Later in his life, a staff member from that period, with strong emotions evident, said that when he arrived in Minnesota, he was told by leadership, "we do not work with the blacks."[9] Interestingly, it would be that same staff member, Jack Bergeson, who would begin to change that prejudicial mindset.

There is no doubt that this mindset not only was a legacy of racial prejudice and indifference, but also an enormous ministry opportunity missed. The religious connections of those Twin Cities' black communities were formed by the 50s. In the 60s and 70s, the opportunities for large-scale partnerships in the black community were over. So, unfortunately, African Americans were simply not invited into the role they could have potentially had in the Minnesota Baptist Conference.

"Every Indian over 50 is already lost!"

It was different with native people. Ministry work among Native Americans became an important part of the mission of the conference in the 1950s, but conference leaders would need to be coaxed into these commitments by two tenacious laymen.

In 1945, William Turnwall was elected as the secretary of Home Missions (1945-1962), to replace R.A. Arlander. Arlander had strongly advocated that the conference not launch its own foreign mission program in 1944. William Turnwall's election would bring national ministries into an aggressive new partnership with the Baptist General Conference districts in church

Art Holmes' story was a compelling diary of an Indian's struggle to find God in a culture of alcoholism.

planting. But starting churches among non-white population groups in America was not yet on the radar, even for Turnwall.

In his unpublished autobiography, Turnwall related an incident where a question was asked of him, "When is Home Missions going to do something about our neglected Indians?" "That question was asked of me," Turnwall wrote, "several times by a Minneapolis layman, Mr. Monroe Killy, a member of Edgewater Baptist Church. I believe he worked in a Kodak store. I felt so guilty about this question that I began to avoid meeting Mr. Killy, if possible. He had invited me to his home and had shown me slides and other pictures and scenes from various Indian tribes. His collection revealed a real love for Indians.... Later, I received a letter from Rev. Sundstrom, pastor in Soudan. He mentioned a young man and his wife, Arthur and Veryl Holmes (Chippewas). They had attended a Bible school in Minneapolis and had hoped to serve as missionaries among Indians but had no support.... Our Board met with the Holmes, accepted them as our first missionaries to the American Indians and they were presented and commissioned at the Centennial conference in 1952." [10]

Art Holmes electrified the audiences where he spoke. "Every American Indian over fifty years old is already lost to the kingdom of God." [11] Holmes went on to explain that after hateful prejudice, oppression, broken treaties, and suffering under military repression, older Indians had lost trust in the white man and rejected his religion. "The only way the old people among them can be won to Christ, is through widespread revival among them, prayed down from heaven." Minnesota was moved and challenged.

William Turnwall thought he was the first in the conference to reach out to Indian people, but he probably was not. Herb Nyquist was the son of a general store owner in Malmo, Minnesota, an early Swedish settlement that had shared life with native people for generations. Herb grew up speaking some Swedish and a few words of Chippewa, the language of the older Ojibwa in the area. In his teens, Herb joined his father in business and moved to Isle, Minnesota, when his father launched a general store, hotel, and restaurant. In the years to come, Herb would buy out his father's business and for most of his life operate a general store in Isle.

Two things would change Herb's life. The first thing was Herb's conversion in 1925. But then came Herb's call in 1947 to minister to native people. Herb and Jesse, his wife, bought wild rice and furs from

Nyquist Collection of Ojibwa Artifacts Given to MBC

The Minnesota Baptist Conference received a significant collection of Ojibwa artifacts from the Nyquist family in the mid-1990s. A lovely display case was built to show the items, many of which were handmade items given to Herb and Jesse as personal gifts. Monroe Killy joined the conference staff, family members and guests for a dedication at the Conference Center. Mr. Killy's stature in the museum world had grown.

Herb Nyquist, a humble man, agreed to have his story written.

Now regarded as a true expert on native artifacts, Monroe shared information with the guests present about the useful and decorative items being put on display. Everyone prayed, thanked God for Herb Nyquist, and rejoiced at what God was doing in Indian ministries. Herb Nyquist died on October 25, 1987. The Isle Elementary School was renamed the Herb S. Nyquist Elementary School and an important scholarship was established in his honor.

them as part of their business. He often traded with them, lending the locals money during lean times and being repaid at harvest. Herb learned Native American ways and values. He sold hand-made decorative and utilitarian items in his store and collected them in his home. He and Jesse were learning the language of the older ones and would deliver groceries to them, telling the story of Jesus when opportunity allowed.

Always humbled by his own lack of education, Herb presented this ministry at the 1950 Annual Meeting. The MBC's Missions Board was amazed at the work and immediately agreed to assist Herb in finding the funds to build a small chapel. Herb was commissioned by the board as a missionary to the Milacs Bands of Ojibwa. Rose Noonday, Frances Sam, Fred and Rose Benjamin, and other native people followed the Lord and became a part of the church. George Johnson assisted Herb and Jesse for several years. Together they traveled to churches and shared the blessings of working in partnership with Native Americans in the state.

Notes

[1] Minutes of the 87th Annual Meeting, 1945.

[2] Minutes of the 88th Annual Meeting, 1946.

[3] Robert W. Olson, "Birth Pangs of a Camp," unpublished memoir.

[4] Bruce Fleming, Kingsley recognition service folder, Sept. 29, 1967.

[5] Orville Burch, "Forward Moves in Missions," *Missions in Minnesota*, Jan. 25, 1948, p. 1.

[6] Maurice C. Lawson, from address delivered Sept. 7, 1956, quoted in *Missions in Minnesota*, Vol. XI, No. 7, September 1956, p. 1.

[7] 97th Annual Meeting Report, Board of Trustees, 1955.

[8] 98th Annual Meeting Report, Missions Committee, 1956.

[9] Truett Lawson, interview with John H. Bergeson, 2008.

[10] Monroe Killy, unpublished letter.

[11] Roger Hedberg, *Missions in Minnesota*, Vol. V, No. 3, April 1953, p. 2.

— Chapter 6 —

The J.G. Johnson Era: The Call for Metropolitan Ministry Grows

Jack Bergeson becomes the co-pilot

In 1960, the Minnesota Baptist Conference was 11 years into the leadership of J.G. Johnson. He was 65 and was enjoying his work. The somewhat concerned board reviewed the executive annually after 1960 and J.G. agreed to retire before his 70th birthday. J.G. retired in 1964 at the age of 69.[1]

Clearly, there was a shift in vision on the Minnesota ministry landscape. Johnson's leadership focus on rural Minnesota churches was a continuation of the role of the district from its earlier history. As an immigrant mission, we had evangelized the recent immigrants in the urban areas of Minnesota, and planted churches in the rural Swedish settlements across the state. This church planting goal was not developing fast enough to include the growing suburban communities. Many leaders continued to feel most comfortable with rural people and smaller churches. But this neglect of the huge cultural and demographic shifts to the growing suburban areas was disturbing a group of Twin Cities pastors and laymen. A new future for the metro was unfolding.

From 1950 to 1968, the five metro counties of Minnesota grew in population from 1,151,053 to 1,778,397, a 54.5% increase. During the same period, the number of Minnesota conference church members in those counties increased by 115.4%. There would be 39 churches in 1968, compared to 18 in 1950. This brought the ratio of MBC members to population down from 1:63,947 to 1:45,600. But in 1968, the metro area still remained a major opportunity for church planting as non-metro Minnesota had one MBC member for each 18,400 residents.[2]

Metro Minnesota leaders wanted to respond to this opportunity. They had formed the Twin Cities Extension Committee in 1956. The committee organized its own funding sources from among its churches and hired Cliff Anderson. For whatever reason, the relationship with Cliff would be short-lived. In 1960, John H. (Jack) Bergeson was called to lead the Twin Cities Extension Committee's church planting efforts.

The Twin Cities Extension Committee must be recognized as a true entrepreneurial endeavor in the state conference. When the Minnesota state leader failed to recognize an unprecedented opportunity for denominational expansion, a group of pastors created a vision and plan, recruited the personnel, and raised a funding base to accomplish what was needed. And they did so outside the structure of the district. There may have been fall out, however. Minnesota has always struggled with two political interests, the metro and non-metro constituents. In the years to come this divided constituency would always be on the mind of the savvy district leader.

Raised by an aunt

The conference had grown in complexity and needed a strong organizational leader. The conference immediately responded to the leadership and administrative skills of Jack Bergeson. Bergeson was a strong personality with an unusual vision for starting churches. He had a passionate social conscience. Jack was raised by an aunt, and then a stepmother, after the death of his mother when he was only 2½ years old. Perhaps it was the brokenness of this childhood that would lead Bergeson to render self-sacrificing efforts to Trout Lake Camp's children's ministry in the years before a paid director was possible. Jack would also be a pivotal leader in the early 60s when the Minnesota conference began looking into its soul as the nation was birthing the civil rights movement.

Bergeson was a change agent leader during his years in the Minnesota Baptist Conference. He would implement the "mother church" concept to the church planting ministry, enlisting Payne Avenue to start South Grove and Snail Lake, Bethlehem with Cedar Grove, Olivet with Northwest, and Willmar with Coon Rapids.

In 1964, with the retirement of J.G. Johnson, the conference enfolded the Twin Cities Extension Committee into its organization. Bergeson would join Lee Kingsley and soon-to-be-elected Bruce Fleming as the staff for another era of Minnesota ministry. As Bergeson loved to put it in the era of Lyndon Baines Johnson, Minnesota had its own LBJ (Lee, Bruce, and Jack).

In 1970 Bergeson left to join the staff of the Columbia Baptist Conference as executive minister and continued to start churches there. By the end of his ministry career, he would be honored for being involved in the starting of 50 churches across the country.

Civil rights and the rekindling of our social conscience

Students of history describe the 1960s as a "cultural revolution." It was perhaps the greatest decade of change in America. The world was quaking. In Africa, nations were freeing themselves from colonial powers. Protests against oppression were becoming worldwide. The Irish Republican Army fought against police repression in Northern Ireland. Italy and other European nations elected leftist governments. Communism appeared to migrate relentlessly in Asia and Africa. The Civil Rights movement was accelerating in America. In 1963, Dr. Martin Luther King Jr. delivered his "I have a dream" speech in Washington D.C. John F. Kennedy was assassinated a year before his dream of a civil rights bill was adopted. There was violence and protest from native people as the American Indian Movement (AIM) was founded in 1968 in Minneapolis. Caesar Chaves was organizing a growing population of Latino workers in America. Women's liberation was a new social movement.

Pop culture was emerging as a power among the young. Gone were the flirtatious rock 'n' roll icons of the 50s. Rock was becoming visceral. Concerts were drug-infested. And rock stars were modeling a lifestyle of moral liberation and social upheaval. Racial integration, changes in morality, anti-establishment protest, and the hated Vietnam War converged to affect every part of American life, including religious life.

A segregated Sunday morning church hour was a conspicuous icon of the past. There was a blurring of the ideal picture of the church-going family. Social change was causing fragmentation in the family, even in church families. Youth culture, even Christian youth culture, was profoundly shaken, polarizing between reactive extremes either for or against popular culture. Eastern religions emerged as non-violent spiritual options. New Christian movements such as the Jesus People emerged in response.

The Minnesota Baptist Conference would be profoundly affected by these fundamental changes in our culture. This would be an era where fundamentalist Christian groups would become more sectarian, and more angry. Other Christian denominations found their relationship to cultural and social change so compelling that they abandoned evangelism for social action and doctrinal truth for moral relativism. The conference had always turned its head away from the flare-ups of its fundamentalist contingents. Once again, the conference would be asked to define itself in the middle of social change.

We Came, We Sang

Renewal movements and revivals often produce strong musical content. The pietist awakening in Sweden produced hymns that have endured into the present day. Lina Sandell was sympathetic with the pietistic revivals around her but remained part of the low Lutheran church. She was influenced by the Moravian missionaries in Sweden who wrote hymns with a sense of intimacy and devotion. She wrote *Day by Day, Children of the Heavenly Father* and six hundred other hymns. Some of her hymns and other favorites were contained in a "Swedish section" in most of the conference hymnals of the 50s and 60s. The conference hymnals also had a large number of gospel hymns. Philip Bliss and Fanny Crosby composed for the ethos of the revival meeting meetings of the 19th century. As D.L. Moody revivals spread across America and Europe, a gospel hymnody evolved.

Another musical tradition that was popular in the 50s was camp songs such as *In My Heart there Rings a Melody* and *If You're Happy and You Know It, Say Amen!* These would be the favorites of one J.G. Johnson.

In the late 60s and 70s, many MBC services became more formal and once again the Wesleyan and Reformation hymns re-emerged.

In his report to the conference in 1963, Warren Eastlund, chairman of the Board of Trustees wrote: "During the past year, the Trustee Board has sought to make a thorough analysis of our total conference efforts… issues have come before our conference relating to so-called population explosion, the migration to urban areas, racial integration, leisure time and problems with the youth age. There is no clear precedent or policy for conference involvement in many of these areas…..The Board concluded that a critical study should be made to determine whether the Minnesota Baptist Conference is accomplishing its mission and purpose."[3]

The board appointed a research committee of five people representing the conference standing committees and the members at large. Their charge was to make a thorough study of our entire conference work and to evaluate the involvement of the Minnesota Baptist Conference in issues of social change.[4]

It is clear in Chairman Eastland's words that a page was about to be turned in our Minnesota conference history. Although J.G. Johnson had not yet retired, the board was already examining the mission of the conference. Haunting echoes of need in our culture were being heard among the youth, among the races, and among the neglected poor.

Already, prototype ministries were heralding a new kind of ministry engagement within a changing Minnesota social landscape. Emmett Johnson was giving exceptional leadership to Elim Baptist in the urban area of northeast Minneapolis. Elim dedicated the Wingblade Educational Center in honor of A.J. Wingblade, whose work with urban children and families set the pace for ministry in the city. First Baptist Church of Cambridge and other Isanti County churches established Grandview Christian Home, a ministry to older adults. Residents moved in on October 22, 1963. The Minnesota conference endorsed the ministry in 1961.

Bethlehem Baptist received the assets of Bethel Baptist Church and began work in an urban property named Bethel Center. In 1964, Al Windom introduced the work of Bethel Christian Center to the conference noting the involvement of Jerry Dahl, Dick Erickson, and a new chaplain, John Sundquist. That year, Bethlehem gave the Bethel Center property to the Minnesota conference to begin an urban ministry. In 1962 David O. Moberg, while a professor at Bethel College, published his highly regarded work *The Church as a Social Institution: The Sociology of American Religion*.

Deep thoughts and re-visioning began to profoundly change the Minnesota conference. This call to change had come from Warren Eastlund, representing the conference trustee board, but it was a deeper call. It was not just a leadership initiative from a new executive secretary. The conference would, in the decade ahead, see the conclusion of the second wave of great growth in its history, as church planting slowed through the late 60s. It would enter a period of self-examination, an inner journey of profound reflection. A fundamentalist critic would see the Minnesota Baptist Conference leaving its conservative moorings and drifting toward the social gospel. But many of the social experiments that lay ahead would actually be re-digging the wells of our forefathers.

Further, one could make the case that this inner journey would prepare the conference for the more holistic ministry that would be required of its churches in the third wave of growth in the 1990s. Through social ministries, we would begin to see the importance of ministry to our broken world. Through targeting urban communities of great need, we would learn the importance of community-based ministry in both city and rural areas. By engaging a more diverse world and a secular world, we would learn to refine our church ministries to consider the growing numbers of unchurched people in our communities. And we would more intentionally seek to reach across cultural barriers.

The retirement of J.G.

The retirement of J.G. Johnson was a joyous affair. He was extolled as one of the most colorful leaders that had emerged in the conference.[5] His hunting, fishing, softball and horseshoe expertise were legendary, especially after shooting a lion in Africa. But mostly, the conference celebrated his deep love for the Lord and his passion to reach lost people.

The crown jewel of the Johnson legacy was, of course, Big Trout Lake Bible Camp. Trout now had grown to nearly 3,000 participants and 300 volunteer counselors and staff. The name was now Trout Lake Camp not Big Trout Lake Bible Camp. The new name was reflective of its broader programming. Retreats, of course, were bringing adults to Trout in large numbers. The camping staff would begin family camps to fill the summer schedule. An inter-camp council brought representatives from Lake Bronson, Waskish, Mink Lake, Ham Lake, and Chub Lake. Mink Lake had been operated by the South Arrowhead area churches. Located on a small northern lake, its proximity to the Boundary Waters

Canoe Area would, in the future, give it a broader ministry because of its unique camping location.

During the Johnson era, Sunday school attendance increased to more than 20,000. The Christian Education board was preparing material and training for "release time" religious training during school hours. Conference Youth Fellowship hosted a State Convention that brought youth together and sought to encourage the formation of local CYF youth groups in churches.

In the period from the mid-40s to the mid-60s, church membership grew by 75%, with 38 new churches started. Every suburban church had one or more building programs and many country churches were rebuilding as well. The Twin Cities Extension Committee was planting one or two churches every year, adding to the efforts of the conference.

Work among the native people in the state expanded during Johnson's era. Ed Viron, even as a young single man, had a great interest and passion for spiritual work among native people. He helped in the Nett Lake church, but in 1953, moved to Grand Portage and organized a church. Two years later, Ed married Donna and for the next 18 years, they built a church and good relationships

In 1957, Wally and Shirley Olson began a life-long relationship with the Ojibwa people of Minnesota.

with the Grand Portage Band of Chippewa. In 1957, Wally and Shirley Olson came to Nett Lake, building a chapel, and starting what would be a lifetime of friendship with the Bois Forte band of Chippewa at Nett Lake.

J.G. Johnson, A.K.A. Happy Johnson, pastored a state and left a legacy.

Notes

[1] 103rd Annual Meeting Minutes, Trustee recommendations, Sept. 29, 1961.

[2] John H. Bergeson, "Minnesota Ministry Memories," unpublished report.

[3] Warren Eastlund, 105th Annual Meeting Reports, Trustees' Report.

[4] Ibid.

[5] *Missions in Minnesota*, March 1964, p. 1.

Churches Started or Welcomed: 1949-1964

1949
Wooddale Church(Richfield)
Ridgewood Church (Minnetonka)

1950
Eagle Brook Church (White Bear Lake)
Lengby Baptist Church
First Baptist (Two Harbors)

1951
First Baptist Church (Glenwood)
Faith Baptist Church (Grand Rapids)

1952
Edinbrook Church (Brooklyn Center/Park)
Cornerstone Church (Litchfield)

1953
Bloomington Baptist Church
Ely Baptist Church

1954
Emmanuel Baptist Church (Duluth)
Bethel Baptist Church (Owatonna)

1955
Lakeside Baptist Church
Elk River Baptist Church
North Haven Church
Calvary Baptist Church (Paynesville)

1956
Babbit Baptist Church
Galilee Baptist Church

1957
First Baptist Church (Coon Rapids)
Pelican Rapids Baptist Church

1958
Grace Baptist Church (Cloquet)

1960
Valley Baptist Church
New Life Community Church (Ortonville)

1961
Oasis Church (Rochester)

1963
Cross of Christ (Eagan)
Berean Baptist Church (Burnsville)
Salem Baptist Church (New Brighton)

1964
Emmaus Church (Northfield)
Rush City Baptist Church (Rush City)

— Chapter 7 —

The S. Bruce Fleming Era (1965-1969): A Voice of Eloquence and a Gift of Administration

From the Klingberg Home for Children to the Minnesota conference

S. Bruce Fleming made a provocative opening statement in his inaugural message to the Minnesota Baptist Conference. Fleming was a golden orator. "I have no neat or pat answers for the complex meaninglessness of this tranquilizer age…but the Gospel, as Paul declared, is the power of God unto salvation." After declaring this great cause, Bruce continued into an area of sensitivity. "Together both rural and metropolitan areas must share in the honest efforts to enlarge the ministry throughout the state."[1]

Abandoned in childhood, Fleming turned the MBC toward a more holistic gospel.

Fleming had ministered in both metro and non-metro Minnesota locations. He pastored in rural communities such as Stanchfield, Minn., and Kiron, Iowa. He also led large churches such as Bethlehem in

Minneapolis and Salem in Chicago. He could make a farmer chuckle at a story or impress a corporate type with his business acumen. He loved nice cars (was given a new Chrysler Imperial in Chicago), but he also enjoyed returning to Cook, Minn., the ancestral home of his wife Astrid, a Swede Finn and a Kronholm.

The Klingberg Children's Home

John Eric Klingberg (J.E.) was born in Sweden in meager circumstances. He immigrated to the U.S. where eventually he became pastor of the BGC church in New Britain, Conn. In 1903, he and his wife took in three young boys who were abandoned and living in a shack. As other children came to light who also needed a home, the Klingberg Children's Home was born. Often living close to the financial edge, the Children's Home became known as the "house that prayer built" because there were many stories of how God met daily needs for food and supplies at just the moment they were urgently being prayed for. The leadership of the Children's Home passed from J.E. Klingberg to his son Haddon (in 1946), and eventually to his grandson 'Don (in 1968). Over the decades nearly 2,000 children were cared for at the Klingberg Children's Home.

Beginning in the 1970s, "changes in the care of orphaned and needy children nationwide prompted a shift from being a 'substitute home' to providing treatment services for children and their families. The Children's Home became Klingberg Family Centers, Inc., a private, nonprofit organization whose goal is to strengthen families, to reunite children and families whenever that is safe and possible, and to assure permanent, nurturing families for children. Today, Klingberg Family Centers provides services to hundreds of persons each year through a range of programs which include residential treatment, a special education school, an acute care unit, extended day treatment, family preservation and reunification services, a parent aide program, respite care for families, a safe home and a specialized foster care and adoption program." (Klingberg Family Centers website)

He shared with Jack Bergeson, his new colleague, a childhood history of brokenness. When Fleming was 3 years old, his family determined they could no longer care for him, so they brought him to the Klingberg Home for Children in New Britain, Conn. The Klingberg Home was an orphanage started by a Swedish Baptist pastor in 1903. It became home for many children, including one Sam Fleming later known as S. Bruce Fleming. Fleming would live with the Klingbergs until he left for Bethel Academy as a teenager. He rarely talked of his childhood. His past would be evident, though, in his clear support of the MBC's growing interest in social ministries. It is interesting in the plan of God, that two motherless sons, Jack Bergeson and Bruce Fleming, would transition the Minnesota Baptist Conference into a more holistic approach to the gospel message.

In the 50s and 60s, the conference had created standing boards – a Board of Education (that also managed camping) and a Board of Missions. With a pastoral leader such as J.G. Johnson, the structure placed initiation and agenda-setting down in the working board levels. But Fleming had no interest in working through the existing silos. He announced in his opening address that his era would be different from the former eras. The Minnesota Baptist Conference had elected an executive leader in Fleming who would direct the work of its staff.

In Fleming's first year, the MBC leadership brought a recommendation that the board of trustees be empowered to debate and act on its behalf when the conference was not in session.[2] The staff (John Bergeson in missions and Lee Kingsley in camping) knew who would be setting the direction, and they liked it. The conference was seeing a new level of leadership and management.

The Mighty Minnesota Quarter

The conference had purchased a small office building on Pascal Avenue in 1956, after renting space at Bethel for two decades. Immediately upon Fleming's arrival, the old brick structure was renovated to provide improved comfort for staff and visitors. A grand opening was held to meet the staff. In addition, the internal systems of the conference were being given the same renovation. Fleming's successor would freely call his predecessor a financial genius.

Minnesota had always been uniquely committed to the flourishing world mission program of the national conference. But with this success, the national office had also found a way of raising its operating budget. The United Mission for Christ was a unified budget that included all ministries and all sources of income. As churches gave to missions in the conference, they also supported both the national conference office and their special missionaries. The districts, of course, had no world missionaries and therefore, no such opportunity to raise their budget. Finances had always been a major challenge for districts. Contribution levels were unpredictable and generally low. Emergency appeals were numerous.

Fleming did two things. He began to talk about giving to the Minnesota conference as a percentage of the church's giving commitment to the national United Missions program. Initially he suggested giving 23% of the national giving level, then simply 25%. He called this the Mighty Minnesota Quarter. To the churches, the math was simple, for every dollar you send to BGC, send a quarter to Minnesota. The other change he recommended was to publish the annual giving levels of the churches in the annual report. So effective were these financial efforts that in 1965 the trustees brought a recommendation that Minnesota proceed with a plan to take no financial assistance whatsoever from the national conference. Although the pure brilliance of this plan would be blurred by Minnesota's continued partnering with Home Missions grants, it showed the confidence of this era.

Four category 4 tornados affect 100 conference families

As if the office had been organizing for such a moment, the Minnesota Baptist Conference and the state faced a disaster on Thursday, May 6, 1965. The spring melt had brought record breaking floods, raising the Mississippi River to a record 26.4 feet above flood level. On May 6th, a massive storm network brought five tornados to the Twin Cities, the worst on record. Four were F4, one F3, and possibly a sixth at F2. The impact was disastrous with 13 people dead and 683 people injured. More than 100 conference families were affected in some way. The MBC and its churches gave generously. More than $10,000 came through the MBC to victims. That did not include many large gifts sent directly. "Three small children in St. Paul emptied their savings bank and gave $4.30 in small change."[3]

Actually, this generosity fostered another crisis. In the urgency of the crisis, the MBC mixed relief funds with the regular Benevolent Fund giving. This would later lead the trustees to clarify these two ministry funds. They declared that the Benevolent Fund's purpose was to assist pastors and their families. Disaster relief would be dealt with through a relief fund and specific appeals.

Fleming's era would rebrand the Minnesota Baptist Conference as a giving option for the churches, and as a mission-driven entity. This was a subtle shift in ministry philosophy. During the J.G. era, with the exception of Trout Lake, most of the ministries in the conference could be defined as serving or extending the ministries of the local churches. Even the starting of churches was defined as church extension. But under the leadership of Fleming, Bergeson, and Kingsley, distinct ministries were promoted as part of the vision to reach the state of Minnesota. This more entrepreneurial approach to denominational ministry would reappear with the third wave of the conference in the late 80s and 90s.

The Penetration Study, prototype for future planning

The MBC's more intentional approach to ministry was encouraged by an assessment/planning process called a Penetration Study. Its breadth dominated the Mission Board's work from 1965 to 1967. Led by Emmett Johnson, pastor of Elim in Minneapolis, and Dick Johnson, chairman of the trustees, the Penetration Study revealed opportunities across the state. Minnesota pastors were asked to assess the geographical region that their churches could penetrate. They were also asked how they felt their churches could affect these areas.

The southeast area had the smallest number of conference members, but had seen a multiplication of efforts with the planting of churches in Owatonna, Rochester, and Northfield. Each area was examined for current and future extension opportunities. The Twin Cities area had 40 churches, but the report called for an increase of 80-100 by 2000. That would require three new Twin City churches a year. These goals were based on our past and future opportunities. The Penetration Report noted that the MBC had grown 85% in the last 25 years but that the future must be faced with even more aggressiveness.

The report also highlighted the commitments of the Minnesota conference to care for those in need through the Social Ministries Committee. The final report saw the study "leading to the penetration of our cities and the lives and needs of many disadvantaged people in our state."[4] This was the first social ministries committee in any BGC district, but it would lead to many more at the national and at the district level.

The Bethel Center, a continuing experiment in social ministry

The Bethel Center was making an impact on the Seward neighborhood in Minneapolis. For two years Dick Plaep had led the center, and then Mr. and Mrs. Westby carried on. A Helping Hand fund had been created. Foster home recruitment was being assisted by Mrs. Clifford Larson. Literacy instruction programs were assisted by Mrs. Virgil Olson. Jerry Dahl had started a Family Counseling Service. For a time, the social ministries committee worked with social worker Linda Waldenstrom to assist in social ministries, especially placement of children in conference foster homes. Eventually this work with foster families transferred to a partnership with North St. Paul Baptist Church. With Mr. and Mrs. Dean James as house parents, the MBC sponsored a group foster home for youth in trouble with the law. Also at this time, the Fort Francis church established a home for Native American boys who had migrated to the city from the reservation.

The north side erupts in riots

In July of 1967, the north side of Minneapolis erupted in riots and violence. Small, by comparison to the disruptions in other U.S. cities, it profoundly affected not only the Plymouth Avenue neighborhood – which was looted and burned to the ground – but also the attitudes of the majority culture who had felt somehow that Minnesota was different. The conference asked Dr. James Holloway, pastor of Zion Baptist Church on the north Minneapolis, to speak at the BGC Annual Meeting in the fall of that year. He spoke with power on "What Caused the Minneapolis Riots?" Delegates at the conference toured the destroyed neighborhoods. Years later, Holloway would be a key link for the MBC in providing help and assistance to the Katrina victims after the 2005 hurricane. He was pastoring an historic church in Mississippi. His son Scotty had become a Minnesota conference pastor. Minnesota's new heart for social ministry would equip us for emergency relief ministries.

In a time of racial and urban upheaval, the Bethel Center became a touch point for Minnesota churches who wanted to be involved with the needs of the city. The center had more than 200 youth involved each week with more than 40 volunteers. It served the increasing numbers of native people migrating from the White Earth reservation. Churches provided clothing and other assistance. The Bethel Student Missionary Project, which the MBC coordinated, would be an avenue for motivated youth volunteers to find service opportunities in the city.

If one includes the work of local pastors in reservations (such as Rev. Reed in Red Lake and Rev. Anderson in Sand Lake), the MBC and Home Missions were actively working in five reservations in the state. In 1972, Native American migration to the city would bring Wally and Shirley Olson to serve the urban native population. In 1970, the Olsons had come under the supervision of the MBC. Prior to this, they had served under BGC Home Missions alone. Eventually the ministry would be supervised by an independent entity that represented both the MBC and the BGC – the Indian Ministries Advisory Committee (IMAC).

In 1969 the Bethel Christian Center was sold. The building was a casualty of urban renewal in the Seward neighborhood. The conference did not try to secure a new location. But this urban institutional social ministry had captured the imagination of many people. MBC leaders encouraged churches to carry on their own opportunities for social ministry in the city. Now was the time for direct partnerships with urban churches. After the Bethel Center closed, Bethlehem, Minnehaha, and Edgewater continued ministries with children on the White Earth Indian Reservation. Nonetheless, many would look back to the bold social efforts of the Bethel Center as a tipping point in the conference's journey to a more holistic ministry of the Gospel.

Calvary Baptist of Roseville and New Hope Church of St. Paul began to partner in ministry together. Rev. Kneely Williams had started an African American congregation on the east side. It was growing in size and stature in the black community. An interesting prelude to this relationship was the fact that the African American community that New Hope served had been the first home of many Swedish immigrants – then called Swede Hollow. New Hope, which had become part of the American Baptists, became dually aligned with the conference. In 1969, both New Hope and North Central, Rev. Gardner's church in Frogtown, would seek affiliation in the MBC. Central Baptist in the midway was partnering with North Central. With the Nett Lake Church and Mt. Rose in Grand Portage, African American and Native American people formed the first racially diverse congregations in a conference. There would be many more in the decades ahead.

In 1968, in the aftermath of the riots in north Minneapolis, a black newspaper in the Twin Cities took a survey of denominational churches asking whether a black family on vacation would be welcome to visit in one's denominational churches across the state of Minnesota. Eighty-three Minnesota Baptist Conference churches responded strongly that they would welcome such a family in their church. This was a very high percentage in comparison with other religious groups. Central of St. Paul and Oak Hill began to advertise their churches in this black newspaper.

So strongly did the board of trustees feel about the issue of racial reconciliation that it brought a special resolution to the floor of the 1968 Annual Meeting. "The Trustee Board, feeling that the burden of today's need must be borne by all of us, recommends that every church and pastor examine their church programs and inner conscience and determine whether or not they are doing all they can to promote and practice racial justice."[5]

Fleming calls up the issues of the day

In the Fleming years, the Minnesota Baptist Conference experienced growth in size as well as maturity. Membership growth would increase to 21,112 in 1969. The 1965 Annual Meeting at Fergus Falls welcomed 540 delegates and friends. Bruce Fleming not only was a clever financial officer for the conference, but he also was an opinion leader and a very savvy promoter of MBC ministries. The venerable MBC newsletter *Missions in Minnesota* was retired, as the *Minnesota Messenger* emerged to promote conference ministries to a wider constituency. At the same time, Fleming created *Contact – A Church Relations Letter* from the executive staff and board of the Minnesota Baptist Conference. *Contact* gave Fleming a pulpit in front of the pastors and key leaders in the conference. He used it homiletically, calling for loyalty and obedience to the cause of Christ.

He also used his writing forum to challenge the district to engage with the culture. A monthly publication, Fleming's monographs were often 40 to 50 pages long. The amazing thing was they were always worth reading. There was always a take-away challenge. During the Penetration Study, Fleming was promoting new strategies in neighborhood visitation. A summary of his writings gives us a look at his heart.

Fleming declared the year 1967 to be a Year of Evangelism in our churches, joining the evangelical energy catalyzed by the Berlin Congress on Evangelism. He cites for the first time the needs of pastors' wives, noting their felt need to gather together as partners in ministry. He affirms their contributions to ministry in the churches and he warns pastors that it is a "mistake to treat them as an addendum to your clever ministry."[6]

He observed the radical transitions being faced in rural Minnesota. School districts were closing, consolidating local schools and districts. Businesses and cafes that were a center of community in small towns were vacant. There was a social and spiritual opportunity for the church at these times. He speculated that there may be a need to return to student pastorates, circuit pastors, yoke ministries, and tent makers. Fleming was a futurist.

The ecumenical movement was burning across mainline protestant Christendom like a wildfire. The United Church of Christ was a merger formed in 1957 and completed in 1961. Many historic doctrines in these denominations were bypassed in the name of tolerance. Vatican II closed in 1965, the year Bruce Fleming assumed leadership of the MBC. Fleming's monographs alluded to the importance of fellowship with Baptists and the Baptist World Alliance. This position for a conference leader was not to be assumed. There were strong voices suggesting separation from the Baptist World Alliance.

In his annual report of 1966, Fleming mentioned the "ecclesiastical demographics" of Dr. Alton Motter, executive director of the Minnesota Council of Churches. He noted the pressures toward church unions in the denominational scene and commented, "One risks tarnishing his own reputation as a straight-lined conservative, yet the spiritual aura we have inherited from our pietistic background will not be violated by facing head-on the great issues which confront the faithful witness of the Minnesota Baptist Conference people. We too are citizens in the amphitheater of the Christian community." He continued by encouraging an open stance toward the Minnesota Council of Churches as well as the National and the World Council of Churches, recognizing that though we have theological disagreements with the leaders of some of these organizations, yet "there remains in these bodies, many evangelical voices that deserve our support."[7] The next year, at the 1967 Minnesota annual meeting, the delegates passed a resolution encouraging participation in local ecumenical ministerial groups, and in the Baptist World

Alliance. Fleming concluded with an appeal that with all prayerfulness, "Churches should evaluate all overtures to unite."[8]

Resolutions in the annual meetings

The role of resolutions in the annual meeting was changing. On occasion, social evils or societal trends brought forth a resolution, rarely dividing the house. As America entered the 60s, our cultural fabric was torn by strife and social change. Increasingly, from within the conference members pointed out issues that needed our unified voice. Resolutions on race, minorities, communism, and ministry to the whole person were brought to the assembly for affirmation. A resolution committee considered the proposed resolutions before they were brought to the assembly. In the late 60s, resolutions became a place for more activism. With an active social ministries committee, our constituency acted to engage with our culture and the issues of the day through the resolution process. Persistent resolution subjects were ecumenicity, church-state relationships, morality/Christian living, and the evils of the day. A 1968 resolution expressed grave concern for the nation's progress into the Vietnam War.

In the 70s, leadership adopted a more orderly process. The resolutions committee created a singular resolution for each annual meeting. These were well-crafted position statements, probably in response to the poorly written ones that occasionally came from the floor. There were resolutions on being friends of the poor, on ministry to older adults, on prayer in the schools, and on church/state relations. Still, resolutions came from the floor. Someone offered a resolution supporting conditional amnesty for draft evaders in 1974. The same pattern was occurring in the national conference. Meetings were becoming political. But this environment would grow tense in the 80s when the religious right found the resolution process to be a platform for their convictions, learning from the religious left of a generation before.

Pastors, parsonages, and retirement plans

Fleming, during his administration, pushed the conference to consider the needs of pastors and their families. Healthcare costs were strongly on the rise. Housing costs were also increasing, and many of the pastors were living in parsonage types of church housing. Most people were depending on the equity value in their home to provide some part of their retirement needs and most pastors did not own their own homes. There was no recognized retirement plan for pastors in the conference. As inflation drove these costs up, the plight of pastors, especially those in very small churches, became more critical. During the Fleming era, the conference created a health insurance plan. The churches were strongly encouraged to enroll their pastors for the protection of the church and the care of the pastor.

This author, as a pastor, drove a BGC representative down to the cities after a missions conference at his church. The worker was nearing retirement and expressed his feelings of anxiety. All his life he had pastored smaller churches. He was working for the conference now but did not own his own home. He was not sure he would have enough money to put a down payment on a mobile home. That conversation profoundly affected this author as a young pastor who later determined to support every effort to help pastors in these areas.

In the late 60s, with the drive of Wyman Malmsten, both Bethel employees and conference pastors were offered a voluntary retirement plan. Fleming strongly promoted these pastoral benefits among the churches and pastors. But his advocacy would go further. In his inaugural message, Fleming challenged the delegates, "Let each church examine itself and make such a determination relative to salary scale…let each minister examine himself, in turn, to merit the unqualified support of his people…"[9] This was a clear shift for the executive minister. Fleming was advocating for pastors. He was challenging the churches to deal generously with their pastors in compensation, health insurance, and retirement. In 1969, Fleming suggested a minimum salary of $6,000/year of which $2,000 was Social Security, hospitalization, and retirement. This was less than a first-year teacher's salary, which was $6,700. He went on to propose that the MBC enter into a three-part, shared subsidy with the church and the pastor on health insurance and a similar plan for pastor's pensions. Although these recommendations seem modest today, they marked a new kind of role for the district.

When Bruce Fleming assumed the leadership of the Minnesota conference, he had made it clear that his executive leadership style was moving well beyond the past role of the executive secretary. There is no doubt that the constituency sat in disbelief, in 1969, as they read the resignation of Bruce Fleming. He was taking a position at Bethel as a director of church relations. Although one could not blame Bethel for picking up a good man, many saw Fleming's move as a great loss for the conference. Fleming's highly competent corporate skills were rare in denominational staff positions.

Strategies for starting churches

The LBJ Team (Lee, Bruce, and Jack) was a strong team. In 1966, newly elected Fleming reported in *Missions in Minnesota* that both Kingsley and Bergeson had turned down prestigious opportunities – Kingsley to become the CE consultant for the BGC and Bergeson declining another position. Both had decided to stay with the new LBJ Minnesota team.[10]

By the closing years of the Fleming era, there was clearly some loss of momentum in the starting of churches. Emmett Johnson would note in his inaugural address that Minnesota started only half as many churches between 1965 and 1970 as it had between 1960 and 1965. Although these trends were being identified, the Minnesota conference could not seem to sustain both a substantive growth in the number of churches and the future challenges of the journey inward.

Jack Bergeson, however, continued to work aggressively in all phases of missions in the state. New models were being tried and prototyped. A mother church approach was employed to assist the startup of South Grove, Snail Lake, Cedar Grove, Northwest, and Coon Rapids. Later Elim of Minneapolis served as a mother church for Salem in New Brighton. It appeared now that Minnesota could also use stronger churches to help weaker ones, so Bergeson found "big sisters" for his needy churches. Bethany of St. Paul came alongside Lakeland and Waconia. Minnehaha and Forest Lake were helped by Calvary of Roseville. The model was applied outstate as Clearbrook sponsored Waskish and Karlstad helped Lancaster.

The Triad Committee, all players at the table

It is not clear how long these church-to-church partnerships survived, but one Bergeson model did endure – the Triad Committee. Actually Jack Bergeson gave credit to Maurice Lawson for coining the term somewhere in the late 50s. During these years, when the conference began working with a new church, a triad committee was formed. The committee included representation from the local church, another interested MBC church, and the MBC staff. The triad guided the church along its path to growth and health. The Triad Committee offered guidance to the church planter through the presence of other local pastors, laymen, and district personnel.

This too would change in years ahead, as churches became more autonomous in planting other churches. But in Bergeson's plan, other churches did have a partnering role, and together with the district, they provided guidance and resources as a "mother" or "sponsor" church. Through Bergeson, church planting became more pragmatic and intentional.

Minnesota, in the years ahead, would illustrate the need for clearer methodologies for starting churches. A church planting movement would offer systems and methods. Church planters would be sought out not only for their skills as good pastors, but also for unique personality profiles and spiritual passion. And the plan they would follow in starting the church would have similarities to the ways that a business prepares to introduce itself to a target customer and a selected retail location.

Churches Everywhere

As part of Jack Bergeson's work with the churches, he published a 46-page booklet on starting and growing churches called *Churches Everywhere*. Editions appear to have been published in the Columbia conference as well while Bergeson was the executive minister there. The volume provided resources for every step in the process of starting a church. A review of the volume gives a good look at the strategies of church planting that were employed in the 60s and 70s.

Bergeson's book laid down a methodology for starting churches.

Bergeson describes the formation of the church from a nucleus usually meeting in a private home. Bergeson lays down some of the pastoral leadership characteristics required in effective new church pastoring. The pastor must know how to pray, must feel called, must be evangelistic, but also must get along with people. He must be optimistic and tenacious and "a small amount of mechanic ability" may be useful.[11]

In 1941, a Building and Revolving Fund had been established with a gift from the bequest of John Abner Hanson of Duluth. In the late

Journey Inward, Journey Outward

Elizabeth O'Connor published *Journey Inward, Journey Outward* in 1968. Through her experience in Church of the Savior in Washington D.C., O'Connor became convinced that church had become all about the numbers and had lost the burden for the individual soul and for the communities in which they existed. Only when a church ministered with equal emphasis on "the journey inward and the journey outward" could it minister with the full expression of Christ in its body. In her book she emphasized that the journey inward must help churches and believers to develop the personal life of devotion, to grow toward God. At the same time churches and individuals should practice servanthood in their communities, expressing the love of God through social ministries. These twin emphases were certainly part of the MBC journey during this era.

50s and 60s, the MBC was able to increase these assets. A trust fund was established in 1962-63. Bonds were sold to increase the assets into the $100,000's. Churches were given loans for building expansions or improvements. The fund would increase in size and importance into the 70s, when the funds were merged with a national conference program with the same purpose. During this period of significant church building, the MBC also co-signed notes for churches. In later years, this practice was abandoned with the warning of the auditors.

Curiously large Minnesota churches

In one issue of *Missions in Minnesota*, Fleming wrote about another noteworthy growth trend in Minnesota. Two churches were experiencing exceptional growth and had recently completed large sanctuary structures for their growing congregations. The author of the article interviewed pastors Peter Unruh at Wooddale and Stanley Starr at Spring Lake Park and compared these exciting churches to the joy of watching a child grow to adulthood. The Minnesota Baptist Conference had large churches in its fellowship. These two churches, both in their size and in the speed of their growth, seemed to be growing beyond the norms for our state.[12]

In the decades that followed, the large church (and then the "mega-church") developed in the Minnesota Baptist Conference, as churches like Wooddale, Bethlehem, Woodland Hills, and Eagle Brook developed huge local ministries and national reputations.

Senior housing continues to find opportunities

In 1968, the board of trustees announced that it was studying the possibility of the MBC actively participating in building a Twin Cities seniors housing facility. A recommendation came at the annual meeting in 1969. The MBC would "give consideration to the development, ownership and operation of retirement homes throughout the state." The conference vote in 1969, however, was that the organizing entity should be the area churches, not the conference. This action would be reversed in the years ahead.

On a parallel track, the east central churches, which had joined together to form plans for a retirement facility in Cambridge, saw more than 1,000 people in attendance at the dedication of Grandview Christian Home. On October 22, 1962, the first resident of the newly built Grandview Christian Home moved in. One would have to describe the relationship between these projects for seniors as somewhat awkward. Both incorporating boards would have many bumps in the road in the years ahead. But both would provide extraordinary service to many aging conference people.

Learning to Serve

Sunday school was entering an autumn season in the churches. Although it was central to most church programs, its energy level was down. It was not promoted like it had been a decade earlier. Lee Kingsley sponsored a one-day Christian education seminar called *Learning to Serve*. He announced that the MBC was forming a film strip library as a resource to the churches.

Trout Lake maintained a consistent number of participants each summer buoyed by the family camps. A north washhouse and a classroom building were built in 1965. The Christian education board was unsure, at points, whether camp programming had been developed and updated to a level that would continue to attract the new generation of youth who had been attending camp summer after summer. So, under the leadership of Pastor Bill Horn, an evaluation was completed with exciting new programming promised.

The camp collaborated with the state CYF to sponsor a youth event on MEA weekend. *Grub-in* was launched with Harold Carlson and Richard Wiens as speakers. Trout Lake and camping had taken its place alongside other ministries in the Minnesota Baptist Conference. Trout was no longer a new experience for many. The conference constituents were quietly raising expectations for camping in its next era.

Rev. Bruce Fleming retired before the final year of his first five-year term. Several years later in an annual report, Emmett Johnson made this observation concerning Fleming's tenure, "Fleming was once referred to by Martin Erikson, then the editor of the *Standard*, as the 'Spurgeon of our conference.' Combining an Irish wit with a great capacity for administration, Fleming brought a stability and cohesiveness to the management of the conference."[13]

Notes

[1] S. Bruce Fleming, *Missions in Minnesota*, installation address, November 8, 1964.

[2] S. Bruce Fleming, 107th Annual Report, Executive Secretary's Report, 1965, p. 36.

[3] Ibid., p. 37.

[4] 108th Annual Report, Missions Board, 1966, p. 47.

[5] 110th Annual Meeting Minutes, Trustee Board Recommendations, 1968.

[6] S. Bruce Fleming, 111th Annual Report, Executive Secretary's Report, 1969, p. 41.

[7] S. Bruce Fleming, 108th Annual Report, Executive Secretary's Report, 1966, p. 39.

[8] S. Bruce Fleming, 109th Annual Report, Executive Secretary's Report, 1967, p. 19.

[9] S. Bruce Fleming, *Missions in Minnesota*, November 8, 1961, p. 1.

[10] *Minnesota in Missions*, September 1965, p. 8.

[11] John H. Bergeson, *Churches Everywhere* (Columbia Conference), 11th edition, p. 13.

[12] S. Bruce Fleming, *Missions in Minnesota*, "From Acorn to Oak," p. 2.

[13] Emmett V. Johnson, 114th Annual Report, Executive Minister's Report, 1972, p. 52.

Churches Started or Welcomed: 1965-1969

1965

Shoreview Baptist Church (Shoreview)

Eden Prairie Baptist Church (Eden Prairie)

Ham Lake Baptist Church (Ham Lake)

Bethel Baptist Church (Fort Francis, Ontario)

1966

Cottage Grove Baptist Church

1967

Mount of Olives Baptist Church (Duluth)

1968

Grafton Baptist Church (Grafton, ND)

Mt Rose Baptist Church (Grand Portage) formally affiliated

First Baptist Church (Ortonville) formally affiliated

1969

New Hope Baptist Church (St. Paul)

North Central Baptist Church (St. Paul)

Pickwick Baptist Church (Winona)

Maple Lake Baptist (Maple Lake)

Koinonia Baptist Church (Farmington/Lakeville)

Trout Lake and Camping

1. A meeting place with God.
2. Everywhere you go, you will find interesting things to do.
3. It takes a village to run a camp.
4. It's always been worth the wait.
5. Buddies mean an enviable safety record at Trout.

1. "Now are you sure it was a bug you swallowed?"
2. The first campers to use the new wash house.
3. Pearl Sorley captures the imagination of young campers.
4. Junior girls gather for chapel, in the years prior to coed camping.
5. "Jer" (Jerry) Healy showing off a future camper.

1. Styles change in swimwear, but smiles don't.
2. The canteen was a camper favorite.
3. Simply a blast – tetherball.
4. Studying together to know God better.
5. Camp programming brings a smile.

TROUT LAKE
and
MINK LAKE

CAMP STAMP
SAVINGS BOOK

1. Pensive staff.
2. Camp Stamps helped families save for camp.
3. The chapel was the last major building in early camp construction.
4. A stone tower marks the chapel hill.
5. It is called a people mover.

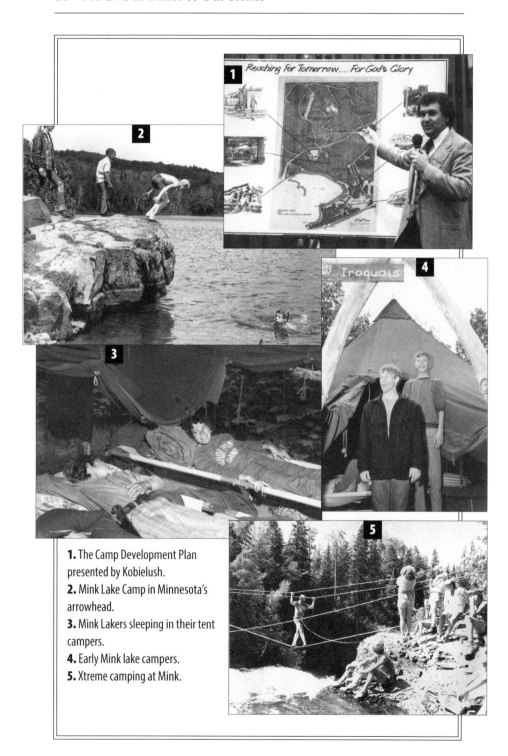

1. The Camp Development Plan presented by Kobielush.
2. Mink Lake Camp in Minnesota's arrowhead.
3. Mink Lakers sleeping in their tent campers.
4. Early Mink lake campers.
5. Xtreme camping at Mink.

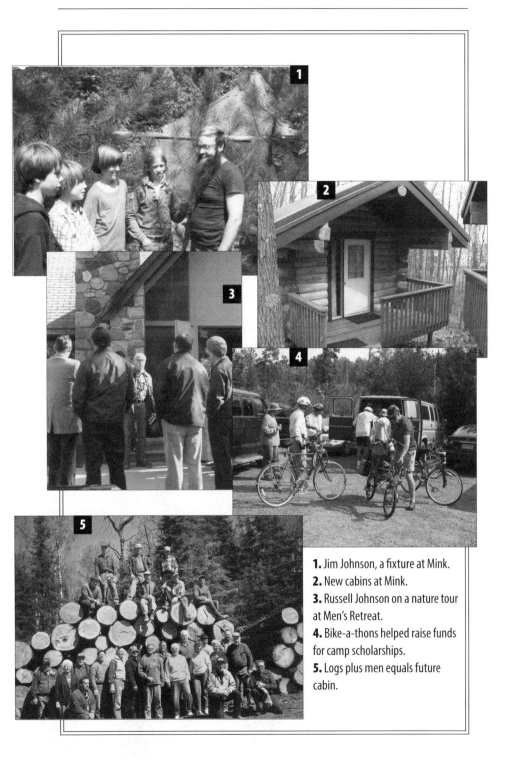

1. Jim Johnson, a fixture at Mink.
2. New cabins at Mink.
3. Russell Johnson on a nature tour at Men's Retreat.
4. Bike-a-thons helped raise funds for camp scholarships.
5. Logs plus men equals future cabin.

1. This sawmill brought logging and building back to camp.
2. Log buildings were constructed with cut logs.
3. All cabins were constructed from logs to create a magical new camp.
4. Timber Ridge, an early vision.
5. Men's Retreat raised a massive barn.

1. Karin Larson formed an amazing partnership with Timber Ridge.

2. Today's campers love camp food.

3. The counselor remains the center of camp's spiritual life.

4. Who says Timber Ridge's hill is for kids?

5. Today's camp activities are amazing.

— Chapter 8 —

The Emmett Johnson Era (1969-1979): The MBC's Master Builder

Revolution in every department

In August 1968, the Beatles released their song *Revolution* and placed it on their famous *White Album*. In his lyrics, song-writer John Lennon expressed his revulsion to destructive change in the process of revolutionizing the world.

America was boiling at the end of the 1960s. Racial tension, political extremism, an unpopular and destructive war, and a youth revolution all added up to massive national anxiety and polarization. An indicator of the national state of mind, the Beatles' *Revolution* did not

After his significant work on the Penetration Study, the conference turned to Emmett Johnson for leadership.

receive a backlash from worried mothers but a kick in the backside from the radical left that viewed the song as a weak anthem of betrayal to the cause. America was still gripped in a decade of social upheaval. Interestingly, when the Minnesota Baptist Conference called Emmett Johnson in 1969, they selected one of the most radical leaders it had generated in this era.

Rev. Emmett Johnson was the logical replacement for executive minister Bruce Fleming, if he was interested in the position. And indeed he was. He had led the Penetration Study which had catalyzed the Fleming era. He had pastored with distinction at Elim Baptist Church in northeast Minneapolis during a time when the Minnesota conference was finding its social conscience. Elim of Minneapolis and Central of St. Paul were working models of churches who avoided the rampant urban flight that saw the majority of historic protestant churches relocating to new buildings in the suburbs. Elim and Central built a strong church core by attracting parishioners from the suburbs, and ministering aggressively in the city. During Johnson's tenure, Elim reached its strongest membership. Johnson was uniquely positioned to lead the Minnesota Baptist Conference in both its holistic inner journey and its continued growth opportunity.

Goodbye to the chief

A student of leadership would quickly observe that Executive Johnson would move strongly in the direction of organizational change. A support staff member in later years recalled that it was clear to the MBC associates that Johnson was nudging them to move on. Indeed, there would be a changing of the guard.

Lee Kingsley had become an iconic leader in Christian camping through his tenure at the Minnesota Baptist Conference. In 1969, he published a book with L. Ted Johnson on Christian camp leadership, *Blueprint for Quality, Administrative Guidelines for Christ-centered Camping.* He resigned in 1972 to take a similar position in camping and Christian education with the Middle East district of the conference, serving there until retirement. At the 1972 annual meeting in Willmar, he was presented with an Accutron watch and a cash gift. His tenure of 20 years was celebrated, though for many Trout Lake without "chief" was a less soulful place.

Lee Kingsley made a significant impact on the Middle East district, as he had in Minnesota. But his influence went well beyond the BGC districts. The *Blueprint for Quality* book was a seminal work in Christian camping and became the accepted guide to leading and managing a Christian camp. Christian camping's founders were entrepreneurs. Few were of a mind to organize their steps to success, much less put them in book form. Kingsley's book was the benchmark guideline for this important and large American Christian enterprise. The camping systems in America had developed from oral tradition – one director telling another director what worked for him. Kingsley's book brought a cohesive operation to camp management – a professional standard.

This made Kingsley something of a guru for Christian Camping International (CCI), the newly formed national organization. He was greatly appreciated by the new breed of camp directors who would understand the basics through Lee and then push the possibilities of camping in the years to come. Minnesota's own Bob Kobielush, after leading Minnesota Baptist Conference camping, eventually became the CEO of Christian Camping International. Kobielush remembers Kingsley's contributions to camping with great respect.

Jack Bergeson remembered

In 1970, Jack Bergeson resigned his missions director position to become the executive minister of the Columbia Baptist Conference. His work ethic, passion for starting new churches, life-long commitment to the conference, and excellent leadership for 11 years was celebrated. A transition committee was created to carry the responsibilities of the vacated position.

There is little doubt that Jack Bergeson was one of the most influential leaders in the Minnesota conference's history. He almost single-handedly assumed the programmatic role for Trout Lake in its early stages. He pioneered church planting in the suburbs. He broke down racial barriers in spite of the entrenchment of the leadership. And he left this author a wealth of files and memoirs on MBC history before passing to his eternal reward.

The second missionary journey for Minnesota

At the annual meeting in 1970, Johnson's friend and colleague Dick Turnwall was called to the missions position. In reflecting on the position, Johnson noted that missions concerned itself with "social ministries, family counseling services, inner city ministries, minority ministries, and church extension." He challenged the conference with these goals as a "second missionary journey." He was completely clear about his new direction, announcing that we have, in the past, been all about starting new churches, and now we need to be about building up and strengthening our churches.[1] These words would mark Johnson's tenure.

Johnson eventually became conflicted with his "second journey" strategy. He increasingly sensed the fact that Minnesota was in a period of reduced church planting. Yet he proceeded with his passion to see the conference strengthened through the transformation of its core. However, in the end, he would express increasing frustration with Minnesota's unsuccessful growth strategies.

Through the lens of a visionary

Emmett Johnson was a visionary leader. He had a unique ability to look at the future of an organization with a view through two import-ant lenses – the position of the organization relative to its past and the position of the organization relative to its changing future ministry. In his first annual report, he revealed his perspective. With regard to the

---

A Tribute to A.J. Wingblade

In 1976 Emmett Johnson paid tribute to A.J. Wingblade, a giant of a churchman, who had gone to be with the Lord at the age of 96. Wingblade, who had been principal of Bethel Academy for many years, had also been a tireless worker in his church, Elim Baptist in Minneapolis. He was Elim's Sunday school superintendent for more than 50 years. At an age when many people were retiring and only making an effort to get to church on an occasional basis, Wingblade spent his week selflessly thinking about the people who might need a special touch to encourage their attendance the next Sunday.

The year that Johnson became pastor of Elim, Wingblade had made 2,300 calls on behalf of the church. He also sent cards, attendance reminders, birthday and anniversary notes...all hand-made with an encouraging verse. "I learned the importance of call-ing." Emmett confessed. "On countless Saturdays, I followed him up tenement house stairs for a minimum of thirty calls a day." For Wingblade, the church neighborhood was his household. (Emmett V. Johnson, *Happenings*, "A Tribute," Summer 1976.)

context of ministry in the conference, he pointed to several areas of profound change.

The conference had a demographically larger and a culturally louder population of youth. Its churches were ministering in increasingly urbanized settings. There was an increased focus on ecology, a waning of religious authority, and a decline in traditional morality. Johnson called for new directions that re-orient conference ministries to reach younger people. More training was needed at all levels, including continuing education for pastors. Leaders must be prepared for the changing world. Johnson called for church cooperation and finally for ministries of healing and reconciliation in an increasingly broken world.

In his annual report for 1972, Johnson looked at the past. He suggested that we must understand the factors that have led us to this point in history. He documented in detail the emergence of a strong and productive evangelical movement within our churches. He saw our identity inherited from our historic pietistic commitments. We are passionate to minister for the cause of Christ in changing times.

According to Emmett Johnson, the Minnesota conference had burnished the following notable characteristics: a practical ecumenicity, an aroused humanness, an irenic spirit in doctrine, a tolerant acceptance of variant life styles, a galloping urbanization, vigorous anti-materialism, and a heightened personal expectancy from church life.[2]

Johnson's concern for ministry in youth culture would be repeated in almost every one of Johnson's annual reports. "The younger generation coming up, are rebels. Some are revolutionaries, set out to destroy the institutions and structures of society. Some rebels are true reformers with good intentions. We cannot discount the latter. They are rightly motivated. We have to come to grips with them and try to understand them."[3]

Johnson's focus on youth

During the 60s, 70 million post-war babies became teens and young adults. It was the age of youth. Emmett Johnson was a student of culture. As he saw the emerging youth culture, he observed the declining conference youth ministry. CYF was a 50s style program that gathered the church young people to separate them from the world. The ministry had been driven by its youth leaders. It had admirably mentored many conference youth into leadership in their churches. CYF supplied leaders in camping. Now, it seemed to be dying. Yes, there were some new retreat events at Trout, and an annual speech and musical performance contest for youth, but we seemed to be reaching only our own kids, not the hard core youth in our world.

Sunday school was in decline. Camping seemed unable to make the programmatic changes necessary to reach the at-risk young person. Teen camps were poorly attended. Johnson was a father. He

Coming from the life of a youth pastor, Bob Kobielush settles in to direct Trout Lake Camp.

and Darlene had a high school student at home – their son Keith. But his passion for youth went beyond parental concern to an appeal for generational transition. Johnson would combine the leadership roles needed in youth work and camping, and hire a promising young entrepreneur to lead both youth and camping – Bob Kobielush.

A new home and a change in the way we conduct our business

Johnson moved into his new job in the Pascal Avenue headquarters building which had served the MBC since 1956. Bethel College and Seminary sold the MBC a two-acre piece of land it had acquired in Arden Hills. The price was $8,000. At the annual meeting in Mankato in 1970, the conference voted to build a new conference center on this site. Gilbert Okerstrom from Quamba was the building chairman and, with the architect, he created an extremely lovely contemporary building that reflected our Scandinavian heritage. At the following annual meeting at Olivet Church in north Minneapolis, the $154,000 building was dedicated with a remaining debt of $73,000 dollars. The $40,000 from the sale of the Bethel Center was invested in the new center.

The Family Counseling Service, which had been started in the Bethel Center, was provided with a private entrance and counseling rooms in the new conference building. The board room, in the center, was an octagonal shape and utilized a custom-designed and built octagonal table. It seemed to weigh about a thousand pounds and required a call to workman's compensation to set up and to store. But it was a delight when it was in place. In the next year, with Johnson's instruction, an unlimited supply of donuts and coffee were provided to welcome Minnesotans from across the state.

In 1971, the trustees recommended a constitutional revision that would modify the governance of the Minnesota conference. One board would carry on the business of the conference, and that board would have the authority to act on behalf of the conference between annual meetings. "Like we had in the Minnesota conference until 1943," Johnson bantered with his readers in *Contact*.[4] The board would be formed through elected representatives from all the areas of the state. Areas would each be given either two or three positions on the board, based on their size. The new board was called the Board of Stewards.

The executive would no longer be called the executive secretary but would be referred to as the executive minister. In increasingly modern times, no one wanted to be called the secretary, especially the CEO. In 1973, the new organizational system was put in place, and toward the end of his tenure, Johnson would write a manual of operation for the MBC.

In 1972, Oliver Kronholm was offered an early corporate retirement from the DuPont Corporation, where he had been the manager for the western regional offices. He was subsequently hired to manage the business affairs of the conference. This staff relationship would not be the easiest for Emmett Johnson. Johnson was the builder and Kronholm, the financial controller. But the conference budgets had grown remarkably. Kronholm brought financial controls and often provided a balance for Johnson's charging entrepreneurship.

He also provided camping personnel with useful mentoring in finance, which Bob Kobielush appreciated. With a resume containing only two years as a youth pastor, Kobielush was on a learning curve with the business side of camping. Kronholm came alongside the camping department, mentored Kobielush in finance and, in spite of a rapidly expanding and experimental camping direction in the Kobielush years, camp closed in the black every year except the last one during Kobielush's tenure. "I front-loaded too many future scenarios in the budget that year," Kobielush would admit as he finished his work at camp with a wash of red ink.[5]

Contact, an intimate conversation with pastors

Johnson created his own printed communication in 1970 and called it *Contact.* It was not a typical newsletter for churches and pastors. Rather, it was an intimate conversation with pastors, which may even "contain some things that are rather confidential."[6] For the wider constituency, *It's Happening* was introduced in 1972. A newspaper for the churches, this new periodical would promote MBC ministries as *Missions in Minnesota* and the *Minnesota Messenger* once did. Though written communications were important to Johnson, he did not send archival messages like Fleming. Johnson's annual reports, however, were serious assessments of the past year's initiatives and a challenge to a refocused vision for the district in the coming year.

Another method of Johnson's communication was the Town Meeting, inaugurated in 1978. The MBC staff traveled to nine areas in the state and reported on the conference ministries. It was the start of what would be a unique staff-to-people connection in Minnesota.

Pastors are my priority!

Emmett Johnson was a natural born leader. He was also an articulate theologian and an ardent churchman. He was unapologetic about his bias to support his pastors in conflict situations. After all, he was called to be a pastor to pastors. Each year, as he began his ministry, he made calls on pastors, sat in their offices, and ate at their tables. In 1972, he made 147 such pastoral calls, for example. During his tenure, he would create many new systems and documents to improve the credentialing and care of pastors. Johnson realized the importance of the pastors to his success and visited them in their church settings – nearly all of them – in the first couple years of his ministry.

In 1974, he wrote, *Procedures in Calling a Pastor.* He created a sample church constitution designed for new churches. Working with Pastor Delmar Dahl, Johnson would publish *Let's Celebrate!* – a resource manual for special days in the church calendar. A *Code of Ministerial Ethics* was produced and affirmed. Johnson worked with a newly formed group representing state pastors, which he named the Pastors' Council. He created an Orientation Day at the new headquarters building which allowed new pastors in the district to become familiar with staff and ministries. He initiated a relationship with the North Central Career Development Center which would help pastors in crisis and enrich pastors with greater self-understanding. He budgeted for scholarships for that program. Many of Johnson's documents and procedures would remain for the next generation.

At the end of his tenure in Minnesota, Johnson commented that above all else, he wished to be remembered as a pastor for the pastors and an ombudsman. Following Bruce Fleming, he laid out in detail the tangible and non-tangible compensations a church should provide its pastor. Johnson often told the story of the bi-vocational rural Minnesota pastor whose church leaders wanted him to move on to another church, so they quit bringing him wood to heat the parsonage. Johnson commented that if they could not get him out, they would freeze him out. It was a bit of humor, but left a listener with a not-so-subtle message.

Johnson inaugurated study leave sabbaticals for MBC staff and recommended it to churches. In four of the pages of his final annual report, he outlines in detail the compensation items that every pastor ideally should be provided. And then he made an unusual demand of his successor: "Priorities in my schedule go to pastors...that role for the next Executive Minister must be taken seriously."[7]

Steps to Ordination, **Emmett V. Johnson**

In 1973, Executive Minister Johnson formed a committee that included Millard Erickson, Frank Voth, John Chisholm, and Bruce Herrstrom. He charged them to examine procedures in the ordination of our pastors. In contrast to other denominational groups, the local Baptist church ordains its pastor. But the local church had very little procedural help for this task. At times, the local churches felt unprepared for their responsibility. Occasionally a pastor came into the process poorly prepared, which was an embarrassment to the pastor and to the church.

Johnson's committee developed guidelines for a rigorous and meaningful ordination process. He wrote these guidelines into a manual called *Steps to Ordination*. This document would remain for decades the guidebook for local church ordinations. What was entirely new in the document was the formation of a Ministerial Guidance Committee. Astute pastors and seminary professors volunteered to spend time with candidates during their preparations. Without shifting the ordination process away from the local church, this committee functioned both as an advocate for the candidate and a pre-examining group to assist the local church in the process of ordination. In later years, a group like this would assist the MBC staff with issues of pastoral misconduct.

SHALOM, a peace and a place

Johnson was a builder. He had completed the building of the new conference center in Arden Hills. In the next years, Johnson and the district would build again. This project would flow naturally from a very effective district small group movement known as Shalom. But the building that was to house this program, Shalom House, would prove to be an incredible challenge to build, even to the inimitable Dr. Emmett Johnson.

The 1960s saw the development of the human potential movement. It was a broadly experienced movement, as it seemed to put some of the tools of psychotherapy in the hands of the individual in small group relationships. Decades before this, Reverend Sam Shoemaker in the Oxford Group experimented with the power of a small group to allow confession of sin and making amends. This kind of giving-in to God in a supportive group could powerfully transform brokenness in life. Shoemaker's work and writings influenced the Alcoholics Anonymous movement.

In the 50s, the Faith at Work organization brought new tools for small groups in the church through the work and writings of Bruce Larson and Keith Miller. Shortly after Emmett Johnson became the executive minister, he and Bob Frykholm from Calvary of St. Paul organized the first "Shalom Retreat." Based on honesty and Christian love in a supportive group environment, the Shalom movement held retreats for conference pastors and lay people to help them find greater "wholeness" in a broken world. Twenty pastoral couples participated in the first Shalom Retreat April 12-13, 1971.

No Shalom found in its building

In 1973, as part of this movement, the Board of Stewards recommended that the conference look for a site for an adult retreat center. King's Ranch in Isanti County, which had been purchased by the conference, was considered but not found to be satisfactory. Sites on the St. Croix River, the Rum River, Sunfish Lake, and Trout Lake Camp were visited. Johnson and others strongly favored a retreat center close to the Twin Cities. It was convenient to the largest group of its potential customers.

After each exploratory meeting, Bob Kobielush would offer his conviction that a Twin Cities area retreat center would never balance its budget. It would always need large subsidies. If the facility was located at Trout Lake, it could partner with the food service and infrastructure of Trout. Kobielush was also active in Shalom House's planning stages when shared bathrooms were being considered. "Think about it! After a long trip up from the cities, do you want to share a bathroom with your friend and his wife?"[8]

Glen Lindberg, a Swedish-American architect who had assisted with the headquarters project, was retained to design the retreat center. But the project came in over-budget, and there were problems with the contractor. Shalom House was completed six months late, and near the end of Johnson's tenure. Shalom House was built on the property of Trout Lake at a cost of $320,000. But the retreat movement it was built to house had run its course. Shalom was stillborn. It would be a financial burden for the next decade. However, being on the property of Trout Lake, the facility would be re-directed to many new purposes in the years to come. It would allow a broad range of adult ministries to flourish. One such adult ministry would be retirement retreats.

With the departure of Lee Kingsley in 1972, a significant amount of special programming fell on the desk of Emmett Johnson. Johnson assumed the Christian education responsibilities of Kingsley. Kobielush was assigned youth and camping. Adult programming was an area of expanding ministry. There was a need to program the emerging Shalom movement.

While keeping his eye on growing opportunities for adult ministries, Johnson's real passion was programming for pastors. The annual pastor's retreat ramped up to a quality expression of appreciation and affection for pastors and pastors' wives. The Trout Lake staff provided their best and attendance was strong. Additionally the MBC now provided multiple continuing education opportunities – preaching forums, seminars on pastoral administration, theology, church growth, town and country ministry, time management, marriage, or social ministries. It was a demanding time of expansion with minimal staff. And there were more challenges ahead.

Notes

[1] Emmett V. Johnson, *Contact*, "From your Executive Secretary," November 1970.

[2] Emmett V. Johnson, 114th Annual Report, Executive Minister's Report, 1972, pp. 32-62.

[3] Emmett V. Johnson, 112th Annual Report, Executive Minister's Report, 1970, p. 30.

[4] Emmett V. Johnson, *Contact*, "From Your Executive Minister," October 1971.

[5] Robert Kobielush interview, 2013.

[6] Emmett V. Johnson, *Contact*, February 1970.

[7] Emmett V. Johnson, 120th Annual Report, Executive Minister's Report, 1978, p. 53.

[8] Robert Kobielush interview, 2013.

— Chapter 9 —

The Emmett Johnson Era: The Burden of Life and Death

Delmar Dahl saves everything he has ever thought or read

In 1976, the Board of Stewards, with an unusual urgency, announced to the conference that we must provide more assistance to our MBC office staff. They recommended that Delmar Dahl be hired as the director of Christian education. Dahl had pastored throughout the Midwest and was enjoyed for his magnanimous personality. He was serving at the Elim Baptist Church in Anoka and was a willing volunteer in many areas of Minnesota's ministries.

Dahl had proven himself to the staff. He had a strong background in Christian education, church administration, and adult ministries. But he was also a detail guy, a nice match for Emmett Johnson's gift for seeing and promoting the big picture. Dahl and Johnson had collaborated on *Let's Celebrate!* At the time of its publication, Johnson commented that Dahl saved everything he had ever read or thought and had a place for it in his extensive files. His ministry would bring continuity to the conference into the early 1990s.

A history to be proud of

Both Emmett and Darlene Johnson were Finland Swedes – their ancestors immigrated from Swedish-speaking communities in Finland. Earlier called Swede-Finns, these immigrants had settled in northern Minnesota employed in mining, lumber, or by the fishing communities on the north shore of Lake Superior. They became an industrious part of northern Minnesota. In the conference, churches in Cook and Chisholm were founded by Finland Swedes.

Johnson had done his historical homework before coming into the MBC office. When reading the written reports of Johnson's predecessors, one has a feeling that references to Swedish heritage were offered cautiously. Or worse, our Swedish heritage was treated with a humorous historical caricature introduced by a smirk or a wink. Perhaps this was simply an unfortunate byproduct of the Americanization of our Swedish denomination. But Johnson would be a vital link in re-connecting the conference with its proud past. In the decades ahead, almost all models of strategic planning would include discovery of our organization's historic identity. The future must be built on the foundation of the past.

Scandia Church finds a new home

The iconic Scandia church is moved to Bethel's campus, with its steeple hinged and folded down.

At the end of 1971, funds were solicited to move the historic Scandia church building from Waconia, Minnesota, to a prominent hill above the seminary buildings on the campus of Bethel College and Seminary. Scandia was the original name for Waconia, Minnesota, and the church had retained that name. The modern village of Scandia is not connected to the old Scandia settlement in any way. Emmett Johnson, together with Warren Magnuson, drove this project which required gifts from the MBC, Bethel, the national BGC, and interested individuals. The *Minneapolis Star* published an article on the plans to move the church building on September 4, 1973, noting that "to move the church's steeple under obstructions between Waconia and Arden Hills, a section of roof including the steeple will be sliced off, hinged and lowered to rest on the church top."[1] In its new location this building has become a historical icon visibly linking Bethel and the MBC with their Swedish immigrant roots.

The district and national, wrestling as friends

Emmett Johnson was not the first Minnesota executive minister to wrestle with the district's relationship with national BGC. And he would not be the last. In 1969, Warren Magnuson left the pastorate of Central in St. Paul to become the general secretary of the Baptist General Conference, replacing Lloyd Dahlquist. Magnuson brought the same strong leadership to the BGC that he had provided as pastor in Willmar and at Central. Magnuson and Johnson – two Minnesota pastors – entered into their strategic positions of leadership in the same year.

Magnuson came into his position with a clear expectation of where he wished to take the conference. He proposed a global vision which stated that the conference departments and districts would be expected to cooperate. This cooperative vision would require the setting of goals for each conference entity. The boards and districts would be expected to provide reports on their progress.

Magnuson saw himself as a team leader for the cause. To implement the vision of the new leader, the BGC's Special Committee on Organizational Relationships (SCOR) recommended constitutional changes in which the BGC Trustees were empowered "to receive reports and review objectives from each department, division and district."[2] The recommendation continued by saying that the BGC board would be empowered to make adjustments to each entity's objectives, including the districts.

The newly elected executive minister of the autonomous Minnesota district was stunned. Emmett Johnson saw this as a move to usurp district autonomy. The board empowered Johnson to speak against the constitutional change at the June 1971 BGC annual meeting, but the controversial wording was removed by the BGC leadership before the meeting convened. However, this would not be the last time the Minnesota district would wrangle with its national counterparts over organizational alignments.

To his credit, General Secretary Magnuson would not give up on the complex relationship between national and district BGC entities. He realized that if there were no authority relationships between national and district, there needed to be cooperative relationships. During this period, Magnuson and the trustees created a District Advisory Council (DAC). Later just called the DEMS (district executive ministers) this group would be an effective cooperative link between the district and national levels of BGC organization. They would meet regularly with department heads and the president. They would formulate strategic plans with home missions.

The Minnesota conference had fully participated in the BGC LIFT capital campaign in 1961. In 1970, the national conference similarly organized Mission Share. As the campaign unfolded, Minnesota churches contributed more than a million dollars of the $3 million campaign – 21% of the population of the conference contributing 33% of its income. Johnson would ask for financial considerations based on Minnesota's outstanding response. He would write that he was seeking "a more viable working relationship with the Baptist General Conference."[3]

Church planters, more of a fellowship group than an action group

Dick Turnwall was a wise and solid complement to the torrid leadership of Johnson. They were clearly on the same page in the district's history. The new associate minister of missions observed in his 1973 annual report that his committee, the church extension committee, "once primarily an action group, was now more of a fellowship group." He seemed pleased that this needed fellowship was evolving in the group. He proposed that the conference start one new church in 1974. The goal of "at least one church a year" was repeated by Johnson and Turnwall during these years.[4] Although there would be significant expansions in many areas in Minnesota missions, it would become clear that starting new churches was not a passionately held staff goal. After all, as had been stated, this was the "second missionary journey." We were more about building up the church in this era.

Passion for starting churches increased toward the end of Johnson's tenure. Missions committee members remembered meetings being very staff-directed. There was lots of discussion on the few projects that were in the works. Later they remember Johnson crashing the party, coming into the meeting at the end with an almost desperate frustration. "Can't we start a couple new churches this year? Just tell me why not."[5]

The church growth movement was gaining a larger audience. Donald McGavran's book *Bridges of God* had been published in 1955. Its principles were going to produce radically new approaches to world evangelization in the following decades. Church growth principles were emerging in American evangelicalism in many denominations. Fuller Seminary and the School of World Missions became a center for such studies. C. Peter Wagner became its next guru. Lyle Schaller began studying denominations in the light of church growth. Dick Turnwall began to examine church growth in the Minnesota Baptist Conference. "We have more churches; we give more money but we are baptizing fewer converts....742 in 1962 and 689 in 1972...4.2 baptisms per 100 members in 1962 and 3.2 baptisms per 100 members in 1972."[6]

Another disturbing marker came when Keith McConnell reported district Sunday school statistics in the annual report of the Christian education committee. Two thirds of our churches had decreasing Sunday school attendance. "Have we come to the end of the Sunday School Era?" he asked. "No!" The answer came from a few churches who had joined the bus ministry era, led by the example of "Brother" Jack Hyles from First Baptist in Hammond, Indiana. A few Minnesota conference churches found busing neighborhood children to Sunday school to be an effective way of reaching children and families. Rev. Dick Wiens led Emmanuel in Mora in this direction, as did Lester Fair in Hastings. Busing was not broadly accepted in the conference. The lack of church growth did remain an ongoing discussion. In 1970, the district conference leadership began forming plans to emphasize church growth in the district.

Gains and losses as the church growth movement arrives

In 1975, the Minnesota Baptist Conference would embrace the new vision of General Secretary Warren Magnuson. The Baptist General Conference in all departments and districts would prepare to "Double in a Decade." The church growth movement would be expressed as a conference-wide goal.

There were financial preparations that went along with the challenge to grow. In 1972, the MBC created a Grant Fund intended to assist churches with special expansion projects. It was funded by loan income from BGC and MBC bequests. The MBC had been burdened by the long-term policy of providing regular subsidies to small churches. In the early 1950s, it was still providing monthly subsidies for 30 to 40 churches. By the Emmett Johnson era, the number was half that (13 churches in 1975), and the BGC contributed half of the grant. The Grant Fund was a step away from monthly support to churches. Churches could apply for one-time grants.

The MBC lost its two Canadian-member congregations (Fort Francis and Sprague, Manitoba) as the Canadian BGC organized as its own national denomination. Although the Bethel Center urban experiment had expired, urban and ethnic opportunities continued to rise. In the summer of 1971, Bethlehem assisted in the formation of the first Spanish-speaking church in Minneapolis. The church was welcomed into the conference in the October 1973 annual meeting. Few would have recognized how important this first step into the Latino community would be.

The group foster home at North St. Paul continued operations with Roland and Rosemary Schearer. The MBC coordinated the Bethel Student Missionary Project which focused on ministries in the White Earth and Red Lake Reservations. The Family Counseling Ministry was now located in the new MBC center, directed by Jerry Dahl, a psychologist from Edgewater church. New interracial links were formed. A triad committee coordinated ministry opportunities between Edgewater Minneapolis and Ebenezer Baptist in South Minneapolis. Elim in Minneapolis did the same with Mt. Vernon Baptist Church. North Central Baptist in Frogtown had a Free Food Day, delivering food and clothing to 50 families and 100 individuals, assisted by Central Baptist, Oak Hill, and Pillager. The MBC assisted North Central by providing financial support for hiring youth pastor Doug Gordh, a seminarian who would develop a youth ministry numbering more than 40 in the church.

Two plane crashes in Native American ministries, one devastating

In the early 1970s, Ed Viron resigned his ministry in Grand Portage after 19 years of work in Native American ministries. Viron and Wally Olson had purchased a float plane with another investor, and were using it to visit more remote tribes such as the Lac La Croix band and the Nipigon areas of Ontario. An unfortunate plane crash took no lives but ended the effort.

Another crash was far more devastating. In late August of 1971, three leaders in the Grand Portage band of Ojibwa crashed, including William (Bucko) Bushman who had held important leadership positions in the band and who was vital to the church's work with native people in Grand Portage. It was 12 years before the site of their crash was even discovered. An Ojibwa game, handmade by Bucko, is displayed by the park service in Grand Portage. In late 1971, John and Dorthea Olson began their ministry at Mt. Rose.

Wally and Shirley Olson continued their efforts to build a Christian Native American community in the Twin Cities. Nett Lake struggled. Doug and Jan Green came to help as summer interns. The goodwill that the Olsons had left was strong, but the body of believers there was weak. Leonard Fineday, a Native American from Squaw Lake, became the pastor. Tragedy stuck the small Christian community in 1973 when the home of Axel and Millie Holmes was totally destroyed by a fire. Bethany of St. Paul and other churches gave major relief to the Holmes, who lost everything.

A miraculous work of God in the lives of Fred and Anna Isham had taken place at Nett Lake. The Ishams were baptized in Fred's canoe in October 1973. The canoe was placed in the front of the church for the service. It was not a gimmick. It was a profound testimony of a man who, through his Native American ways, would deeply affect the witness of Christ at Nett Lake and in the Minnesota conference. Cross-cultural ministries of the Minnesota Baptist Conference gained strength through the 1970s.

A chapel house becomes the standard

Attendance at annual meetings remained near the 500 mark each year. The "Mighty Minnesota Quarter" was raising more money for district ministries. Bethlehem, Central, Trinity, Calvary, and Edgewater were the top contributing churches during these years. Possible extension sights were identified in Rochester, Mankato, St. Cloud, and North Branch. In 1975, the district called Robert Dischinger to start a new church in East Bethel. The birth announcement was placed in *Contact* with these words: "The Minnesota Baptist Conference is back in the church extension business again."[7]

A chapel house was constructed in East Bethel. Although it seemed to be a progressive idea at the time, it would not be an enduring model. The plan was to design a first unit which would be converted into a family home as the church grew. Perhaps it would be used as the pastor's parsonage or sold as a single family home at the time that the church was relocating to a larger facility. The new church in Lakeville (Koinonia) would replicate the East Bethel plan. Dick Turnwall announced that this house/church plan was now the standard for all new works in Minnesota. This announcement has a between-the-lines message. The "plan" must have also been that these new churches would grow slowly,

Providing a Serious Look in the Mirror

Pastors have various ways of remaining fresh and focused while facing the pressures of ministry. One pastor reported that he would page through the help wanted ads in the Sunday paper and think to himself, "I could do that job." He said it made him feel that, although he could successfully do many things, he was choosing to be in ministry.

In 1973 the Minnesota Baptist Conference became a covenant partner with the North Central Ministry Development Center (NCMDC). Since its founding in 1970, the center had pioneered an effective psychological and vocational assessment with counseling. In order to provide these valuable professional services to MBC pastors, the district committed annually to a significant number of full scholarships. Of course the center also was vital for pastors in conflict, in transition or trouble. But the MBC staff boldly promoted the assessment as an intentional look in the mirror that could make a good ministry better.

as these chapel houses were hardly able to accommodate 100 worshipers.

Tragedy struck the East Bethel church as Dischinger died suddenly, leaving wife Virginia and their large family without a husband and father. The church attempted to move on with another pastor but eventually closed. The building was sold. Ginny was an extraordinarily bright light for the MBC as she remained a cherished member.

Later in the Emmett Johnson era, Olivia and Grand Forks were prepared for church planting. For someone who studies these things, one cannot help but notice that in the Johnson/Turnwall era, the district office was back as the main player in the church planting business. The district was buying property in East Bethel and Grand Forks, even building buildings, but none of this contributed greatly to the success of church planting in those sites.

Grandview Christian Home, from expansion to crisis

Grandview Christian Home was a pioneering institution in the Minnesota Baptist Conference. Its presence in the quiet little town of

Cambridge, full of conference Baptists, would lead to many perceptions. Jerry Sheveland would later quip when someone talked about an upcoming retirement in the national office that, "Yes, he's close to the decision to move to Cambridge." Retirement meant moving to Cambridge.

But in 1973 Grandview, which had started out with an extraordinary flurry of energy, faced its first crisis. Orville Johnson, who had grown up in the area and pastored Minnesota churches, had effectively led the institution since 1961. Marian, his wife, was a nurse. Together they were a caring symbol for a Christian facility. In the early 1970s, Grandview built a nursing home addition to their facility in Cambridge. This addition, however, required a *Certificate of Need* from the State of Minnesota. Grandview had failed to apply for this certificate before it began to build.

In the 1960s, nursing homes and hospitals were being overbuilt. State and federal reimbursements made them very profitable. To control this proliferation, the states cooperated with the federal government to require state approval through regional boards before building. Minnesota put into place this required step in 1971. A *Certificate of Need* was not so much a license to operate as a building permit for this kind of nursing home facility. The fact that Grandview had gone ahead with its nursing home building without this certificate was a serious violation.

Grandview was in serious financial peril. Skilled nursing type rooms were not designed for other levels of care, so these rooms were producing no income to offset their expense. Additionally, the overwhelmed Grandview board, unable to manage this crisis itself, was forced to hire consultants and lawyers to influence the appeal for the *Certificate of Need*.

Deeply concerned, the MBC placed Oliver Kronholm as the home's administrator on the board and proposed that a management committee be established by the Board of Stewards to solve its legal and financial problems. There is little doubt that Grandview was being taught a lesson by the authorities for its brash building project. It is also true that Grandview may have been victimized by a St. Cloud-based board, eager to consolidate healthcare in their region. But in December 1975 Grandview was granted a *Certificate of Need*, a relief to everyone. Daniel Bolhouse would become Grandview's CEO and bring financial stability.

In the meantime, Twin Cities Christian Homes was having its own challenges. Underfunded, it was unsure how to implement its vision. It was looking seriously for an existing nursing home to purchase, as it was very difficult to get a *Certificate of Need* to build one. It was considering various government-assisted senior housing programs. In 1977, these inquiries got a warning from the Stewards that if they were to receive federal funding for their proposed facility, there would be issues with the policies of the conference. Federal funding was an issue of grave concern for the conference as it crossed a line in the separation of church and state.

The Kobielush era begins

Camping was entering a period of expansion. Bob Kobielush was hired in 1972 based on his excellent leadership potential. He was youth pastor at Trinity in St. Paul and was a strong supporter and participant in Trout's program. Bob grew up in north central Wisconsin, raised by his mother and extended family. He and his brothers all went to Bethel College and were exceptional young men. As a youth, Bob's spiritual life was profoundly affected by a life commitment he made at Forest Springs Camp in Wisconsin. This experience left him with a hidden dream of becoming part of Christian camping. After college, he entered Bethel Seminary but not to become a pastor. Bob's dream would require a theological education. An overwhelming number of Christian camp directors in the early years of camping were seminary trained pastors.

When Trout Lake Camp's director position became available, Bob did not apply, convinced that he lacked the necessary experience to lead a camp. Pastor Bill Hamren, the chair of the search committee, saw it differently. Hamren asked Bob to apply. Bob Kobielush today remains amazed that he got the job. "I figure they liked me in spite of the fact that I probably showed up in my leather moccasins and afro hairdo."[8] Bob invested 10 years in Minnesota conference camping and went on to become a part of Christian Camping International (CCI). He eventually became the CEO. In 2002, he was chosen Bethel University's Alumnus of the Year.

In 1972, Trout Lake had 3,210 youth campers and staff, as well as many hundreds of retreat attendees. The next years would bring strong expansion of ministries in camping. There was significant experimentation with camping methodologies. Although Trout Lake was always the central ministry in Minnesota camping, several area fellowships were operating their own camping programs and Minnesota camping always sought to encourage them.

Mink Lake, unique and adventurous

One of those camps, Mink Lake Camp near Grand Marais, had been operated by the south arrowhead area and was given to the MBC in 1965. It was included under the camping operation in 1966. Kobielush, in his first report, refers to Mink as "a camp of the future with the demands for a unique and adventurous camping experience…but which currently, except for its novelty, is not sufficient to capture the attention of the youth."[9] Mink Lake would be developed.

Phil Bjork invested himself in Mink Lake during the Kobielush years. Dale and Alma Bjork had returned to Minnesota after their missions career in China was cut short by the communist takeover. They re-entered life in the Cambridge area and their family became part of conference life. Their children would contribute in amazing ways. Phil Bjork entered into developing Mink Lake camp. Strong loyalties among the staff and campers developed, in spite of modest numerical gains. Phil developed a leadership program with Bethel College and Mink. However, in spite of its successes, Mink remained a financial burden to the overall camping program.

Kobielush, in the same 1972 report, announced "trip camping." Minnesota was moving offsite with new youth adventures. Campers had alternative camping opportunities such as backpack trips to Isle Royale or canoe and rock climbing adventures in the BWCA. Considering that the conference would approve the building of Shalom House on the Trout property in 1974, this was indeed a period of expansion for camping.

Adjacent land, a hope and a future

King's Ranch, the 71-acre site near Cambridge, had been purchased for $35,000 as Minnesota's third camping location. However, the location did not seem to satisfy the vision for an adult retreat center. Youth groups who rented it rarely returned. It was sold in 1974, as unviable.

In the fall of 1971, the conference was able to purchase 40 acres of adjacent land across the bay at Trout Lake. Called the Seaquist Property, the conference men quickly raised a $4,500 down payment on the $12,000 cost, and finished off its purchase through Men's Retreat offerings in the next years. In 1975, an additional 80 acres of wooded land and hiking trails came up for sale behind the Seaquist Property. It contained the highest point in Ideal Township. Professor Russell Johnson surveyed the land and declared it a unique asset to Trout. It included a defunct ski hill with a tiny warming house. It was purchased by the conference for $29,900, but no one could then foresee how important the property would become in the new millennium. Bob and Karl Smith redesigned an old rope tow on the hill to invite winter adventurers. Every year Russ Johnson took men on nature hikes through the property. Children rode its trails on horseback.

These land purchases must be seen as powerful steps of faith. The Minnesota conference was building a new office center. It was planning to build a new adult retreat center, and yet it stood by Trout, when adjacent land became available. Bob Kobielush recalls being introduced numerous times by Emmett Johnson as he asked for financial support to purchase these properties. "As far as I know," Johnson would say, "God is not making any more land….and we all also know that you cannot pay too much for adjacent land when it comes available."[10] Johnson's endorsement and Kobielush's excitement always made a sale.

Upgrades at Trout, but more is needed

Upgrades in the Trout Lake village continued. A soda fountain from the Falcon Heights drug store was purchased and installed on a site below the dining hall. Expanded recreational programming, such as horsemanship, was introduced. Camp activities were redesigned to fit the different interests of individual campers. In the past, the church group was the epicenter of the camp and the pattern of cabin assignments. Under Kobielush, there was an effort to serve individual interests and yet maintain and develop a sense of community in the cabin, beyond any church connections. Kobielush's youth director background helped him to strengthen the large group energy in chapel, and in all-camp games. In the 1970s, lead counselors were hired for the summer season. This too was a move toward a changing future. Volunteer counselors needed accountability and training. Eventually the camp would realize that volunteer counselors would present too many risks to the camping program.

Trout saw annual increases in attendance throughout the mid-1970s. Mink increased in numbers modestly as well. Mink developed a fierce group of loyal staff, committed to its unique brand of camping. Trip camping was a growing edge but proved too expensive. Camping found that it could partner with the churches in outfitting their trips into the Boundary Waters.

In 1979, Kobielush took his best people and put together a Master Site Development Plan with the help of a consultant and a planning committee. His leadership strengths were attracting a strong group of people, some of whom had cut their teeth in ministry at Trout. The Long Range Planning Committee would include Roy Anderson, Phil Bjork, Maynard Frost, Bill Malam, Don Sension, Marilyn Starr, Bob Swanson, Howard Wallin, and Kobielush himself. Paul Olson had been on the camping staff in recreational programming and was giving leadership to the camp committee. This committee's work would test the vision of the conference in a way it had never been tested before.

That same year Shalom House became available but brought a serious operational deficit in its first year of operations. Overall attendance figures took a slight drop. Women's retreats saw a downturn in numbers. Church rentals did not meet expectations. Camping was in a challenging situation, having to manage an economic downturn at a time when it was also making serious commitments to facility expansion.

Emmett Johnson and Bob Kobielush provided extraordinary leadership to the district's programs. These accomplishments are all the more stunning in the light of the personal and health challenges being faced daily in the lives of office staff. After all, this was a decade of death.

The decade of death

In the late 60s, Emmett Johnson was diagnosed with Hodgkin's disease, a cancer of the lymphatic system. At that time, the required treatment was to surgically remove the severely affected areas and to undergo radiation to stop the progression of the cancer from node to node. Eight years later, while still in office, Johnson had a recurrence of Hodgkin's. It was a severe relapse that required more extensive surgery and more damaging radiation and chemotherapy.

In the spring of 1976, Johnson's wife Darlene was diagnosed with cancer and began radiation and chemotherapy also. With serious hopes, and regular setbacks, Darlene ("my lover of 25 years, my honest critic and best friend") ended her struggle at the close of the year.[11] Her memorial service was held on December 30, 1976. Johnson saw the loss of Darlene through the eyes of his son, Keith, a first year dental student. He is "the strong one in the family these days," Johnson added. As a lad, Keith had experienced loss when his dog Andy ran away. After much praying, Andy surprised everyone by coming home. Now, of course, they both knew that Darlene would not come back. But they also knew that God's grace would be sufficient for them.[12]

A staff member remembers the energy and fun of working at the MBC in the Johnson days. She also remembers the many days when, without a word, Johnson came in to his office and closed his door, unable to deal with the personal burdens, loss, and confusion in his life at that particular time. Another staff member recalls that Johnson had always been a bit intimidating to work for. You might, at any time, be called into the office to be told what you were doing right and what you were doing wrong. In his later years, there would be memories of his impatience with people and his frustration with those who opposed him, particularly his fundamentalist friends. It was the beginning of the end. To some of his closest friends he would confess that he wondered if he had outgrown the conference. That perhaps his talents could better be contributed elsewhere.

Our Give and Take with the American Baptists

There is no doubt that the conference owes much to the Northern Baptist Convention (the American Baptists). Like a mother hen, they assisted in our birth as a denomination and nudged us along in our growth. They financially supported many of our Swedish-American church planters and international missionaries. Our separation from the ABC is remembered as painful to many.

But down the road of separation, there was genuine return of talent from the conference to the ABC. When Emmett Johnson left the Minnesota conference, he became national director of evangelism for the ABC. He later assumed responsibility for their church planting programs. He initiated *Ministry of Caring, Kerygma, Inviting New Neighbors* and *ABC-Find.* Another outstanding American Baptist leader, John A. Sundquist, also had conference roots. John was first a district executive in the ABC and then, in the late 80s, led *Alive in Missions,* the largest missions fund campaign in the denomination's history. He served as executive director of the ABC Board of International Ministries from 1990 to 2003.

In 1970, Dick Turnwall and Emmett Johnson had been asked by the Board of Stewards to agree to a proposed Board policy limiting tenure for a Minnesota executive to two five-year terms. Both agreed. Johnson resigned in December 1978, effective March 1979. He was called by the American Baptists to provide national leadership in evangelism. The two-term policy was later eliminated with Bob Kobielush's continued tenure in mind.

The conference too had its sharp edges

The conference too had its sharp edges at this time. Johnson was passionate about his theological and social platform. Social conservatism was on the rise in many evangelical churches. Ecumenism, the Baptist World Alliance, the separation of church and state, and prayer in the school were controversial issues. Johnson had the strength and persuasive ability to pretty much get his way. But that often left his conservative pastoral colleagues angry.

In 1978, almost reflecting Emmett Johnson's suffering, Scott Peck published *A Road Less Traveled*. He begins with the words, "Life is difficult." In the book he unfolds the power of love in relationships during difficult times. Emmett Johnson would not disagree with Peck's observations. Life was difficult but love would overcome. "His grace is sufficient for us."

Earlier, in 1973, after an eight-month struggle with cancer, Lindon B. Karo had died in the prime of his life while pastoring Salem church in New Brighton. "He left his church for the last time," Emmett Johnson eulogized. He also left Nancy, his wife, and three children. In the next years, Nancy recorded her journey in her book *Adventure in Dying*, published in 1976. Her ministry to the grieving during that period was profound.

The blessing side of sharing this story is that Emmett and Nancy, two souls adrift with the loss of their spouses, found each other. In November 1977, Johnson wrote: "a pretty, vivacious, high energy widow knew the way I had taken…one day I fell in love."[13]

Although there was surprise and a measure of confusion among some of the people of the district when they learned of this courtship, eventually Emmett and Nancy were married and enjoyed many happy years of marriage together – a testimony to God's continuing grace.

Notes

1 *Minneapolis Star*, quote by David Guston in "Happenings," Tuesday, September 4, 1973, p. 1b.

2 Proposed Trustee Bylaw Change, Article II, "Conference Organization," A,c, "Duties" (1).

3 Emmett V. Johnson, 113th Annual Report, Executive Minister's Report, 1971, p. 29.

4 Emmett V. Johnson, 116th Annual Reports, Executive Minister's Report, 1974, p. 35.

5 Truett M. Lawson, author's recollection.

6 Richard Turnwall, 115th Annual Report, Mission Director's Report, 1973.

7 *Contact,* February, 1975.

8 Robert Kobielush interview, 2013.

9 Robert Kobielush, Annual Report, 1972.

10 Robert Kobielush interview, 2013.

11 Emmett V. Johnson, 119th Annual Report, Executive Minister's Report, 1977, p. 44.

12 Emmett V. Johnson, *Contact*, January 1977.

13 Emmett V. Johnson, *Contact*, November 1977.

Churches Started or Welcomed: 1970-1979

1971
First Spanish (Minneapolis)
Baptist Fellowship (Marshall)

1975
Basswood Baptist
Friendship Baptist (East Bethel)

1976
East Grand Forks

1977
Stillwater
Olivia
Midway (St. Paul)
Maple Grove
St. Cloud

1978
Friendship Baptist Church
   (Prior Lake)

— Chapter 10 —

The Dick Turnwall Era (1979-1984): With a View to Kingdom Growth

A serious mood for a new beginning

On July 13, 1979, the Board of Stewards met at newly dedicated Shalom House for an unprecedented two-day meeting. Leading the group was the newly elected executive minister William Richard Turnwall. The atmosphere among the leaders of the MBC was hardly what one would expect on the inaugural year of a new Minnesota executive. Board chair Roger Camerer described the mood of the day as he considered

After serving as missions director, Dick Turnwall stepped into executive leadership.

the events of the year in his annual report. "Finally, I want to share a burden that the Stewards, Dick Turnwall, Delmar Dahl, and Bob Kobielush all share. It is the concern that we have not done all that we could as Minnesota Baptist Conference churches for the cause of Jesus Christ. The spiritual fervor of our conference is the collective impact of each of us. We have asked ourselves as Stewards if our collective concern for the cause of Jesus Christ is starting to wane. While the evidence may be mixed at this point…the greatest need is for faith to believe God for the impossible."[1]

Certain factors contributed to these serious thoughts for the staff and board. There had been internal fractures in the office, one leading to the resignation of Oliver Kronholm. Emmett Johnson's final years had many challenges, to say the least. There was existing debt from the building of the conference's new center. The men's brotherhood had failed to fund the purchase of Trout's adjacent camp property which added more debt. The expansion of programs and facilities had brought operational debts. Now the board was facing the grim reality that due to a contractor's financial problems in building Shalom House, this project also would bring a significant new debt to the conference.

But to listen to the words of Roger Camerer and others during this period, the shortfall that seemed to be worrying leaders was more than operational debt. One is mindful of the adage that leaders carry the pain of an organization. There was a sense that the extraordinary two decades of ministry expansion that the Minnesota Baptist Conference had experienced seemed to be ebbing away. The search for answers to this burden was turning thoughts inward. What is wrong with us? Have we lost our spiritual energy or our passion to see kingdom growth? These questions would create an uncomfortable itch during the Turnwall era that would continue to the very end.

A member of the Executive Minister Search Committee recalls the committee's work. "Yes, we looked outside of the district for our next leader, but as we looked, we became more and more convinced that we had our next leader in Dick Turnwall. When you have a man of this quality on the staff who wants the position, that person becomes your number one candidate."[2] W. Richard Turnwall was an intense, spiritual man. He was now elected to the most challenging leadership role in his ministry life. Without question, for Turnwall, one must begin such a challenge on one's knees in an attitude of prayer.

As Turnwall was being installed in his new position, Professor J. Edwin Orr was retiring from the faculty of the Schools of World Missions at Fuller Seminary. Both Orr and Turnwall were Baptist historians. Orr gave his life to the study of Christian revival. He documented American and European revivals, and during his lifetime challenged the church to pray for and expect revival. Turnwall would cite Orr's findings on spiritual revival.

Orr's foundational thesis was that all of the Christian revivals had started with two ingredients – prayer and confession. The words of

Chairman Camerer were no doubt part of Turnwall's journey. If you believe that your people need revival, you begin your journey and theirs with prayer and contrition. With this humility, the power of God can bring transformation.

William and William, a family legacy

William Richard Turnwall, or "Dick," was born in Gowrie, Iowa, to Rev. William and Nettie Turnwall. His father was a pastor. With the same first names, the family called dad "Bill" and son "Dick." Many of the conference's excellent leaders after WWII were the sons and daughters of pastors. Bill Turnwall was elected Home Mission's director for the Baptist General Conference in 1945 and served until his retirement in 1962. He can fairly be described as the architect and builder of the second wave of BGC growth. The conference under Bill Turnwall saw a 50% increase in the number of churches, and a 70% increase in membership. Dick Turnwall enjoyed this family legacy, as he also enjoyed the Swedish Baptist history that produced him. He, like Emmett Johnson before him, felt good in both his Baptist and Swedish skin.

Dick and Marge (Johnson) found each other in Duluth. After Turnwall completed advanced theological degrees from Bethel and Wheaton, the couple served churches in Hartford, Conn., and Moline, Ill. At the time of his call to join the district leadership, he was serving Salem Baptist in New Brighton where he was the founding pastor. Turnwall was called to join the staff of the Minnesota Baptist Conference by Emmett Johnson. He served for nine years in missions until his election as executive minister in 1979.

In 1979, newly elected executive minister Dick Turnwall was working through a challenging Doctor of Ministries program in organizational leadership. He used the July Steward's meeting as an opportunity to sharpen his planning skills. A new mission statement was adopted and moved forward for conference approval.

The Minnesota Baptist Conference exists to link together its constituent churches. Its mission is to anticipate and identify needs in the churches, and to develop services by which those needs can be met.

Somewhat surprisingly, this first expression of the mission says very little about church planting or camping. This statement would be expanded in 1981 with more precision.

*The Minnesota Baptist Conference is a district association in fellowship with the Baptist General Conference. The mission of the Minnesota Baptist Conference is fourfold. It is to **link** its member churches in terms of shared values, inter-church fellowship and communication. It is to **activate** its member churches, both the lay and clergy leaders, through consultations, seminars and workshops. It is to **initiate** new churches by means of providing skilled leadership, financial assistance and meaningful information. It is to **facilitate** programs for evangelism, training and recreation through its camping and retreat ministries.*

This statement is indeed comprehensive. Some of the well-chosen words ("link," "activate," and "initiate") would survive well into the MBC's future.

A comprehensive planning process ends with a question

It was apparent already, that Dick Turnwall had a passion to analyze, classify, and articulate with precision. At his 1979 planning retreat, Stewards brainstormed 34 needs, but selected five as most important. The MBC needed to develop cooperative local activities focusing on evangelism, outreach, witness, ministry, and church extension; to develop cooperative activities and resources for personal and spiritual development, and renewal; to work with search committees in pastoral calling and pastoral supervision; to help churches recruit, train, and supervise lay administrative leaders; and to provide information resources, such as "how to," "where to find it," and "how do we compare?"

These five driving needs would be noted by Turnwall in his annual report in November 1979. His statement acknowledged God's direction in the conference. "We are a God-directed organization with a spiritual mandate to link and to activate churches, to initiate new churches, and to develop programs, facilities and staff in order to resource the above," he wrote.[3]

Dick Turnwall's conceptual work on the mission of the MBC was enfolded into a board handbook which, in the main, would endure for the next generation for training and orienting new Stewards.

In spite of what appears to be good group process, the year of long range planning appears to have raised an unanswered question with the Board of Stewards. In the Stewards' report, the concern was summarized with a question. "How can we say we care about these matters (church planting), if we do not have an associate minister whose basic job is to lead the district in the meeting of this need?"[4] This was indeed the "itch" that would not be satisfied until the end of the Turnwall era when Neal Floberg was hired as the Associate Minister of Evangelism and Church Extension.

In his first executive report, Turnwall laid out his leadership commitments, missional plans, and biblical convictions. But then, with evident pain, he reveals a burden and a frustration. "I want you to look at some of the problems with which we are trying to cope. There is a set of problems that share the common denominator of expectations and their fulfillment. These problems show up as interpersonal conflicts. I have intervened in several such situations…"[5] Executive Turnwall then went on to find the source of these problems in unrealistic expectations and eroding values and standards in ministry. At this early stage in his tenure, Turnwall felt the brokenness of both his congregations and his pastors. He found himself in irresolvable pastor/church conflicts. He may have been overwhelmed by it. Many district workers have found pastor/church mediation to be the most exhausting part of leading a denominational district.

Gathering around the mission to serve churches

In the years to come, the Turnwall era saw the conference gather around the mission of serving churches. Turnwall personally sought to provide learning opportunities for pastors. Emmett Johnson's personal strength had put him in a position above pastors. He sought to advise and mentor pastors. One senses a somewhat different motivation in Turnwall's approach to pastors. In his opening annual report, Turnwall salutes the pastors, dedicating them with these words: "Together we can become colleagues at a much higher level of significance than we have known before."[6] The MBC's financial environment was tight, so there were fewer funds available to help pastors. But Turnwall still saw the MBC contributing to pastors by gathering them together. He saw his role as coming alongside pastors.

A significant Turnwall initiative was the reconfiguration of the Pastors' Association. Emmett Johnson had convened this group but Turnwall would take it to a new level. Advocacy for pastors was new to the conference, although the pastors' organization was more symbolic than functional in its early years. With Turnwall's re-design, the 12 area pastors' fellowships each selected a representative for the district Pastors' Council. The council met regularly through the year and worked with district staff on issues related to pastors and ministry.

In the first years of its organization, the Pastors' Association through its Pastors' Council produced a studied approach to the ordination of ministers called *Policies and Procedures for Ordination*. Johnson had done significant work on ordination in his Doctor of Ministries degree at Luther Seminary. Turnwall and the Pastors' Council would put those ideas into guiding procedures in the district. The Pastors' Council would be an effective working group in the Minnesota Baptist Conference for many years to come. The Minnesota district would set an example of excellence in ordination procedure.

The new facility of Shalom House was providing the district with expanded opportunities to serve pastors. During the winter, the MBC and camping would provide a midweek escape at Shalom called Pastor's Study Break. This time was intentionally unstructured, and many pastors took the opportunity to catch up on some reading or plan a sermon series. The MBC continued to sponsor an annual pastors' retreat. The MBC staff would also target younger pastors in a Timothy Retreat. Recipe for Renewal was a retreat for pastors' wives. The number of pastors' wives in the workplace was increasing significantly. For many wives, in the years to come, Recipe for Renewal provided valued support and encouragement in their lives and ministries.

Stretching staff in cautious times

Delmar Dahl had been added to the staff by Emmett Johnson in 1976. His primary function was to work with churches in evangelism and Christian education. Dahl's interpersonal skills made him a valuable asset for any leader who wanted to stay in touch with his constituency. He had a large "Rolodex," as they would have said. When Turnwall became executive minister, Dahl was assigned new responsibilities in church development – a shoe that did not quite fit him. Through this period, Dahl would report that he had been assigned to church planting because there were not adequate funds to hire a church extension director. Now the "itch" was delivering some discomfort.

In 1981, Turnwall expressed appreciation for the observations he received from the Personnel Committee on the occasion of Dahl's five-year evaluation. He then quoted Chairman Dwight Jessup and the Minnesota Task Force who suggested that Dahl "should return to Christian education only."[7] Dahl was the epicenter of Shalom House programming. For Dahl, church extension was in the class of "other duties as assigned."

Truett Lawson was pastoring Elim Baptist in Isanti at this time. He met a young lay couple from the Milaca church at an "East Central Town Meeting." Mark and Sherrie Krueger lived in Princeton, and the Kruegers and Lawsons began to talk about starting a church. After several weeks of Bible studies in the Kruegers' home, four key couples were enlisted and services were started in a nearby dinner club. Lawson led the services for three months and the group became viable. In a meeting with Delmar Dahl, the new work was handed over to the MBC for supervision. Dahl was thrilled. Frank and Shannah Evans were called to pastor the Princeton work.

In many ways, this model was replicating the classical model of starting churches in the conference. A pastor looks over the fence at the next town, which had no church. But it also represented a methodology that exploded in the 90s, where churches, not denominational offices, would become the incubators for the formation of new churches. In his report in 1981, an overjoyed Dahl expressed his feelings. "Twenty-five years ago I was hoping that I could have a part in the formation of a new church in Princeton." Dahl had been a pastor in Milaca. "That dream has been fulfilled and it is a good feeling!"[8]

Why does God allow us to come so close?

In 1981, a task force within the Board of Stewards recommended that the MBC have three separate staff departments and executives: camping, church extension (new churches) and Christian education. In 1982, Chairman Dennis Mattson confessed, "One of the most difficult struggles for the board this past year was relative to the calling of an Associate Minister of Extension."[9] He then attributed the Stewards' failure to act on this recommendation to poor support from the churches and MBC budget constraints. "Why does God allow us to come so close to calling an individual and then give us direction to delay the addition to our staff?" But there was another accruing deficit. The board's ambivalence reflected negatively on the leadership of Dick Turnwall and Chairman Mattson.

In the 1982 Annual Meeting in Minnetonka, the failure to hire additional staff in church planting provoked a motion from the floor. Mark Coleman, a pastor from Mount of Olives in Duluth, brought a resolution called *New Beginnings*. If the Stewards did not feel that the employment of a full-time church development staff member was possible, might they consider using consultants? Rev. Coleman's resolution called for three consultants. The first would assist urban churches to work more effectively in their neighborhoods. Another would provide research for the MBC on possible church planting locations in the state. A third would be hired as an evangelism strategist to spend two months a year providing training to church leaders in evangelism strategies. No doubt stunned at this unusual approach to the need, the conference tabled the action and then removed it from the table without conference action. Interestingly, Rev. Coleman's recommendations would mirror the district's staff pattern in the 90s. Practitioner pastors and laymen with special skills were often employed by the district with an annual stipend instead of a salary.

On February 15, 1983, Rev. Neal Floberg started his ministry as associate minister of Evangelism and Church Extension. But a growing number of MBC constituents would attribute the delay in this hire to a lack of conference leadership. For 14 years, the Minnesota conference seemed to have lost the required ingredients to start new churches. Several of the new churches that were initiated during the period would not survive. One cannot point to lack of financial support as a reason. Many of these churches were generously provided with land and pastoral salary grants. The district simply could not find a clear path to church planting success.

The notable exception to these observations was Doyle Van Gelder and Friendship Church in Prior Lake. Coming out of the Bloomington and Burnsville churches, Prior Lake was a carefully selected site of great opportunity. This project had a mother church. It had a gifted pastor, passionate in his spiritual message and driven in his leadership. Within a year, they were in a building and growing at a very fast rate. Friendship Church was a model for next generation church plants in the Minnesota Baptist Conference.

Wally and Shirley Olson and a quarter century of Indian partnerships

Wally and Shirley Olson were honored at the 1982 Baptist General Conference Annual Meeting in San Diego. They had completed 25 years of service to Native American people. On April 30, 1977, at the age of 60, Fred Isham of Nett Lake (who was baptized in his canoe) was ordained to become the pastor of the Nett Lake Church. It was a great moment for the Bois Forte Reservation and the native church. A leader had been born spiritually and organizationally from within the church.

Gene and Bonnie Mitchell were helping at Grand Portage. Pastor Ron Menges was ministering at the Red Lake reservation, but without compensation. Each year, five to eight MBC churches sent teams to work with projects on the reservations. Vacation Bible School programs were held on the reservations each summer.

Lac La Croix had welcomed Wally Olson and Ed Viron in 1959. In the 70s, a new chief of the band asked them to leave. In 1985, that chief was replaced by Justin Boshey. His memories of attending Bible classes with Wally and Ed were very positive. He invited the IMAC (Indian Ministries Advisory Committee) to return to Lac La Croix. Although our cultures were at odds at this time, for the conference, this work with Native people was a matter of the heart.

On the road with the MBC Town Meetings

Serving the existing churches was a priority for the Minnesota Baptist Conference under Dick Turnwall. The staff continued the pattern started by Emmett Johnson of holding Town Meetings in all of the area fellowships of the state during the month of March. Staff members greeted people, gave reports, and promoted coming events. Herb Skoglund, the head of BGC World Missions, joined the staff several times bringing reports on the latest books on world missions. It was a massive commitment of staff time and energy. However, listening to staff give reports became predictable. A change was needed.

That change began in late 1984. It was announced that the Town Meeting program would be reformatted. The area gatherings would be called Family Get-Togethers and would be preceded by a selection of workshops on Christian education, evangelism, and camping. A dinner would be served, and after an audio-visual presentation on MBC ministries, the executive minister would bring a challenge. There is little question that this new format was influenced by Donna Sahlin and the newly formed Growth Resources Department. There is also little question that this format change would bring new energy to the final years of Dick Turnwall's leadership.

During this era, the ministry to churches was the shared responsibility of both Turnwall and Delmar Dahl. Turnwall was a thinker and analyzer. Dahl was a program developer. He had entered ministry as a Christian education director. Training was in his blood. Dahl was also a "touch" kind of person. This quality would create a demand for him in situations that required a relational touch. Because he was accessible, Dahl became the go-to guy for pastors and lay people during this era. He was also in demand as a speaker. He kept a full calendar of preaching and speaking opportunities in the churches. He was the staff representative on the Men's and Women's Board, which placed him in the middle of retreat and event planning for these organizations. It was Delmar

We Came, We Sang, but the Choir Did Not

If we were singing Reformation and Wesleyan hymns in the 60s and 70s and enjoying the choral anthem, all that was about to change. Two musical movements moved into conference worship in the late 70s and 80s. In 1964, Bill Gaither released his breakthrough song "He Touched Me." Bill and Gloria Gaither continued to perform as the Bill Gaither Trio but more importantly to write songs and hymns that would enter the conference worship experience. "Let's Just Praise the Lord," "Because He Lives" and many other songs brought an easy, intimate southern gospel style into worship. At the same time, large charismatic West Coast churches brought many talented musicians into fellowship from the "Jesus People" movement. They were writing worship music and Chuck Smith at Calvary Chapel in Costa Mesa founded Maranatha Music to distribute their work.

The compelling nature of this new worship music, from these groups and others, elevated congregational singing but began to displace the traditional choir and soloists. It also led to dozens of phone calls to the MBC office wondering if some small church could use a church organ - free!

Dahl who scheduled and programmed the Town Meetings.

During the early years of the Turnwall era, Dahl was conducting between 10 and 12 mini-conferences on Christian education annually. But as his job responsibilities broadened, Christian education became a lower priority. When Dahl hired Donna Sahlin as his secretary, the department experienced a resurgence. The audio-visual library had more than 500 filmstrips available. Because they were accessible through a catalogue, library materials were in regular circulation.

Shalom House finds serious success

Shalom House had been deployed without the retreat movement that created it. With a developing operational debt in camping, there was a great hope that Shalom might bring in paying rental clients. But alas, the clients were mostly Minnesota churches who expected the fees to be

Eventually Shalom House became a favorite gathering place.

reasonable. The Camping Committee tried other approaches, among them vacation rentals. For $25 per night, individuals could enjoy a short or long stay at Shalom House at any time during the summer. There were few takers.

Without Shalom retreats, the MBC staff had determined to aggressively use the facility for other MBC adult retreats. The goal was to provide at least a dozen district-sponsored retreats for various target groups. Although this goal would prove illusive in the early 80s, some very interesting programming developed. The very last of the Shalom retreats was a couple's retreat lead by Keith and Brenda Johnson, Emmett Johnson's son and daughter-in-law. Crossroads Retreat provided inspirational spiritual growth opportunities. Recipe for Renewal, the retreat for pastors' wives, was consistently well attended during the 80s. Special-interest retreats were attempted. Berkeley and Alvera Mickelsen led a retreat on a woman's changing world. Tom Johnson led a retreat on parenting. A Day of Conversation about Marriage was held at Bethel and proved to be an attractive pre-marital experience for many young couples in love. It would be

Retirement Retreats at Shalom that would change the value of Shalom House in the years ahead.

The MBC's greatest generation retreats to Shalom

The 1970s and 80s brought with them a greater consciousness of the presence of older adults in American life. The AARP was formed in 1958 out of the National Retired Teachers Association. Ethel Percy Andrus's philosophy of *productive aging* formed the basis for the organization. The organization's financial power came when Andrus and AARP aligned with an insurance provider to sell insurance and use its influence to lobby for more government programs for poorer retired Americans.

With AARP's financial success, marketers began to see potential in the growing population of aging adults. Seniors felt comfortable, even insistent, in asking for a discount. The number of senior adults compared to the overall population would double over the 50 years from 1958 to 2008. This number was significantly less than in Europe. Demographically, a massive increase in the percentage of older adults was predicted after 2008 as post-war babies reached retirement.

In 1998, Tom Brokaw published *The Greatest Generation,* and the nation offered a hearty *Hip Hip Hooray.* Brokaw was right. The generation that was born in the baby boom of WWI, grew up in the depression, saved Europe in WWII, and built America with their character and work ethic in the economic expansion of the post war, may well have been the greatest generation.

The Minnesota conference had its own greatest generation. This generation saved the denomination in 1944, built strong churches and a strong conference in the 50s, 60s and 70s, and after that, began to look for new ways to fellowship and serve in their retirement. District and national resolutions called the churches to serve this generation with older adult ministries and staff. The conference and its churches entered into the senior housing business.

If Andrus was looking for "exhibit A" in her philosophy of *productive aging*, she could well consider the Minnesota older adults who gathered for three decades at Shalom House for their retreats, and then for the service opportunities that would follow. It provided a brilliant model.

In 1974, the Minnesota Baptist Conference held its first retreat for retired people. Dick Turnwall was the speaker. In a few years, this ministry to the *Greatest Generation* would multiply. Interest in this retreat became so strong that by 1980 there were three retreats, and five in 1982. In later years, up to 10 retreats were held. The Fred Tumas and Gordon Sundbergs came alongside this ministry and it flourished with their skills.

Fred Tuma was nearly a professional choreographer in programming his own church's adult retreats. Often Fred and the MBC team built on Ham Lake church's adult retreat programs as a basis for the retirement retreat programs at Trout. Retirement Retreats created a generation of older adults who supported the MBC and Trout Lake with their financial gifts. Many learned to love Trout and served as volunteers. They became an important leg on the stool that would allow the MBC and camping to flourish in the decades ahead. Delmar Dahl also provided his own special panache for the retreats.

Sahlin and Wicklund become a new team

During the course of Delmar Dahl's service to the Minnesota Baptist Conference, a staff pattern evolved. As Dahl was assigned more responsibility in Minnesota missions, he had less time for Christian education. He coordinated with the BGC on grants to new churches. He served as the MBC liaison to the BGC in the work with Native people. Dahl accepted these responsibilities, but his plate was full. And he was not hiding his concern.

During this period Linda Wicklund, a member of Calvary in St. Paul, became a steward and a member of the Christian education committee. Linda could see that Dahl was overextended, but she was also aware that with all the additional missions-area responsibilities, little was being done to resource the local churches in Christian education, especially the smaller church.

In February 1981, Donna Sahlin became Dahl's secretary. Donna and John Sahlin had returned from mission work in Papua, New Guinea. John was working at Bethel as a development officer. Donna was raising three children, but was ready for another ministry. She knew the conference. She was organized, and in Dahl's words, she "remembers details." [10]

In late 1982, Dahl submitted his resignation to become senior pastor at First Baptist Church of Cambridge. Linda Wicklund stepped forward in the committee with a proposal. Christian education could be repackaged using a consultant and a team of volunteers and the existing staff from the MBC. In the early stages, Ed Buchanan of Bethel Seminary led a survey of church needs. But it became clear that the key person on the team was already in place – Donna Sahlin. With enthusiasm, Dick Turnwall reported that the MBC would soon see "one of the most aggressive and effective networks of assistance to the churches that exists anywhere."[11]

Turnwall had been aggressively seeking to resource the town and country churches. As the new Christian education model was emerging, Turnwall was writing about the uniqueness of the small church. David Rey had published a book, *Small Churches are the Right Size*. The book was being read by pastors of smaller congregations. In November

The Children's Shelter of Cebu (CSC)

As Dick Turnwall entered his leadership term in the conference, two young adults were wondering if they were indeed discovering their spiritual destiny. Marlys Danielson had visited the Philippines with her father as part of a support team for an evangelist. She was smitten by the plight of the street children of Cebu and returned to Minnesota on fire to help them. She persistently communicated her vision to start a shelter there, attracting friends for the vision. One of those friends was Paul Healy who would become her husband. They would say that their early fundraising efforts might be grouped together under the title "What Not to Do!" However, after they shared their vision with a group of Bethel students, a student approached them about his desire to give them half of a trust fund, $40,000. This would be enough to buy the first residence home! Their first supporting churches were Central of St. Paul and Elim of Isanti.

Today CSC's campus includes three large residences for children, a youth dorm and center, and Hope School. As children arrive they are nourished and loved until they are ready for adoption across the world. There is an extraordinary sense of God's presence and love in the Philippines, at the Children's Shelter of Cebu.

1983 and again in January 1984, pastors and wives of churches with memberships of less than 110 were invited to a retreat at Shalom, compliments of the MBC. The conference used funds from the Decade Growth capital campaign. David Rey affirmed the special opportunities of ministry in a small church in two special retreats with 48, and then more than 100, participants.

The Sahlin/Wicklund team created a Christian Education Resource Center in the conference center. They arranged regional training seminars. Ideas for children's and youth work, Sunday school, club programs, and adult ministries were promoted in these gatherings. A large Christian education fair was held in conjunction with the annual meeting. All of this training targeted the needs of the smaller church. Christian education professionals volunteered to provide instruction and resources for these training programs. Stan Olsen, Joyce Fifield, Penny Zettler, Craig Dahl, and other CE professionals assisted.

Another byproduct of this Christian education revolution was that it freed up funds in the operating budget that could be shifted toward the church extension staff position. This emboldened the Stewards to fill that position. Dick Turnwall, however, was never given credit for this turn of events.

The seeds of disillusionment

Midway through Dick Turnwall's first term, the Board of Stewards was fielding questions on the leadership effectiveness of the executive minister and the board. There was "the itch" that had been there since the beginning. Was the MBC's ineffectiveness in church planting attributable to a lack of vision? Then there was a somewhat persistently restless Delmar Dahl who felt spread too thin. Camping and the other ministries of the MBC seemed to be drifting apart.

An early effort on the part of a board chair encouraged members to listen to their area constituents and bring feedback to the board. Board members brought responses into a discussion. The discussion admonished executive Turnwall. He was spending too much time in the office, and he needed to get out with the pastors. Turnwall indicated that his first responsibility was to keep churches healthy. He suggested a reapportionment of staff assignments could address these perceptions. Dahl would devote 60% of his time to church extension and 40% to Christian education. Turnwall would devote 30% to church assistance, 30% to clergy support, and 40% to organizational functions.

Turnwall's renewed calls to kingdom growth

Dick Turnwall had a passion to see kingdom growth in the churches. He analyzed church statistics in the Minnesota Baptist Conference, and especially their growth patterns. He did not like what he saw. In his second annual report, he observed that our total Minnesota church membership had declined 121 members in the past year – the second year of loss. Worship attendance was down by 261. Sunday school attendance had declined for the third straight year, losing 500 attendees in 1980.

Turnwall was also calculating the rate of the baptisms in Minnesota churches. There was a slowdown in the number of baptisms recorded per 100 church members. We were only holding our own in attendance and membership, but we were losing the battle when it came to reaching people for Christ and bringing them into baptism and membership. In his 1981 annual report, Turnwall indicated how much he deplored the individualization of Christianity and its effect on the church and the Minnesota conference.

In 1982, Turnwall reaffirmed his commitment to setting a vision of growth for the conference. He asked the question, "What is wrong with us?" He saw the churches ministering in a changing environment. He also saw many churches unable to muster strength for their situation in ministry. "What can we do about it?" he asked, and then answered. "Repent! Think present and future rather than past… be truthful with your situation. Use today's technologies to analyze and solve organizational problems." What can the churches expect from Turnwall, the leader? Spiritual integrity, a diligence in remembering our roots, truthfulness, and finally a commitment to apply the skills of our organization through goal-setting, planning, and evaluating. He invited the MBC on this "pilgrimage into the future."[12]

Nationally, the BGC was observing a growth slowdown in the conference as well. Warren Magnuson announced his Double in a Decade challenge to the churches. Turnwall reacted to this challenge with disbelief. In *Take Five*, Turnwall reasoned that a doubling goal for Minnesota would mean a five-year increase of 7,200 in additional members, or a total membership increase from 23,700 to 30,900. "That would require revolution, not reformation; an explosion, not growth; fanaticism, not zeal; militaristic control, not participative planning."[13]

Turnwall's assessment of Double in a Decade was understandable based on the current growth trends. Warren Magnuson would later say that his doubling goal was not intended to be a measurable goal. But it only underscored the growth paralysis of the Minnesota district at this time.

Saber rattling in the BGC silos

During the Turnwall years, the Minnesota conference participated with the BGC in the Decade Growth Fund capital campaign. National ministries had sweetened the financial benefits to the districts for participation. Minnesota hoped to receive several hundred thousand dollars for camping and church planting.

In the 80s, the organizational relationship with the BGC became a matter of discussion again. Through the 1971 SCOR committee, the national Board of Trustees was expanded to include district-elected representatives on the board. Districts were becoming stronger and more autonomous in their ministry agendas. The 1971 SCOR process would raise many issues concerning BGC organizational alignments.

In 1982, a Committee on Organizational Planning (COOP) was formed to revisit structural issues in the conference. It must be noted that this new effort at reorganization was not directed at the districts. The world missions department was demanding more autonomy to manage its finances and set its agendas – a societal model of organization. There were tensions among the various departmental silos in the national office. COOP did not offer autonomy for the world missions department, but they did recommend that the all boards be permitted to raise their own funds.

This was a radical change in funding policy. Previously all of the income sources of the conference were adjusted into one United Mission for Christ budget. Initially the decision to raise designated funds looked like a big win for world missions. They had been encouraging designated giving to missionaries for years. Indeed, their percentage of the BGC dollar initially increased. Home missions had been supported by its share of the United Mission for Christ. They were important to Minnesota because they had partnered with districts by providing 50% of a new church support grant. With the new financial system, those funds were drying up.

This outcome would change when home missions announced Missions USA and TeAMerica, a cooperative district/national effort to deploy and support its own church planting missionaries in the United States.

Camping, we are still working through the shock!

When Dick Turnwall took the reins of the Minnesota Baptist Conference, camping was completing a decade of expansion. But in April 1981, Bob Kobielush resigned. "Those of us who are his colleagues are still working through our shock."[14]

Why? Kobielush was deeply invested in the future of Trout Lake Camp and had been preparing for its next great advance. It was clear from the circumstances that this was not a move to a different job. Actually there was no "other job" available immediately to him. Four months later, he took a position with Christian Camping International and eventually become its CEO. But that was still in the future.

Even though his successor was secured by the end of the year, Kobielush's resignation rocked the boat for the conference. Executive Turnwall found himself managing the disappointments of many highly effective lay people who had joined Kobielush in his next steps toward the camp's future. And it created some shifting sand for Roger Camerer, the new camp director. Finally, it left a question as to why Kobielush resigned, a question that was difficult to answer.

The Camp Development Plan, ahead of its time

On July 26, 1981, four months after Kobielush resigned, the Stewards met to hear a presentation from the Camp Planning Task Force. For 24 hours, the Steward group examined the camp plan in detail. Over a 10-year period, the entire housing scheme of Trout Lake would be rebuilt and transitioned to winterized year-around housing. The entrance to camp and recreation areas would be reconfigured. The uses of all campsites would be redefined to reduce the serious erosion occurring on the property. All projects would be constructed to conform to public safety and health codes. Camp would need to move away from its use of volunteers. With the safety of campers becoming a key focus of customers, it was becoming more critical than ever to have trained staff and more difficult to produce a safe environment with volunteers. Camp was facing health and building codes it needed to meet immediately. The price tag would be substantial and would require major capital fund raising. It would also require a broader marketing reach for Trout Lake Camp, both inside the Minnesota conference and outside.

Two months later at the September Steward's meeting, the Camp Development Plan was not approved. The Stewards, clearly ambivalent, informed the Camp Planning Task Force that they had decided to display the plan at the annual meeting without comment. No one interpreted this as anything other than a total rejection.

After assuming his position in January 1982, new Camp Director Roger Camerer recommended to the Board of Stewards that the development plan not be implemented and that two of its foundational assumptions be categorically rejected. First, that the concept of Trout as a year-around facility, be rejected. And second, that the idea of expanding Trout by marketing outside the conference be rejected. Dick Turnwall and the Stewards agreed.

In their separate leadership situations, one can understand why Bob Kobielush chose to resign, and why Roger Camerer chose to walk away from the Camp Development Plan. Kobielush moved into Minnesota camping with modest camp experience. He worked hard to create a quality camping experience on the beloved campgrounds. He did this by improving programming on all MBC camping sites. Program directors had been selected from the pool of state conference people. A program director would be a pastor or youth pastor. A Christian education director might supply the program leadership for the junior girl's camp.

Kobielush began to restructure camp programming to position camp to provide a higher quality camp experience. In 1976, Ralph Gustafson directed the program as a staff summer hire. Lyn Gustafson was the staff head counselor. These were key transitions from the past tradition of volunteer program and counselor personnel.

Kobielush knew that camp customers, whether young or old, were expecting more from their camp or retreat experiences. He centralized the administration of the camp, increasing the effectiveness of camp promotion, program creation, fundraising, and financial management. He created a middle level of management so that the camp would not collapse with the loss of a director.

What Kobielush could not fix by his limited operational budget was the widespread deterioration of the camp structures. He needed agreement that the conference would need to invest major capital dollars in the camp to see improved quality and expanded ministry. The

Camp Development Plan was essentially a big vision to raise big dollars. Kobielush also saw great potential for Trout in markets outside the conference. He needed agreement that the leaders of the conference saw Trout as a ministry beyond its local churches and conference young people. Finally, Kobielush recognized the limitations of the Trout Lake site. Camp had already maxed out the facility for its three-season use, and that expansion would require preparations for year-around camping.

At first, the Stewards seemed to agree. In a July 1980 planning meeting in preparation for the Camp Development Plan, the Stewards affirmed a dozen resolutions that indicated their support for these planning imperatives. In other words, every supporting assumption in the plan had the Stewards' agreement before a professional site planner put a pen to paper.

Decade Growth Funds provided the services of Wehrman-Chapman site planners. A blue ribbon Camp Development Task Force provided the organizational guidance and accountability as the plan was developed. In spite of a solid affirmation of the underlying principles, and in spite of a high level of professional development of the plan, it appears that the resulting plan to re-envision Trout Lake's sacred grounds simply overwhelmed the MBC staff and board.

Several observations are relevant. The climate in the MBC was such that any strong movement forward was often met with ambivalence. Clearly there was organizational and financial anxiety. It had taken nearly four years to agree to hire a church extension staff person.

The public documents are silent on the Camp Development Plan. If executive Turnwall was supportive of this carefully crafted planning process, he did not write about it or promote it in any way. The Stewards' discussions are a matter of record, but staff leadership is strangely silent. One would have to assume, best case, that Turnwall was holding back to see which way the river would flow.

In his summary report, after the resignation of Kobielush and the hiring of Roger Camerer, Turnwall reflected on the issues faced in the camp development proposal. He summarized the history from his point of view. "The crossroads at which we stand in relationship to our camping program involves us choosing whether our camping program will continue to be a ministry of, by and for the churches of the Minnesota Baptist Conference, or whether it will become a business providing services for conference churches and many others besides."[15]

From the perspective of history, this critique is surprisingly short-sighted. But it is the only way to understand the indecisive ending of the camp development proposal. No one in MBC leadership at this time was standing up for a future camping vision of this kind.

Camerer enters an unstable landscape

Roger Camerer entered an unstable landscape. He had been a candidate for the camp position nine years earlier. He knew the conference, having served churches in Milaca and Minneapolis. He was extended a call after a search committee process. The call was an invitation to serve until the next annual meeting. At that time, the Stewards would decide whether Roger would be hired for a regular five-year term. Clearly for the Camerers, who were leaving a successful pastorate, this was a tenuous beginning to an MBC staff leadership position. The chairman of the Stewards resigned during this period over the issue of camping and the Camp Development Plan. Life was feeling politically unsafe for many.

New Associate Minister of Camping Roger Camerer attempted to defuse the tense political environment created by the rejection of the Camp Development Plan. His natural response was to try to return the camping program to its core roots. Not only would two of the controversial components of the development plan be removed by Camerer (winterization and marketing outside the conference), but the plan itself would be ignored for years.

Roger Camerer was a good manager. Without the huge capital challenges of a new direction in Minnesota camping, he moved forward to stabilize the ship. In the first year of his administration, the number of participants in camping programs decreased by 13.7%. In the last year of Kobielush's leadership, camp had ended its season with substantial operating debt. Camerer raised fees about 5% a year in order to reverse the red ink. Camping seemed to be in a recovery mode.

It took several years, but camp started to stabilize financially. A "revised development plan" called for staff training, improvements to conform to codes, spending controls, aggressive promotion of camping in the churches, and excellence in programming. Special fund promotions were created. A camp scholarship fund was designated to address the "haves and have nots" clientele. Bike-a-thon fundraisers and camp alumni phone-a-thons were tried successfully. Camerer was a hands-on leader and the camp staff functioned as a family. The middle levels of management were pruned, which contributed to budget health. One of Camerer's great strengths would be his use of volunteers in all areas of camp life.

Kobielush, always a friend of Trout Lake Camp

A period of turmoil in any organization calls for reflection. Kobielush, after his rise to CEO of Christian Camping International, always was an encourager of the Trout Lake staff. He returned to Minnesota at key times and blew the trumpet for Trout. On three occasions this author heard the same comment from Kobielush: "This place is doing unbelievable. Denominational camps are dying."

There is little doubt that comment reveals a deep seated belief that Kobielush brought to the table. The best camp, and most successful camp, would be a camp without the entanglements of denominationalism – an autonomous camp. Trout never became that camp for him or anyone else. Yet, over time, it is interesting to note that almost everything else that Kobielush advocated in the Camp Development Plan became a reality at Trout.

Roger Camerer moved to make Trout a year-round facility. Marketing was broadened to include customers outside the conference. Counselors and most staff became trained and compensated employees. The site and its building would be radically reoriented to an entirely different kind of camping. When asked about the Camp Development Plan in preparation for this book, Roger Camerer reflected, "It was ahead of its time."[16] One thing did not change. Trout continued to be owned and operated by the Minnesota Baptist Conference.

Grandview and TCCH, a magnanimous gesture

On another front in conference ministry, Grandview Ministries and Twin City Christian Homes saw remarkable advances during the Turnwall years. In the late 70s, the Minnesota Baptist Conference had co-signed a note for $150,000 which allowed Grandview to operate through a period when public health agencies would not allow usage of their skilled nursing facility. Grandview would stabilize financially, and purchase land across the Rum River to begin plans to develop independent living housing for seniors.

Twin City Christian Homes (TCCH), which was started under the umbrella of several local churches, had aligned with the Minnesota

An Archive and a History Center

In 1898, the Swedish Baptist conference established an archive to preserve historical materials relevant to its church life. Over the years, key leaders in the conference collected facts and published important history. Martin Erikson, editor of *The Standard*, published a 110-page, photo laden book of *Centenary Glimpses* for the centennial celebration in 1952. Adolf Olson published the exhaustive review of the BGC titled *A Centenary History* that same year. Seminary librarian and historian Norris Magnuson produced the wonderful *How We Grew* booklet a quarter century later, and many scholarly studies besides. Librarian David Guston, co-archivist with Magnuson, helped to move BGC history out of the cloister with a table display called *The Conference in the Early Years*.

But it was the duo of Diana Magnuson and Dick Turnwall that brought added professionalism to the collection and a new public awareness of our history. In the early 1990s, the name of the archives became the BGC History Center, and was later renamed The History Center, archives of the Baptist General Conference and Bethel University. Diana Magnuson, history professor at Bethel and daughter-in-law of Norris Magnuson, became director of the History Center. A supporting group, the Friends of the History Center, was established and Dick Turnwall became the first chairman of the Friends Steering Committee. The Friends raise awareness and support for the archives, publish a newsletter called *Trail Markers*, hold occasional events of historical interest, and publish related books. Two of their recent books are *5 Decades of Growth and Change*, a 50-year history of Bethel and the BGC, and *Give First Priority to Jesus Christ*, about the life of Carl H. Lundquist. Both were by Jim and Carole Spickelmier.

Currently the archives are housed in the Bethel Seminary library building and are financially supported by both Bethel and Converge/BGC. Information about the History Center is available at www.bethel.edu/history-center.

Baptist Conference in 1978. The organization had made several failed attempts to enter the ministry of residential care of older adults. After a challenging search, an opportunity arose in 1981. Castle Ridge Nursing Home in Eden Prairie was available. The Board had sold some property in Arden Hills the year before, but they had experienced little hope of finding an opportunity for the ministry. With land sale funds, a $250,000 loan guarantee from the Minnesota Baptist Conference, and gifts from churches and individuals, TCCH purchased and launched its initial 60-bed operation.

In a magnanimous gesture of goodwill, Grandview lent TCCH its outstanding new administrator to assist the facility in its first steps of operation. In 1984, TCCH opened Edendale Retirement Residence, also in Eden Prairie, a HUD project. Bruce Farrington piloted the board through the Castle Ridge project. Long-term board member Howard Wallin took the helm in the mid-80s. Minnesota was in the retirement housing business.

A painful end of an era

A casual reader of the Minnesota conference's 1983 annual report might turn to the report of the district executive minister and be shocked, as many no doubt were, to read this sentence: "The Board of Stewards has received notice of my decision to terminate my call as Executive Minister."[17] It was the end of a painful year for Turnwall and for the Minnesota Baptist Conference.

In the April 1983 issue of *Take Five*, executive Turnwall had listed several personnel matters that the MBC leaders would address, including requesting input regarding "certain aspects of my performance as Executive Minister."[18] A performance review survey had been brought to the Board of Stewards by the Personnel Development Committee. It contained some significant concerns from constituents and colleagues regarding Turnwall's leadership and relationship to the pastors and churches. In the memory of one Steward, there was a dominant feeling that Turnwall's strengths were integrity, management, and organizational analysis, whereas the conference at this time had a need for vision, energy, and direction. Turnwall informed the board that he intended to conclude his ministry with the MBC, but would remain available to serve the coming year. The board recommended to the annual meeting that Turnwall be elected to continue service until December 31, 1984.

Turnwall was a huge and godly persona in the Minnesota Baptist Conference. This ending left many saddened for him and for Marge. They had given so much for Minnesota. However, the final year of Turnwall's service to the MBC turned out to be a great period. He gave enthusiastic leadership. Neal Floberg ramped up church extension. Donna Sahlin transformed Christian education in Minnesota with Growth Resources. Roger Camerer had brought stability to camping and was pushing forward with a capital campaign – *40 More*.

In his report in his final year as executive minister, Turnwall expressed pride in his accomplishments. There was a new and uniquely functional Pastor's Council, a participatory caucus system of election for area Board of Steward's representation, and a much improved and computerized office system in the MBC.

Most of Minnesota was delighted that the Turnwalls remained in Minnesota, and that Dick would find an amazing leadership role in the transformation of the BGC archives into the Baptist General Conference History Center.

Notes

[1] Roger Camerer, 121st Annual Report, Board of Stewards Report,1979, p. 35-36.

[2] Search Committee member interview, 2013.

[3] Annual Report, November 8, 1979 p. 39-40.

[4] *Contact*, "Board of Stewards Report," July 1979, p. 1.

[5] Richard Turnwall, 121st Annual Report, Executive Minister's Report, 1979.

[6] Richard Turnwall, 122nd Annual Report, October 1980.

[7] Delmar Dahl, 123rd Annual Report, Associate Minister of Church Ministries Report, 1981.

[8] Ibid.

[9] Dennis Mattson, 124th Annual Meeting Report, Board of Stewards Report, 1982.

[10] Delmar Dahl, 123rd Annual Report, Associate Minister of Church Ministries, 1981, p. 76.

[11] Richard Turnwall, *Happenings*, "It Seems to Me," June 1983, p. 4.

[12] Richard Turnwall, 122nd Annual Report, Executive Minister's Report, pp. 37-38.

[13] Richard Turnwall, *Take Five*, June 19,1981, p. 1.

[14] Richard Turnwall, *Take Five*, April 24, 1981.

[15] Richard Turnwall, 123rd Annual Report, Executive Minister's Report, 1981.

[16] Roger Camerer interview, 2013.

[17] Richard Turnwall, 125th Annual Report, Executive Minister's Report, 1983, p. 44.

[18] Richard Turnwall, *Take Five,* "Two and Half with Turnwall," Vol. 5, No. 12.

Churches Started or Welcomed: 1979-1984

1980

East Grand Forks

New Life Bible Church (Bemidji)

1981

East Bethel

Princeton Baptist Fellowship

1982

Gethsemane Grove (Inver Grove Heights restart)

1983

Koinonia (Lakeville)

— Chapter 11 —

The John F. Anderson Era
(1985-1989):
A Surge of Forward Movement

The religious right enters through the front doors of the church

In the last months of 1984, while the Minnesota Baptist Conference was making the transition from the Turnwall era to the tenure of newly elected John F. Anderson, a profound change in the American political climate was emerging. This political agenda would boldly walk through the front doors of churches and onto the platforms of Minnesota's annual meetings.

In 1980, fundamentalist pastor Jerry Falwell borrowed the term "Moral Majority" from the Republican strategist Paul Weyrich, founder of the

John F. Anderson brought to the MBC a heart for the small church and experience from large ones.

Heritage Foundation.[1] Falwell began to call on conservatives and evangelical Christians to take a more activist role in their churches regarding social issues that were important to conservative Christians. In a video, Falwell offered a challenge to emerging evangelical political activists. You need to "get them saved, get them baptized, and get them registered," he said.[2] Falwell's swagger rubbed many conference folks the wrong way, but there was a resonance with the issues. It seemed like every moral issue was getting hammered by activism on the other side – the sanctity of life, creationism, pornography, family values, and secularism in the schools.

During the same period, Pastor Tim LaHaye formed the American Coalition for Traditional Values. Beverly, LaHaye's wife, began organizing women as the Concerned Women for America. LaHaye served on the board of Falwell's Moral Majority and would be a major donor to his Liberty University. LaHaye also aligned himself with Henry Morris and the Institute for Creation Research. LaHaye became an advocate for the literal seven-day creation theory being taught in public schools as the biblical view.

At the annual meeting in Rochester, October 29, 1981, Dr. Russell Arndts a member of a conference church, presented four resolutions for adoption at the annual meeting. All were political issues of the emerging religious right. After meeting with Arndts, the resolutions committee convinced him to bring one resolution to the assembly rather than four. Arndts brought a resolution mandating that the Stewards appoint a panel of theologians and scientists to study the subject of "creation and origins" and bring a report of their findings to the 1982 annual meeting. After consideration, the motion was tabled until the next annual meeting. The next year, the resolution was taken off the table. The motion was defeated by a voice vote. Arndts would bring similar resolutions to the national annual meeting during the same period.

Resolutions had always had a part in Minnesota annual meetings. Their origins seem to be more about courtesy than controversy. A resolution would be made to thank a host church or honor a volunteer or retiring staff member. The conference passed a resolution supporting the Billy Graham crusades in the 1950s. There were resolutions on social evils such as alcohol. In the 60s, resolutions became more activist in their orientation, reflecting social/political issues of the day like racism, ecumenism, or social justice.

In the first years of the Emmett Johnson era, a resolution committee had been formed to bring a single, well-crafted resolution. Resolutions that challenged and extended the ministry vision of the Minnesota Baptist Conference had always been welcome. However, the constituency became disturbed when the maker of the motion clearly was bringing an outside agenda for action within the conference, especially if the resolution threatened to divide the house.

In 1986, four resolutions were again presented to the annual meeting by the same group of individuals. One was on pornography, another on abortion as a humiliation to women. There was also a resolution calling our denominational and educational leaders to educate on the subject of abortion. And finally, a resolution was presented to encourage our churches and members to be politically active on these issues. In 1987, once again, resolutions on obscenity, abortion, and homosexuality were offered for action. By this time, a fatigue was setting in.

The delegates sought recourse in a parliamentary action called the *objection to consideration*. It would be used often during this period when the assembly felt it did not want to act on a resolution. The Minnesota Baptist Conference started a policy that resolutions must be submitted in advance of the annual meeting, thus avoiding the hastily written or ill-considered motion. Arndts brought activist resolutions until the early 90s.

After a discussion with the district executive ministers, a quite disturbed Truett Lawson met with Arndts and his pastor. He asked if Arndts' resolutions were endorsed by his local church or if they were coming from Arndts alone. Arndts was a fine and respected man in his local church but, after that inquiry, the resolutions ceased.

The fallout of public debate

Local churches in Minnesota during this period handled the rising call to activism from the religious right in different ways. Some became highly engaged. Individuals pressed forward with their concerns to school boards, advocating for school choice, church schools, and home schooling. Some became active in prolife movement or crisis pregnancy centers in their communities. A lesser number of churches, especially those in urban areas, viewed these issues very skeptically. For these, the issues of racism, the plight of the poor, and social justice were being ignored by the religious right.

The majority of Minnesota churches, however, tried to make church a neutral place for differing views on these things. This "silent majority" maintained that activism on these issues was an individual Christian's responsibility. At many points, the Minnesota Baptist Conference seemed to embrace both the issues of the left and the issues of the right. Newly elected Executive John F. Anderson, although passionate about social issues, led the district with maturity and fairness during this explosive period.

In 1985, Arndts convened a Committee on Social Concerns at Calvary in St. Cloud and invited other churches to participate. Other individuals joined him. In March 1987, the executive minister and the Stewards enfolded the committee into the organizational life of the MBC. It appears from the record that the committee considered both the issues of the right and the issues of the left. It sought to educate and create awareness. Many of the issues dealt with were issues that communities were struggling with on the local level. Churches were beginning to realize that concern for the soul is better received when a church exhibits concern for the local community. Arndts chaired the group at first. Pastor Rick Sturm, a Board of Stewards member, then took leadership.

Many core conference people viewed the resolution process as a dangerous political process, without wisdom. They saw it as an opportunity to seize a moment in the conference. Resolutions brought division. Unity was what was needed. Others showed detachment, and commented that a conference without a great debate was a boring gathering. It is doubtful anyone could have imagined where the vehicle of resolutions would take the conference in the 90s, when the issue of Open Theism would become a matter of public debate.

John F. Anderson, born and bred in Houston

At 9:15 a.m., Saturday, October 27, 1984, the delegates of the Annual Meeting voted to elect John F. Anderson as their district Executive Minister.

Anderson was born in Houston, Minnesota, on the Root River, where the earliest Swedish Baptist church had convened. John's father was a Swedish Baptist but his Norwegian mother was a confirmed Lutheran. Anderson would write, "So when Curtis and Una started a family, they had a decision to make about church."[3] But Pastor Hugo Bersell reached out to the family during the difficult times of the depression, and with humility and care brought the family into the Swedish Baptist congregation.

Anderson came to Bethel College shaped by the farm families and working class people he grew up with. At Bethel, he found his spiritual convictions confirmed, but he also found his social convictions stimulated by great professors like Walfred Peterson and Roy Dalton. He felt a nudge toward ministry and entered the seminary. Here too, he found role models like Anton Pearson and Virgil Olson who integrated authentic Baptist faith with a heart for the poor and oppressed. In seminary, it was clear that John Anderson's leadership skills and winsome personality would open many ministry doors of opportunity.

Anderson pastored in Galesburg, Illinois, followed by a distinguished ministry at Central Baptist in St. Paul. He served Bethel on the Board of Regents and chaired the board in 1975. At the time of his call to lead the MBC, he was serving as senior pastor at La Crescenta in California. Fuller Seminary had conferred a Doctor of Ministry degree on him. The Southwest Conference had elected him moderator. It did not hurt Anderson's candidacy that he brought a bit of humor, a winning smile, and a lovely life-partner named Barbara – a strong ministry woman herself.

Pastor Bruce Petersen led the Call Committee. They were impressed not only with Anderson's understanding of large churches, but also with his sensitivity to the small church. As they interviewed him, they sensed a confidence in his thoughts and commented on his perceptive observations concerning ministry in the culture of the 80s. His name had been suggested twice as often as that of any other candidate.

Ministry in Minnesota began for John and Barb Anderson on January 1, 1985. The overnight temperature was -18 degrees Fahrenheit, a reminder that their ministry in California had been concluded. The inside temperature at the Minnesota Baptist Conference was very warm.

The obvious pain experienced by the Turnwalls during 1984 had been transformed by their compelling graciousness. Every expression of appreciation from all parties was very heartfelt. The MBC and its departing leader had found an amicable closing. It had also found a great sense of expectation in the ministry of John F. Anderson.[4]

Bruce Petersen communicated a feeling of excitement in his first report as the chairman of the Stewards. "There is something about a change in leadership that seems to make even the 'housekeeping' items of business take on new life and meaning. The Board of Stewards experienced this during the past year due in large part to the arrival of John F. Anderson as Executive Minister, with his freshness of perspective and his dynamic, positive attitude. There were changes in the format of board meetings…. time was given to brainstorming and the periodic sharing of 'joy stories.' It was a pleasure to serve on a board which spent time being celebrative and creative."[5]

Happenings! More than a periodical, more like a reality

As the Stewards recognized a new freshness in leadership, the staff would renew its dedication to excellence. Public events became colorful, contemporary, and appealing. Constituents sensed newness. And yes, the staff could be approachable and fun. Annual meetings and Family Gatherings would all feel the pressure for change and upgrade. Camp would start hearing the call for greater excellence.

The monthly communications from the MBC staff would be written in *Of One Mind*. *Happenings* was published through 1990 for the wider Minnesota conference constituency. Growth Resources began to produce a quarterly newsletter in 1987 called *Creative Equipping*. It provided resources for Christian education leaders in local churches.

Some staff transitions had occurred in the office the year before Anderson's arrival. Neal Floberg had joined the staff as the Associate Minister of Church Extension. Donna Sahlin had been Delmar Dahl's secretary. She became the epicenter of a department that would be named Growth Resources.

Sidney B. Nelson and Life-Long Learning

Sidney B. Nelson spent 31 years as pastor of the Oxford Baptist Church in Stacy, Minn., retiring in 1989. Early friends of Sidney B. recall that for most of his life he struggled with the fact that he had only a minimal education for his ministry. However, those who had the opportunity to hear him knew of his giftedness. As he drew near retirement, Sidney B. Nelson returned to the University of Minnesota to receive his baccalaureate degree and then to complete a master's degree in ancient

Pastor Nelson followed his dream and earned a Ph.D. in retirement.

history. Delighting in his studies, Sidney B. pressed on to finish a Ph.D. in Sumerian languages in 1982. He passed his orals in the first review, and became a teacher on the university level. But being a pastor was his first and greatest life calling.

Anderson recalls, "One of my accomplishments was recognizing the talents of Donna Sahlin and elevating her to a staff position as Director of Growth Resources. This position was equal to the other Associate Ministers. I gave her a leased car like the rest of us. In a perfect world Donna would have been my successor."[6] Roger Camerer continued in his position as Associate Minister of Camping. In 1986, Will Youngquist, a Steward and a retired administrator of a medical clinic, joined the staff to assist the executive minister with matters of business. Barb Johnson had worked in finance, but now Steve Whitehouse and his assistant Kathy Nelson would provide financial services.

In summer 1988, Delmar Dahl would return to the staff of the Minnesota Baptist Conference. He probably still had his coat in the closet. In an interview with Dahl, Florence Johnson refers to his legendary Rolodex. "Almost everyone in the MBC knows you, Delmar, or is it the other way around?"[7]

Dahl was given a new assignment. He was to enlist Waymakers in Minnesota. A Waymaker was a representative of the district who served by linking the ministry to its local churches. Waymakers would represent the financial needs and ministries of the district to pastors and lay people in their area. Waymakers was such a powerful concept that Anderson's successor would regret letting the program lapse with Dahl's retirement. Dahl was also assigned to assist camping with 1986's *40 More* capital campaign. The campaign was having some issues.

Growth Resources, a prototype for the next two decades

The formation of Growth Resources created a new brand within the district's ministries. Camping always had the potential for being an entrepreneurial brand. But in its developing years, camping revolved around the staff. Camping was "Chief" – Lee Kingsley, its staff member. Christian education was Delmar – Delmar Dahl. Ministry to pastors was the executive minister – the pastor to pastors. But Growth Resources almost felt para-church. It was an attractive ministry epicenter and a prototype of ministry for the MBC in the next two decades.

Donna Sahlin was passionate about Growth Resources. She had a team of professionals who were ready to provide assistance to churches. Sahlin also excelled in event planning. Suddenly, MBC-sponsored events were festive. Balloons and flowers decorated tables. Presentation areas were nicely staged. Human needs for water and food were considered in advance. In hiring Donna Sahlin, the MBC had acquired both a planner and a promoter. Many ministry expressions would benefit from her touch.

But in her annual report, Sahlin salutes Linda Wicklund. "For the past six years Linda Wicklund has served on the C.E. Committee. Linda is a volunteer who has given hours and hours to the ministry of the Minnesota Baptist Conference through Growth Resources and Adventure Club. She has traveled across the state of Minnesota, led workshops, developed new programs in Christian education, led the C.E. Committee meetings, consulted over the telephone. She has many dreams of what could happen in our churches in Christian education."[8] However the affirmation was offered, these two gifted women were instrumental in providing a whole new level of service for the churches. More than that, they created an entirely new way of re-energizing ministry in the Minnesota Baptist Conference.

At the annual meeting in 1984, Growth Resources sponsored a C.E. Fair, a large undertaking that made the annual meeting more than a gathering for delegates. The C.E. Fair became an event with many levels of interests for worker bees in the local churches. Additionally, in the years that followed, dozens of regional workshops would feed into both the annual meeting and the newly formatted Family Get-Togethers. The film strip library was obsolete. The VHS video format was winning over Sony's Betamax. Growth Resources would be on the cutting edge of this available technology. More and more, Christian teaching series videos were made available to Minnesota churches through a catalogue and reasonable mailing cost. The MBC was definitely doing new things.

Adventure Camp, from home-grown to amazing

A remarkable project during this period was the collaboration of Linda Wicklund and Donna Sahlin in Adventure Club. Historically, the MBC had strongly promoted and resourced available club programs like Pioneers and Awana. With a background in children's work, Wicklund began to write a club program for children in grades 1-6 with the smaller church in mind. In the fall of 1984, Sahlin and Wicklund launched Wicklund's first year of curriculum. Sahlin's department assisted in training as early adopters were implementing this new program in their churches. By 1986, when a third year of curriculum had been prepared, 50 churches were participating. The number would increase to 70. In order to support and assist the churches, six to eight Adventure Club trainings were held annually in those early years.

Wicklund's Adventure Camp material was eventually purchased by the Evangelical Free Church, and after that, became part of the club curriculum of David C. Cook Company, where it existed until the 1990s. No one could have anticipated the transformation of Adventure Club when clubs would become the basis for the Ukrainian Adventure Camps in the sister church movement.

A broadening ministry at Growth Resources

Donna Sahlin also assumed the promotion of the MBC's retirement retreats. The number of retreats offered would increase during the Anderson and Lawson eras. These retreats ushered in an exceptional decade in ministry to seniors. Marilyn Starr, a Minnesota resident, was leading the BGC Gold ministries. Many events for older adults were coordinated by Starr and Sahlin.

Women's ministries had, in recent years, existed to sponsor Trout Lake Women's Retreats. Donna became a consultant to the women's work but as her leadership expanded, her creativity entered women's work. More and more, the women's events were assisted by Growth Resources. A significant change in the leadership format of the women would be made in the mid-80s. Shannah Evans became the director of Women's Ministries, giving the state women a strong figurehead for the next several years. Christine Kolb replaced Evans at the end of the Anderson era. With Kolb and Sahlin, one of the strongest eras of ministry to women was launched. The women were occupying two fall weekends for their retreats. With expanding ministry in the department, Diane Wicklund joined Growth Resources in November 1989, and would become a key long-term member of the MBC team.

A setback for Twin Cities Christian Homes at Brightondale

Minnesota's two home-grown senior housing ministries were betting the farm, as they entered the world of independent living seniors' facilities. Grandview had fully recovered from its issues with the regional health planners. It would build on land it had acquired across the Rum River. Mill Ridge Commons provided one and two bedroom independent living apartments for seniors, opening its doors in October 1988.

In the same year, Twin Cities Christian Homes (TCCH), now an affiliate of the MBC, would complete its independent living project in New Brighton. Brightondale was a lovely middle-income senior residence facility. TCCH was having great success with its Castle Ridge Care Center and the Manor House. Edendale, a federally subsidized housing facility, was also very successful in the marketplace. But, for whatever reason, the strong predictions of marketing success for Brightondale did not prove accurate. After filling only partially, the facility was saved from receivership in 1990 by a discount sale. A $150,000 loan from the MBC was repaid in the transaction.

Emerging women leaders

The Minnesota conference evolved in its view of the role of women, as society changed. More women were working outside the home. Church was a place to come together as a family. Sunday was a much needed day of rest and renewal. Gender roles were traditional in most churches. There was the Deacon board and the Deaconess board. Each had its traditionally defined roles. If someone should suggest that there was inequality in these roles, you might find some agreement but you would also be reminded that it was not intentionally so.

In the 50s and 60s, churches became more corporate. Churches organized to effectively lead and administer their ministries. In some cases, the biblical roles of Deacon and Deaconess were sidelined from the administrative roles. A church board ran the church and the Deacons tended to their spiritual callings of prayer, visitation, and spiritual welfare. For many churches in the conference, this more administrative reorganization of the church allowed women to emerge in leadership. Their gender perspective enriched the church board, the advisory board or the management team.

Strong theological discussions of gender equality began in the 70s and continued in the 80s. Bethel Seminary Professor Berkeley and his wife, Alvera Mickelsen, members of the Minnesota conference, were producing groundbreaking theological perspectives on biblical gender equality. They were also writing adult studies on the subject, organized into 12-week adult class curriculum. After Berkeley's death, Alvera continued to write on biblical gender equality. She became a resource for organizations like Christians for Biblical Equality (CBE).[9]

A counterpoint to church gender equality would come in the 80s with the resurgence of the elder or elder rule in conference polity (church organization). The strength of this movement cannot be denied. Quite simply, it was being fed from many sources. John MacArthur led a seminar in his Shepherding Conferences outlining how to successfully restructure the congregational church into ruling elder governance. The charismatic movement brought strong teachings on authority and submission. Finally, the new megachurches modeled ruling eldership and were especially attractive to new churches.

As many churches organized their own elder governance, leadership opportunities for women were often limited. Some of these churches believed that the gender distribution of leadership in the early church needed to be replicated in the contemporary church. Male headship in the home and in the church was reaffirmed. Of course, there were many exceptions to this trend. Willow Creek had women elders from its inception. But in the main, churches that did not walk down the eldership road were more likely to welcome women into their leadership roles.

During the Anderson era, a woman pastoral staff member would be ordained in a Minnesota Baptist Conference church. Penny Zettler was ordained to the gospel ministry by the Central Baptist Church of St. Paul. Penny became the first woman lead pastor in the 1990s. She served as senior pastor of Elim Baptist Church of Minneapolis from 1996 to 2005.

Earlier, Emmett Johnson had written about the ordination of women in his Doctor of Ministry thesis. He believed the ordination of women was not something the district would see soon, but that it was in our future. The majority of the Minnesota conference embraced the view that the ordination of women was a local church decision. This pattern affirmed our traditional Baptist polity that the whole does not speak for all the parts. The local church is autonomous.

Minnesota's gatherings gain rock concert energy

Under Anderson, public events would become one way for the conference staff to communicate its vision. Annual meeting attendances had decreased in prior years. John F. Anderson would invest his network of talented people in the annual meeting. They created events that people wanted to attend. Bubba Laudermill, vocalist extraordinaire, came in 1985. Larry Ward, in 1986, brought an international missions message. Vera Schlamm, a holocaust survivor, told her compelling story. That year the C.E. Mission Fair was introduced. Growth Resources provided a high level of children's programming for the meetings.

In 1987, the annual meeting set a standard that would never be repeated in district history. Annual meetings had always been located in local churches. During the Anderson era, there was a shift to hotel and resort venues, a financially risky venture. Delmar Dahl oriented the new executive minister in 1990, humorously explaining the financial challenges of hotel-based annual meetings. "We basically load up a trunk full of cash when we leave for the meeting to pay for the event and all the add-ons. We just hope that the numbers aren't too bad when we get home." [10]

In 1987, the Arrowwood Resort in Alexandria renovated its facility. A powerful program was arranged, featuring popular author and lecturer Gary Smalley, dramatist Richard K. Allison, and an excellent group of seminar leaders. A record-breaking 787 registrants attended this 129th Annual Meeting. There were 225 kids in a children's program. Out of 148 MBC churches, 126 were represented. This annual gathering will probably always be regarded as the grandest annual meeting ever.

In the years to come, as the mid-winter Family Get-togethers picked up steam, more than 2,000 would attend with nearly 1,000 attending the Twin Cities gathering alone. The Anderson era would package MBC ministries in an exciting event-filled format. Yet, in spite of good programming, the next two annual meetings (1988 and 1989) would have more typical attendances. This would continue for the next generation. These are the realities of event promotion.

The MBC is Family! A new face for district gatherings

The Minnesota staff had been making a strong commitment to its churches by bringing Town Meetings to their churches each year. In the last year of the Turnwall era, the name and format of the meetings was changed to create new energy. John F. Anderson introduced the motto, *The MBC is Family!* Ten *Family Get-Togethers*, as they were now called, were held during the winter months. Anderson told his successor when he was describing the Family Get-Togethers, "You'll get out to the churches and meet some of the greatest people in the world." He was right.

With Donna Sahlin, Delmar Dahl, Roger Camerer and then John

What Came to be Known as M&M

The retired Ministers and Missionaries retreat (M&M) was established as a ministry to those who had served faithfully as pastors or missionaries in Minnesota and worldwide. In 1988, the MBC welcomed 44 men and women to Shalom House. They ranged in age from 62 to 82 and represented 1,200 years of ministry. There was a "warmth of fellowship, oneness in Christ and sharing of burdens and the Lord's Supper" said John F. Anderson as he expressed the feelings of all the MBC staff and retreat participants. (John F. Anderson, *Happenings Digest*, "Expansion at Trout Continues", Midwinter 1988.) In the years to come, these annual M&M retreats would provide a profound experience of collegiality for both the MBC staff and the retreat participants.

F. Anderson, these events began to do more than gather the loyalists. They allowed the staff and their ministries to penetrate deeper into the local churches. The classical mission statement, "Doing together what we cannot do alone", was making an impact on younger people and newer people in these events. Of the 10 events, the Twin Cities Family Get-Together was the largest. It included three area fellowships in one large event. Bethel's Founder's Week changed its format during this time. The MBC's event became the Twin Cities' annual gathering to meet old friends and find new ones.

The staff began to develop creative ways of presenting new and continuing ministries at these events. The meal, often provided by the ladies of the host church, became the center of fellowship. A program often mimicked TV game shows like "Wheel of Fortune" with MBC staff taking the roles of the television personalities. Churches were given awards for the best attendance at the event. But the attendance numbers were computed as a percentage of Sunday morning attendance. Small churches often received the award with great enthusiasm. The MBC's prize was candy and free use of the video library for a year.

The Twin City event stretched the staff. There were challenging technical issues connected with presenting their program in a hotel ballroom to 600 to 1,000 people. Once again the financial director found himself bringing the proverbial trunk load of money and hoping that the offerings covered the bill.

Minnesota church planting, calling up the reserves

The MBC was clearly walking with new swagger. But could this new confidence be used to reverse the negative growth indicators that had weighed down the previous years? It certainly had with the creation of Growth Resources. But could the same transformation occur in evangelism and church planting?

Rev. Neal Floberg had been called to provide leadership in evangelism and church extension. Floberg was a pastor, with ministries in Wisconsin, Pennsylvania, and Minnesota. The MBC called him to his position in early 1983. During the Turnwall years, it is clear that Floberg's priority was the resourcing of the churches in evangelism. Conference leader Dick Turnwall had been profoundly influenced by his discovery that the MBC churches were showing signs of decline, as evidenced in reduction in the number of baptisms. If baptism is an indicator of a disciple made, then the churches needed to be about reaching the lost, not feeding the saints. Early on, Floberg urged the staff to promote evangelism.

In 1984, however, the home missions staff at the BGC were praying and planning for some new way to stimulate church growth and church planting in the United States. World missions would be freed from the restraint of a unified, planned budget. Cliff Anderson, Mahlon Hillard, Vic Winquist, and Rob Boyd represented a strong home missions team with a commitment to partner with the districts. It was clear that the old systems of financial support would no longer exist.

In 1985, Home Missions presented a new vision: Mission USA. The conference would be challenged to see America differently. The unchurched population in the U.S. was growing. The world's mission field was coming to us with immigration. Many ethnic populations in our cities and towns were unevangelized. The traditional church was not speaking to new generations of younger Americans.

The vision of Mission USA took root across the country, and in Minnesota. National and district leaders gathered to consider aggressive new goals. The years of the mid-80s to early 90s brought a great collaboration between national home missions and district missions.[11] Church planters began to share resources. The Great Lakes district at this time was one of the more innovative church planting districts. Home missions hired church planters Steve and Paul Johnson as practitioner facilitators. Dave Olson, also a church planter, brought wisdom and direction from his unique statistical studies. Training schools were held regionally to present the latest church growth strategies. Home missions developed financial support policies, and offered assistance in the methods of personal support-raising.

With the financial policy changes of COOP, the BGC would now allow "personalized" missionary fund raising. Donors much preferred to directly support missionaries and missions projects. But to everyone's surprise, as world missions stepped through the door of individual missionary support-raising, home missions and the districts were right by their side. Church planters and ethnic pastors began raising support. Church missions committees were overwhelmed with requests and proposals.

Minnesota, learning from World Missions, set up accounts for the church planter to raise a certain level of monthly support. Home missions offered a $10,000 start-up grant to a new church in the late 1980s. Minnesota would pick up these grants into the 1990s. The old "welfare" system of providing monthly support for five years was abandoned. New churches knew they must become self-sufficient quickly.

Minnesota also established operating accounts for the new churches within the district's ledger of accounts. Church planters brought weekly offerings as deposits and the districts paid the new churches' bills and salaries. This was immensely helpful to the new church as banks were reluctant to open accounts for a new church until the church had actually incorporated their congregation. Many church planters looked to the office personnel to help them with incorporation and creating a constitution.

Joining a national church planting movement

Minnesota was not the only denominational entity ramping up new church development. Success stories began to emerge. "How-to" materials provided step-by-step guidance on making good decisions at all points in creating a new church. Bob Logan would copyright an immensely helpful *Church Planter's Toolkit*. Win Arn and C. Peter Wagner contributed church growth perspectives.

Norm Whan, a telemarketing specialist, used home calling to start a Friends church in Southern California and developed a template for others to do the same. Telemarketing and direct mail media blitzes helped church starts to get past the critical mass necessary for churches to continue to grow. In the Lawson era, Whan would speak at an annual meeting, encouraging the young church planters to "above all else, do something."[12] Minnesota would purchase an automatic dial-up machine for telemarketing and make it available to its churches. Soon, however, the public would sour on these somewhat intrusive calls and church planters would move on to other ways of creating attention.

The Johnson Brothers and TeAMerica

Paul and Steve Johnson in the 1990s.

If you were to scan the United States with a church planting seismometer in the mid-1980s, you might be surprised by where you were getting earth-shaking activity. The Great Lakes district was being led by Minnesota transplant Larry Seiffert. Paul Johnson was planting a new church in Fond du Lac, while his brother Steve was pastoring in River Falls, and preparing for a church plant in Hudson. Under John Dickau in Home Missions, these catalytic leaders would be given a national platform in the BGC and a new era of district/national cooperation in church planting began through TeAMerica. The Johnson brothers understood organizational growth and charted BGC church planting as a movement rather than a program adding a sense of team to every level of participation. They modeled the practitioner leader. They created an assessment center for church planters built on the functional demands of the job. They empowered an extraordinary procession of influential church planting leaders, such as Dave T. Olson, Tom Nebel, Steve Smith, Dave Mobley, Dan Maxton, Greg Heinsch and Gary Rohrmayer.

Paul Johnson became a denominational leader in the BGC under Jerry Sheveland while pastoring Woodridge Church in Medina, Minn. Steve Johnson founded the visionary interdenominational church planting movement called Vision 360.

During the period from 1984 to 1989, a total of 16 churches was started in the MBC – compared to five from 1978 to 1983. The infirmity in the churches had been diagnosed by Dick Turnwall in his era. But the treatment recommended was more emphasis on evangelism. The local churches were in step with this, as was Dr. Robert Ricker, the new president of the BGC, who made it clear that his tenure would feature evangelism as the clarion call. During this era, churches often hired their second or third person on staff to work in evangelism.

But emphases on evangelism did not seem to bring transformation. Down the road, in 1991, C. Peter Wagner would stun the church with a new perspective on contemporary evangelism. "Church planting," he said, "is the single most effective form of evangelism under heaven."[13] Church planters began to quote Wagner like Scripture. Indeed, new churches would open a wider door for evangelism than had been seen in generations.

The Anderson era set the district on a path that would see a third wave of extraordinary church growth in Minnesota. The starting of 16 churches is no small achievement. But it went beyond that. The district began to grow in church attendance totals, after several years of decline. In some senses, however, Minnesota was a late bloomer in the church planting movement. Only a few new churches were targeting unchurched people. Of the 16 new churches, six were rural or small town churches. Neal Floberg had a heart for these communities. Four of the churches were urban or ethnic. These, too, would propel Minnesota on to its future ethnic prospects. Of the remaining six church plants, three were daughters of Minnesota churches and three were district initiated works. There was a potential for so much more.

Churches with an extraordinary capacity for growth

During the Anderson era, several churches began to evidence capacities for growth that had never been seen before in the Minnesota district. California was always regarded as a fertile church growth area. In the Minnesota conference, churches of more than 1,000 were virtually non-existent. And yet in the next decade, the Minnesota Baptist Conference would see the emergence of the megachurch. It would also see models of church multiplication so significant they would be emulated across the country. With those multiplication models in mind, it is interesting to observe several churches in the early steps of their extraordinary journeys.

In 1981, Wooddale church in Richfield purchased 32 acres of land in Eden Prairie. Under Pastor Leith Anderson's leadership, Wooddale was approaching 1,000 worshipers each Sunday. From 1983 to 1990, the church moved through three building phases. They completed their campus with a magnificent new worship center topped with a remarkable contemporary spire. Attendance doubled through the period. Wooddale became a national model for a megachurch. Wooddale had an extraordinarily strong organizational foundation and an unusually gifted pastoral leader. Lyle Schaller, one of the great analysts of church growth in the 90s, would call Leith Anderson the "finest senior pastor in America."[14] Anderson encouraged many churches with a lecture he called "Relocation as a Strategy for Revitalization." Wooddale's growth accelerated in the 90s. Anderson revealed his vision for the future of the church in two widely read books: *Dying for Change* (1990) and *A Church for the 21st Century* (1992). Additionally in the 90s, Wooddale aggressively started strategic new churches with extraordinary resourcing and preparation. In 2007, worship attendance was approaching 5,000.

In 1980, John Piper became the pastor of the historic Bethlehem Baptist Church of Minneapolis. John left his position as a popular Bible professor at Bethel University. Many Bethel professors during the 80s and 90s tried their hand at pastoring large churches, with mixed results. Often, they retained a full or part-time teaching responsibility in academia. Piper, with no experience as a pastor, immersed himself fully in shepherding and leading this declining downtown church of 450 weekly worshipers. The church had grown nicely to 800 when, in 1986, Piper's book *Desiring God, Mediations of a Christian Hedonist* was published. This fresh and award-winning meditation would refresh many duty-bound Christians, challenging them to delight in the glory of God. Readers found Piper's theology to be a new Calvinism with a face of joy. The response to Piper's book led Bethlehem to sponsor a Pastors Conference in 1988 that would become a powerful annual experience in worship and teaching for pastors, nationally. It also led to the founding of Desiring God Ministries in 1993, a non-profit to distribute Piper's teaching and writings. Bethlehem grew to 1,600 by the year 2000, at which point it established a new vision for a multi-campus church. They added sites in Moundsview in 2002 and a south campus in Burnsville in 2006, doubling attendance to nearly 4,000 in 2007.

On March 12, 1985, Pastor Jerry Sheveland of Berean Baptist

Church called together pastors from the Twin Cities churches to discuss "dreams, hopes, plans, and in some cases, actual progress toward the establishing of mission churches."[15] Other pastors must have felt the tug as St. Paul area pastors also met, in late 1986, to discuss church planting sites in St. Paul. Berean, under Sheveland's strong preaching, had grown to 1,200 attenders. But, whereas Wooddale would relocate to stimulate new levels of growth in the 1980s, Berean focused on establishing new churches in its growing region of the Twin Cities. Wooddale would add church planting to its repertoire after its relocation. Berean was a partner in establishing Friendship in Prior Lake which would, in turn, start a new church in Savage, and then a second campus in Shakopee. Berean invested heavily in the starting of Chapel Hill in Eagan. Berean remained a large and effective church under Pastor Roger Thompson, multiplying its ministry through the starting of other churches.

America's top multiplying churches

One cannot find a better example of a contemporary reproducing church than Grace Fellowship, established in Champlin by Dave Reno, an associate from Salem Baptist in New Brighton. With a strong media effort and telemarketing, Grace gathered 270 at an opening service in December 1988. It would sustain attendance in the 200s, which was an archetype goal for "quick start" new churches. In the years to come, Reno would lead his church to well over 1,000 in attendance. This is exceptional, but it is not what would make Grace Fellowship an icon for the church planting movement in America. Reno asked a question of almost anyone who would listen: "If a denominational office can start churches on a regular basis, why can't a local church do the same?"[16]

In a multiplication process, Grace Fellowship set out to plant a new church each year. It came close to doing that. At the same time, it challenged its new churches to start a church of their own every three years. Grace created a support network of its own called the Minnesota Grace Network. In 2007, Leadership Network sponsored a national survey of churches with a priority ministry in church planting. The survey examined a church's growth, the number of churches started over its lifetime, the percentage amount of its budget set aside for church planting, and the level of esteem held for the church in the national church planting movement. In 2008, based on the survey, *Outreach* magazine published a list of America's Top Multiplying Churches. Grace Fellowship, the only

BGC church on list, was #18 on the list, having started 17 churches in its short history.

The People's Choice Award, Rev. Brown and Philippi Baptist Church

If America's Top Churches had a Minnesota division and a People's Choice Award, the choice would be the Philippi Baptist Church and Rev. James Brown. Established in a rental storefront property at 26th and Bloomington in July 1986, the Philippi Baptist Church and Rev. Brown would daily reach into the Phillips neighborhood with a grace-filled message and tangible love. The Phillips section of Minneapolis in 1986 consisted of 11,000 Caucasians, 4,500 Native Americans, 1,100 African Americans, and 450 Hispanics. Jim and Diane Brown stated their vision to bring hope in their neighborhood and to build a church that would be a physical symbol of God's presence.[17]

The last half of the 1980s would mark the return of many MBC churches to active social ministry. As with the years of the Bethel Center, churches from across the state stepped forward to join North Central in St. Paul and the Philippi Baptist Church in feeding programs, tutoring ministries, clothing drives, and youth outreaches. Volunteers came from Worthington to Ely. In the weeks before Labor Day, Jim Brown poured his energy into his Minnesota State Fair concession Sir James Bar-b-que. Cooking and selling ribs those weeks kept the pastor and the church afloat for the year.

Philippi was able to purchase its building in the late 80s. To the delight of many, the Philippi Baptist Church established itself as a vital church in the Phillips neighborhood. To the huge sadness of all, the MBC would lose Rev. James Brown to a heart attack in 1991.

Other than Philippi, the conference in the 80s had not yet moved to replant the church in urban areas. But there was certainly a greater consciousness toward racial reconciliation developing with many churches, urban, suburban, and out-state. John F. Anderson's personal passions nurtured these convictions. President Reagan declared the third Monday in January as Martin Luther King Jr. Day, a federal holiday. A year later, the President recognized February as national Black History Month. The MBC staff for years to come met and invited others to gather on MLK Day, in recognition of Dr. King. African-American pastors brought thoughtful challenges to the attendees. Pastors James

Brown and LeRoy Gardner brought chilling stories of growing up in a racist America. Pastor Gardner would record his story in his 1996 book *Prophet without Honor*. During his years at Philippi, Brown featured Black History Month events to reach out to both whites and blacks with his message of Christ and racial reconciliation.

Ethnic church expansion to the tribal grounds of Lac La Croix

Cross-cultural church planting opportunities increased in the Minnesota Baptist Conference in the late 80s. The Roberto Trevinos established Willmar's Iglesias Evangelical Bautista. A Laotian group, meeting in the Bethlehem building, called Pastor Phou Littana to lead their group in the early 1990s. Phou would become a valued partner in the district's work. Missionary Kevin Walton took over a Southeast Asian ministry when its pastor returned to Thailand. The church established outreaches to the Vietnamese and Hmong communities and took on the name of the United Hmong Baptist Church. It partnered with Calvary of Roseville. This church would leave the conference in the 90s to seek more fellowship with other Asian congregations in the Christian Missionary Alliance denomination.

There is a principle here. To survive, ethnic ministries require an ethnic church community within the denomination. The districts and Home Missions would advocate in the late 80s for greater community and more representation for ethnic churches. The result was the formation of Ethnic Associations within our denominational family. This action would contribute to the amazing growth of ethnic churches within the conference in the 90s.

The partnership with Native people saw advancement in Lac La Croix during the Anderson era. Lac La Croix is a Native tribal village in the Boundary Waters Canoe Area (BWCA). Wally Olson had visited Lac La Croix as early as 1959. But as years went on, that early openness was repressed by tribal politics. In 1984, the seed that had been planted took root again and Olson was invited to return to the village and build a mission center. The Indian Missions Advisory Committee (IMAC) approved the new building and Olson turned to the conference for financial help. Minnesota churches contributed generously and Rob Boyd in Home Missions secured a loan so construction could begin. Lloyd Mattson, a conference pastor and Christian men's work leader, suggested

Oden Alreck as the contractor. Alreck was a member of the North Shore church. Olson and Alreck began building the modest home/center.

Art Holmes and his wife Betty moved to Lac La Croix and ministered until the early 90s. Holmes had a lifelong struggle with alcohol but, in spite of his challenges, he and Betty profoundly affected the lives of both white and Indian people. In 1991, Holmes wrote his life story in a book called *The Grieving Indian*. He traced his call to ministry and his lifelong struggle with alcohol. He is what Art Holmes has always been, direct and honest about what it is like to carry the marks of his Native grief, and yet aspire to bring his Savior to his people. This book has had a great impact on many in the Native community.

These were difficult years for the Nett Lake church. Fred Isham was having serious health problems, and Nett Lake was depending on interim pastoral help. John and Dorthea Olson, after an extended interim period, relocated to Grand Portage. The Olsons' ministry was followed by their daughter and husband who also gave leadership to the Mount Rose Church.

Trout's *40 More*, something to celebrate!

Trout Lake Camp celebrated its 40th anniversary in 1986. But to those who understood, the next year brought a truly newsworthy celebration. A strong presence of God in the ministry brought 297 recorded spiritual decisions in 1987. Camp had welcomed 7,783 people to events at Trout, 750 to Shalom House and 214 to Mink Lake. This brought the total level of participants to 8,747, a record for the camping program. But there was more to celebrate. Operational debts that had followed camp for seven years were paid. The purchases of additional land and a building debt from Shalom House had encumbered both the MBC and Trout. But now, in 1987, the camp declared "All debts paid off!"[18]

Roger Camerer and camping leaders were managing other challenges. Neither camping nor the MBC had ever initiated its own capital campaign. The national conference had cycled through four national capital campaigns. The districts were made active partners in these campaigns, but the results were often considerably under expectations. Both camping and MBC ministries benefitted from these campaigns but also expended great energy participating in them.

Before the arrival of John F. Anderson, Camerer and the camp committee brought a request to the Stewards that camping be allowed to sponsor a capital campaign that would benefit camping only. The Stewards, who had never approved a district capital campaign, agreed. When Anderson arrived, he enthusiastically joined the campaign. The campaign was christened *40 More*, celebrating the 40 years of successful camping that the MBC had completed. The campaign proposed upgrading camping facilities, putting in place needed safety codes and expanded programming.

Camping and the MBC staff expended tremendous effort toward this campaign. More than 110 churches held "birthday parties for Trout" – nearly 75% of the MBC churches. This was a stunning level of participation. Yet, after this extraordinary effort, camping reported $130,000 in pledges and contributions, a small fraction of the funds they were hoping to receive. This delayed the building of the Quad cabin, the one specific outcome of the campaign.

The consultant pointed to certain critical parts of a capital campaign that camp's leaders had not wished to make a part of its effort. Trout's leaders reflected on poor procedures recommended by the consultants – namely that commitment cards would be passed out, but not collected, at the event. People took them home and were asked to send them back to Trout or the MBC.

From the view of fundraising strategies today, the campaign card confusion may not have been the only opportunity lost. There was no real proposal for local church participation other than having a party. There was no reason for people to participate who were primarily interested in other MBC ministries. There appears to have been little effort to make the case for camp with people who had significant financial ability. The good news was that Camerer and camping learned from this disappointment. In the next decade, camp would partner with the MBC in very successful campaigns.

Bringing resources to pastors

Pastors who were active in ministry in the Minnesota conference during the Anderson era report that Anderson's leadership was exceptional in providing resources for them. Yes, MBC still provided the Pastor's Study Breaks, the Recipe for Renewal for pastor's wives, and the Pastor's Retreats. During the Turnwall era, the Pastors Council became very influential in representing the interests of pastors in the state.

Anderson utilized the potential of the Pastors Council to ascertain the educational interests of pastors. His recent ministry in California, and his pursuit of a D.Min. degree at Fuller Seminary, put him in contact with gifted professors there. He also had a close relationship with Bethel and President George Brushaber. He had twice served on Bethel's board. Bethel's faculty was a valued resource for pastoral continuing education through the years.

During the Anderson era there were clinics on preaching. Classical preaching was covered by the impeccable orator Ian Pitt Watson of Fuller Seminary. Nils Friberg presented professional materials for pre-marital counseling. There was a continuation of the small church consultation. This round focused on vision for a small church. Dr. H. Newton Malony from Fuller Seminary brought insights into *Managing the Local Church*. Actor John Holland brought an unforgettable seminar on the rare topic of the *Public Reading of Scripture*. He came with an unknown preacher as his Exhibit A. The preacher's name? John Ortberg. Other notables like Lyle Schaller, Gary Collins, John Burkhart, and Carl Dudley also brought continuing education seminars.

The exceptional nature of these events raised a question as to how, financially, the MBC was able to deliver such outstanding opportunities during the Anderson era. A benefactor, who was actively part of the conference and saw his business success as an opportunity to make an impact on pastors, provided the Minnesota Baptist Conference with financial gifts that allowed such educational opportunities. His father had been a pastor, and he had a heart for the demands of pastoral ministry. His passion and John Anderson's vision provided a unique mission match. May his tribe increase! Indeed it would.

The good, the bad, and the ugly

In September 1989, John F. Anderson began his article in *Of One Mind* by quoting from a *Newsweek* article about flagrant sexual misconduct by well-known preachers. He referred to the church's recent embarrassment with Swaggart and Bakker, who once represented success in worldwide evangelism but now represented hypocrisy, duplicity and immorality. But, he continued, "we need not turn to the television preachers to find examples of moral failure. Evangelicalism, and yes even BGC life, has ample evidence of the problem."

He then announced that a special task force had completed a five-page statement called *Guidelines for the Restoration of Ministers*, and that within its preamble were these words: "…there are certain areas of moral failure that bring a particular disgrace upon the church and the name of Christ." Anderson continued by saying that these sins are named in this document to encourage all of us to commit to a lifestyle of moral purity.[19]

Anderson's *Guidelines* were one part of a process in the conference to both rightly judge sin and graciously care for the repentant and the injured. Historically, churches were inclined to deal with these embarrassments quietly. This approach appeared to avoid embarrassment to the church and protect the pastor's wife and family. However, it left open a frightening choice of options available to the offending pastor. He could slip away to another district or denomination and continue ministry activity – and some did. The perception of the pastor being a repeat offender did not exist in most minds, although experience would show that it was a real possibility.

In 1986, the Minnesota State legislature adopted Statute 148A to protect patients from sexual exploitation by psychotherapists and counselors. The statute allowed that a patient could sue the therapist, and in some cases the employers of the therapist. It was also clear that the statute applied to members of the clergy. In many ways the law made pastors especially vulnerable to criminal charges because they were on duty as a pastor all the time and the entire congregation may be viewed as a counselee. A therapist on the other hand had specific hours of appointments and clear lines of who are patients and who are not.

The law raised legal liability questions for church organizations. If there was misconduct by a pastor, when did the congregation know of the misconduct and become culpable for the pastor's activity. Was it when one member knew, when a staff member was informed, when a board member was told, or when the matter came as an official complaint to the board or the church? For any number of attorneys, any one of these situations was sufficient to name a church in a suit. A Minnesota attorney would develop a national reputation for his litigation against the Catholic Church, and would find quite a market for leading seminars for other attorneys on how to sue a church and denomination.

The law would be a wakeup call for church organizations, including the Minnesota Baptist Conference. Clergy sexual misconduct was now more than a moral failure of a pastor and a threat to the reputation of the church. There were psychological implications in the pastor's conduct that had to be considered in his future ministry. There was a growing awareness that the damage caused by this sin was acutely felt by victims of the misconduct. And indeed, a court of law might find not only the pastor but also the church and the denomination responsible.

Is there a road back from the abyss?

Several years earlier, a Minnesota pastor had left the pastorate after sexual misconduct. The pastor removed himself from ministry and left the area to submit to the discipline of another church and pastor in another state. A decade later he returned to Minnesota with his wife and family as a layman. He was asked to preach and help out in a small Minnesota conference church. The chairman of the church talked to the conference office and expressed the feeling of the church who wished to consider this man as a pastor for their church. Prior to this time there had been no procedures in place for responding to this kind of request. When, if ever, could a pastor who failed return to ministry?

The new *Guidelines for the Restoration of Ministers* provided a framework for considering the issues at stake in the restoration of a pastor. It included a mandatory removal of the pastor from all ministry positions or roles for at least two years. A restoration process could only be put in place by the request of the offending pastor. This was followed by a period of discipline, reflection, counseling, and accountability. There was never a suggestion that re-entering ministry was promised in the end. Regular supervision would be carried on under the direction of a restoration committee, appointed and qualified to lead this process for the MBC. It was an important first step in managing the unimaginable.

So long...too short, Dr. Anderson

The BGC annual meeting was held at Bethel in June 1987. The national conference would receive the recommendation of its search committee to elect Robert Ricker as its General Secretary, now called President. The search committee had approached John F. Anderson about his availability to be a candidate. He had turned down their inquiry.

Contested elections were unusual for such positions in the conference. After the announcement of Ricker's candidacy, there were concerns expressed in many places. Although his father was a conference pastor and Robert Ricker had pastored two conference churches in the beginning years of his ministry, his two most recent churches seemed to be more in the tradition of independent Bible churches. Would he cater to our fundamentalist minority? Would he represent the conference in diverse groups such as the Baptist World Alliance?

In the midst of these discussions, several pastors and lay leaders approached Anderson about reconsidering his decision not to be available as a candidate. Anderson agreed to be nominated as a candidate for election on the ballot with Dr. Ricker. The day of the election, there was uneasiness among the assembled BGC delegates, in spite of the fact that John Anderson was a hometown candidate. When John Ortberg, a friend of the candidate, came to introduce Anderson, he spoke out with a Billy Graham-like southern accent. It was a sincere effort at a bit of humor for a tense moment, but few people were laughing.

A vote was carried out and Bob Ricker became the president of the Baptist General Conference. In all fairness, many of the concerns about Ricker's candidacy proved to be unfounded during his presidency. He actively served in leadership in the Baptist World Alliance. He cooperated with districts, and promoted a balanced home and world missions program. He maneuvered the conference through two very difficult theological issues – baptism/membership and the foreknowledge of God.

Two years later, in 1989, it was a genuine disappointment for the district when Anderson resigned his position as Minnesota executive minister to accept the pastorate of the historic Third Baptist Church of St. Louis, Missouri. Five years seemed too short.

Several years later, when Anderson retired from Third Baptist Church, he was immediately recruited to minister part-time back at Central Baptist of St. Paul. Central was the strong church John had inherited from Warren Magnuson and had continued to reshape into an urban ministry.

Dick Turnwall, John F. Anderson and Virgil Olson at F.O. Nilson's grave in Houston, Minnesota.

In 2006, John Anderson presented a monograph on F. O. Nilsson for the Friends of the BGC History Center. Perhaps some saw parallels between John F. and F.O. They were both passionate about those oppressed by societal or ecclesiastical structures. They both lived in Houston, Minnesota, and will no doubt be buried there. They were both free thinkers, although Anderson fortunately did not have to endure Nilsson's doubts and depression. They both would draw their circles of fellowship widely. Delmar Dahl teased Anderson, suggesting that his many references to F.O. Nilsson and Houston, Minnesota, were "way over the top."

However, Anderson's legacy of ecumenical cooperation would continue when he returned to Minnesota. Like Bruce Fleming, he and Central Baptist enjoyed the interdenominational fellowship of the Minnesota Council of Churches. And the Council was increasingly interested in building more bridges to evangelical judicatories. When the annual meeting met in Duluth in 2007, Minnesota's First Lady, Mary Pawlenty, was the featured speaker. But the Rev. Peg Chemberlin showed her evangelical Moravian roots and brought a strong greeting to the Minnesota conference from the Minnesota Council of Churches. Chemberlin had visited the MBC center and she had included Executive Lawson as a guest in discussion with council sessions. She would be elected as the president of the National Council of Churches. John Anderson was the key link for these two church organizations, fulfilling Fleming's call, "Churches should evaluate all overtures to unite."[20]

John F. Anderson left an enduring mark on the Minnesota Baptist Conference in his five years of leadership.

Notes

[1] Moral Majority cofounded by Paul Weyrich and Jerry Fallwell, 1979.

[2] Video produced by People for the American Way.

[3] John F. Anderson, *The Baptist Pietist Clarion*, "Why I Am a Baptist," p. 6.

[4] Richard Turnwall, 126th Annual Reports, Executive Minister's Report, p. 37.

[5] Bruce Petersen, 127th Annual Meeting, Board of Stewards Report, p. 25.

[6] John F. Anderson, interview, 2013.

[7] Florence Johnson, *Happenings Digest*, "Turning Opportunites into Realities," Summer 1988.

[8] Donna Sahlin, 127th Annual Report, Director of Growth Resources, 1985.

[9] Alvera Mickelsen, *Women, Authority and the Bible*, Intervarsity Press, March 1986.

[10] Author's recollections.

[11] From an unpublished memoire of Victor Winquist.

[12] Quote by Franklin Delano Roosevelt.

[13] C. Peter Wagner, *Church Planting for Greater Harvest*, Regal Glendale, 1990, p. 5.

[14] Lyle Schaller, stated in a national denominational executive briefing in the early 90s.

[15] *Of One Mind,* March 1985.

[16] Author's recollections.

[17] *Happenings Digest*, Winter 1987.

[18] *Happenings Digest*, Winter 1988.

[19] John F. Anderson, *Of One Mind*, September, 1989.

[20] S. Bruce Fleming, 109th Annual Report, Executive Secretary's Report, 1967, 19.

Churches Started or Welcomed: 1985-1989

1984

Bruno Bible Fellowship (Bruno)

Faith United Fellowship (Federal Dam/Boy River)

Bethel Bible Fellowship (Gaylord)

Calvary Baptist Church (Redwood Falls)

1985

Calvary Baptist Church (Madison)

Berean Baptist Church (Glencoe)

Warroad Baptist Church (Warroad)

1986

Cornerstone Church (Savage)

Hmong Central Baptist Church (St. Paul)

Phillipi Baptist Church (Minneapolis)

1987

Majestic Oaks Community Church (Blaine)

Grace Fellowship (Brooklyn Park)

Iglesia Evangelical Bautista (Willmar)

1988

Emmanuel Community Church (Oakdale)

Little Mountain Community Church (Monticello)

The MBC and Missions

1. J.G. Johnson at the end of his term along with MBC leaders at the beginning of theirs.
2. The Annual Meeting remained the gathering place for the conference.
3. First Spanish of Minneapolis became the first Minnesota Latino congregation in 1972.

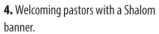

4. Welcoming pastors with a Shalom banner.
5. Emmett Johnson with every executive's task of raising the budget.

1. Emmett breaking the bread in an early Shalom Retreat.
2. Staff and board members at groundbreaking for the MBC office center.
3. New Conference Center at 1901 W. County Rd. E-2.

4. Jack Bergeson's work ethic kept his appointment book full.
5. At North Central Church's welcome in 1969, Rev. Leroy Gardner addressed the conference.

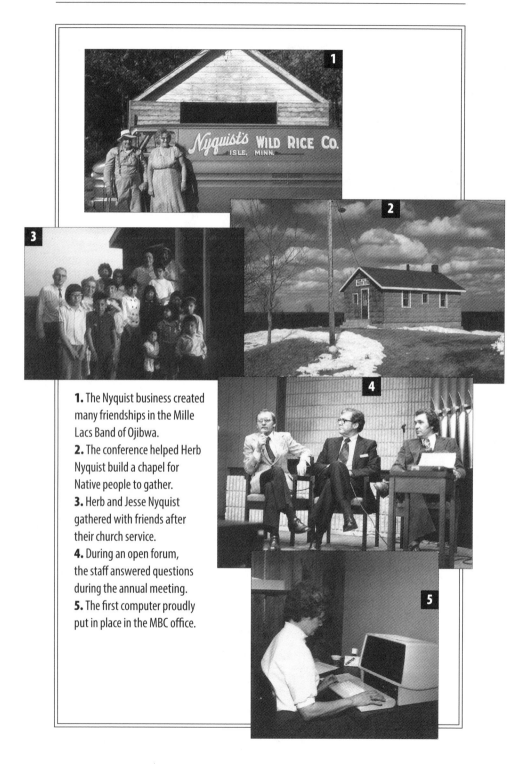

1. The Nyquist business created many friendships in the Mille Lacs Band of Ojibwa.

2. The conference helped Herb Nyquist build a chapel for Native people to gather.

3. Herb and Jesse Nyquist gathered with friends after their church service.

4. During an open forum, the staff answered questions during the annual meeting.

5. The first computer proudly put in place in the MBC office.

1. The staff gathered during the Anderson era.
2. Neal Floberg directed missions from Turnwall to Lawson.
3. Art Holmes and Betty pioneered ministry among the Lac La Croix Native village.
4. Wooddale's vision for the future.
5. Wooddale, the first MBC mega-church.

1. Roger Camerer led camping for 23 years and could lead a song service besides.
2. Wally Olson became part of the Nett Lake Native community.
3. In Wally's final weeks the Bois Forte tribe presented him with honorary membership.

4. Several MBC churches spent a week creating day camps for Nett Lake children.
5. Nett Lake Fellowship gathering. The group now meets in a new center.

1. Grandview Christian Home, Cambridge, Minnesota's first retirement home.
2. The Conference became a financial partner in Scandia Shores in Shoreview.

3. Rob Boyd collected fire truck toys, and every pastor would agree Rob was MBC's early responder.

4. Cristo La Roco, our Latino church, represents several Spanish-speaking churches in the north.
5. Latinos in Minnesota enjoy meeting in statewide gatherings.

1. Family Gatherings grew to almost 2000 attenders in 10 statewide meetings.
2. Family Gatherings brought the staff into many roles directed by Dale Rott.

3. First Baptist White Bear with humble origins would become a "turn-around" church.
4. Bob Merritt delivers a message to a growing Eagle Brook Church, the revisioned White Bear Church.
5. Eagle Brook now ministers on five campuses with one administration.

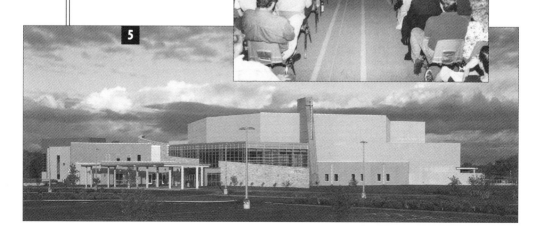

1. Joel Nelson, often wrapped in technology, has led Minnesota's church planting ministry.
2. True Spirit Church came out of Rev. Gardner's North Central Baptist Church.
3. Chris Reinertson started River Church in the Mall of America.

4. Signage transforms malls, schools and theaters to houses of worship.
5. It's always important to provide a welcome to the Journey.

— Chapter 12 —

The Truett M. Lawson Era (1990-2007): The Tipping Point

On a new wave of growth for the future

A tipping point in the growth history of the Minnesota Baptist Conference came in the early 90s. There had been a net growth of about 3,500 in average church attendance in district churches from 1970 to 1985, but a net decline of nine in the number of churches. The inevitable closing and merging of distressed churches was not being balanced by the starting of new churches.

Truett Lawson joined the MBC after directing church planting in the Southwest.

Church growth demographers would suggest that unless a denomination is increasing its total number of churches by 2% each year, it would be facing decline.[1] For the conference in Minnesota with many older churches, this number (which amounted to about three new churches a year) had been a challenge for two decades. The Anderson era had seen a turnaround in both attendance numbers and the number of new churches started.

David T. Olson, in his significant study of American churches, suggests that new churches provide more for a denomination than the sum of their attendance. They lower the age profile of the group and increase its multi-ethnic character, better preparing it for the future. They provide the best approach for reaching an emerging generation. They attract passionate lay and pastoral leaders who can ignite new energy and ideas. New churches often become the research and development factory for models of ministry that can transform existing churches. They are very effective in growth through conversion and therefore contribute strongly to kingdom growth. They will also provide a foundation for continued ministry in the denomination during their mature years – as the new churches reach age 10 to 40.[2] The turnaround in church planting in the era was encouraging.

The 1990s produced significant church growth movements that affected Minnesota. Evangelicalism in America was beginning another metamorphosis. Several new "evangelical" movements had stimulated growth in the 70s and 80s. In the 70s, the charismatic movement swept through evangelicalism. Renewal movements broke out among the Episcopalians. These new expressions of the Holy Spirit began to affect the evangelical churches with prayer groups, healing services, and spiritual gifts. Charismatic churches were formed in most communities in Minnesota. Traditional Pentecostal denominations, like the Assemblies of God and Four Square were seeing growth. In the 80s, new associations of charismatic churches were formed. Groups such as Calvary Chapel and The Vineyard saw significant growth.

Churches of the Minnesota conference responded to these movements variously. Some expressed great openness to the gifts, if not to classic Pentecostal theology. A few aligned with cessationist theology, maintaining that the miraculous gifts ceased with the end of the New Testament era. There is little doubt, however, that the charismatic movement awakened the Minnesota Baptist Conference in the power of authentic God-centered worship. Jack Hayford told the Minnesota Baptist Conference annual meeting in the early 1990s that true Christian worship touches the non-believer, not just the believer. Several Minnesota churches would follow in this Hayford tradition.

Another church model would be embraced more broadly by the Minnesota Baptist Conference in 1980s – the teaching and equipping church. Based strongly in the biblical culture of the evangelical church, this model saw the church as a classroom for the teaching of the Word of God, often presented in verse-by-verse exegesis and exposition. The teaching and discipling that was then accomplished would send the believer out to serve and evangelize. Ray Stedman at Peninsula Bible Church in Palo Alto, California, through his Discovery Papers, demonstrated with eloquence that Bible teaching could come alive in preaching. Charles Swindoll, whose radio program promoted his preaching, built Fullerton Free Church in California around expository preaching. John MacArthur, the pastor of Grace Community Church in Sun Valley, California, joined this group during his lifetime, teaching and writing reformed theology with a bent to a purer gospel message.

The challenge of this model, however, was always the equipping part. President Bob Ricker's call to evangelism was timely, based on the disappointing decline in adult baptisms in the conference. But how do you equip a church to do evangelism and then see them doing it? The actualization is the problem. In 1985, Frank Tillepaugh (*The Church Unleashed*) of the Bear Valley Community Church in Colorado, shared his passion for getting the believer out of the "fortress." Two large churches in Minnesota brought him to speak to all interested churches. It was appreciated by all, no doubt, but there were fears among many that teaching and equipping churches did not seem to produce new converts.

The unsettling movement that seemed to be working

In the mid-1980s, this author was asked by *The Standard* magazine to write three articles on California super churches. Garden Grove Community Church, (Crystal Cathedral), Charles Swindoll's Fullerton Free, and the Mt. Zion Missionary Baptist Church of E.V. Hill were selected. Nearly 97% of the members of Fullerton Free came to the church as believers, in contrast to 62% at Robert Schuller's Crystal Cathedral. Schuller's success in reaching the unchurched was admired by many pastors. Rick Warren and Bill Hybels were greatly influenced by Schuller's effectiveness in reaching the unchurched. Their churches would lead the Seeker Sensitive Movement in the 90s on similar principles.

In an interview on his *Grace for You* program, John MacArthur criticized the seeker movement. "Robert Schuller started it!" he stated. "Bill says his guru is Robert Schuller….and Bill Hybels then was drawn to the success pattern of this. He was drawn to the numbers and, of course, the wealth that came with it."[3] Elsewhere, MacArthur recounted that shortly after seminary, Rick Warren and his wife attended Schuller's leadership seminar and were blown away by what he was doing in Garden Grove. MacArthur and many others saw the connection of Warren and Hybels with Robert Schuller as a disqualifier.

Although no Minnesota Baptist Conference churches tried to replicate Schuller, many MBC leaders believed his ministry was using cutting edge principles to reach America's unchurched culture. Their interest was not Schuller's television program or the possibility-thinking rhetoric of his messages, but the philosophy behind the church and its passion to reach people. During the Johnson/Turnwall era, many MBC leaders and pastors attended Schuller's leadership seminars. But it was through the influence of Hybels and Warren that the seeker movement became imbedded in the ministry DNA of many Minnesota conference churches.

Who are the unchurched?

In 1978, the Princeton Religion Research Center published findings from the largest study ever conducted on the unchurched in America – their values, interests, and backgrounds. Males dominated the unchurched group. A higher percentage lived in western states. Three-fourths of unchurched people indicated that for some extended period they had once been part of the church but had given up on that part of their lives. Surprisingly, most of these still believed in God (83%) and many in Christ, as they understood him. Unchurched people were a significant and increasing percentage of America (41% in 1978; 44% in 1988; and 47% in 2002).[4]

In 1991, demographic researcher George Barna, who had been working for the Disney Channel for six years, decided to dedicate his talents in demographic research to assist the church in reaching a changing country. Conference leaders, especially pastors of new churches from the 1980s on, began to understand their target audience in a more complete way because of Barna.[5]

Robert Schuller had started his new church in 1955. Without modern demographics, he surveyed his community to see what the neighbors felt about church and why they had chosen not to attend. He found that they had preconceptions that were quite different than Schuller expected. They felt that the churches were always fighting each other, that they were begging for money, that it felt conspicuous attending church, and that they rarely saw, in church, the culture and quality that they liked when they went to concerts. Schuller would disclose in his seminars that he used these hang-ups to form his strategies in building his church.

Bill Hybels also organized a survey when he started. Teams of three people visited homes asking people why they did not go to church. He, too, found people were bothered by being asked for money. They were bored and did not find the messages relevant to their lives. They disliked the guilt-inducing challenges. Hybels created a profile of just who "unchurched Harry and Mary" were.

Rick Warren surveyed the neighborhood in his California community. In his pastors' conferences, he recommended that church leaders get out in the community to hear how the people feel about church, asking questions like: What is the greatest need of our community? Are you a church attendee? Why do you think most people do not attend church? What could I do for you as a pastor? And do you have any recommendations for me?[6] It was through his surveys that Warren developed a sense for the felt needs of Saddleback Sam – the average unchurched guy in his city.

The churches Warren and Hybels led became stunning examples of church growth. Beyond that, they demonstrated that a church could grow by reaching unchurched people, and thereby fulfill the Great Commission. Warren wrote *The Purpose Driven Church* and founded the Purpose Driven Network for pastors. Hybels created an annual Leadership Summit that brought pastors and their lay leaders into thoughtful planning for their church. Rick Warren became the most prominent evangelical Christian voice in this age. Bill Hybels invited churches with a match in mission to join his Willow Creek Association in 1992. His annual leadership seminars went global.

Experimenting with seeker sensitive

The Minnesota Baptist Conference became an early adopter of seeker movements. Dick Daniels started Christ Community church with Mike Gray as a purpose driven church in 1990. And there were others. Most Minnesota church plants were inclined to incorporate seeker principles into their plans. In the jargon that would develop, they became "seeker sensitive" rather than "seeker-directed." The seeker-directed church generally abandoned all traditional church elements to provide a comfortable place for the seeker.

The passion to reach unchurched people would also transform some existing churches. Early on, Brooklyn Center Baptist Church sold its large edifice and moved north to a school in the next ring of suburbs in Brooklyn Park. They had resources and a competent staff where they had ministered in Brooklyn Center, but the church was in decline. They began meeting in a school, practicing seeker sensitive principles. For a time it appeared that this experiment would fail and that the conference would lose this new congregation, just as it had lost the old. But with a leadership core of tenacious laity, the church made a transition, graciously sending their visionary but aging staff on its way and calling a younger pastor to lead the church. Edinbrook church would flourish under Ivan Veldhuizen as a traditional church, but one with a large door to the unchurched in the community.

Some churches, looking for a shortcut, sought to become a seeker sensitive church through a name change. Most would be awakened to a cruel reality that "a name change doth not a transformed church make."

The most stunning turnaround church in the Minnesota conference was Eagle Brook church. Seeker principles and effective leaders would transform First Baptist of White Bear into Eagle Brook, a multi-campus seeker church. After a strong resurgence in ministry with the interim preaching of Greg Boyd, Pastor Bob Merritt in the next several years, at great personal cost, redirected the church to become the most successful seeker congregation in the Twin Cities. The quality of leadership at Eagle Brook was outstanding, and the innovations of Willow Creek were evident. Eagle Brook became the site for the Willow Creek's Leadership Summit video simulcast. Eagle Brook committed to multisite ministry and would realize a potential few American megachurches had achieved.

What is in a church name?

Selecting a name was a key part of the seeker sensitive process. After the late 80s, virtually no startup churches incorporated the word "Baptist" in their names, unless they were ethnic congregations. Baptist in the African American community still had a strong message of substance and position in the community. For many recent immigrant groups, Baptist defined the belief systems they had suffered for in their home countries. But most church planters in the majority culture felt the name "Baptist" brought up negative associations – hard-shell Baptists who don't dance or go to movies. This was deeply troubling

Your Basic Name Groups

Executive Lawson, in a tongue-in-cheek article in the *Relate* publication, noted various themes emerging in MBC church names:

- *The Woodland Group* – Woodland Hills, Woodridge, Wooddale, Woodcrest, Westwood, Riverwood, Basswood, Majestic Oaks, Oak Hill
- *The Food Group* – Ham Lake Baptist, Hayfield Fellowship, Mount of Olives, Fish Lake Baptist
- *The Directions Group* – Memorial Drive Bible Fellowship, Country Roads Church, North Isanti/South Isanti Baptist
- *The Existential Group* – The Crossing, Journey North, CrossPoint, Connections Church, Crosswinds Community Church
- *The Religious Group* – Cross of Christ, Cross of Glory, Grace Fellowship, Word of Grace, Calvary (times 7), Faith (times 3)

(Truett M. Lawson, *Relate,* Jan/Feb 1998.)

to many traditional conference people and also to those who knew and honored the great history of the Baptist movement. To these, it seemed like the ship was being set adrift on an uncertain ecclesiastical sea. And indeed, there were risks.

In his seminars, Robert Schuller talked about naming of the Garden Grove Community Church (later known as the Crystal Cathedral). "We are a denominational church," he would say, "part of the Reformed Church of America. Would you want that word in your church name? Reformed? You know what everybody in the community thinks? They think we are saying, 'We want to reform you!'"[7] So in the 80s and 90s there were quite a number of "community churches" in the Minnesota conference.

A few churches headed in a different direction, calling their group a "fellowship" rather than a church. Although this name added a contemporary casualness to the name, most unchurched people were not really against "church" per se. Some were likely confused about what a "fellowship" was. So that name quickly became arcane.

The historic honor of being named the "First Baptist Church" was largely ignored as modern thinking arrived. Biblical geography or theology had dominated the naming trends during most of the 20th century – Bethany, Gethsemane, Bethel, Grace, Calvary, or Glory. City names were always popular – Littlefork, Waskish, Litchfield, Lake Sarah, or Alvarado. But now other themes prevailed.

If creativity were the criteria for naming, the honors must go to Jeff Gauss who pastored two churches in the Lawson era: Lounge Divine, a post-modern church on Grand Avenue, and Epiphany Station, a highly successful new church in Thief River Falls.

A group of churches ready to dream

Between 1990 and 2008, the Minnesota Baptist Conference would grow from just under 25,000 attendees to just under 60,000. It would start 61 new churches in Minnesota, many of these through the vision of its local churches. There was a failure rate of 10%, which was extraordinarily low when studies indicated a national average of 50%. In 2008, these newly established churches contributed almost 15,000 worship attendees to the 35,000 increase in overall growth. This growth was noted in the year 2000 when the *Minneapolis Star* referred to the Minnesota Baptist Conference as the fastest growing religious group in the State of Minnesota.[8]

It must be made clear, however, that all of this growth did not come through seeker sensitive church strategies. Quite the contrary, two of the faster growing churches in Minnesota had real issues with the market-driven nature of the seeker movement. Greg Boyd, pastor of Woodland Hills in St. Paul, was emphatic in his reservations about the seeker approach. Similarly, John Piper led Bethlehem Baptist on three campuses without a name change. They were not alone in their suspicions of the seeker movement.

This was the Minnesota Baptist Conference's historic third wave of growth. The first wave came in the last quarter of the 19th century through a deep passion to reach Swedish immigrants. The second came through the re-visioning of the conference as an English-speaking American evangelical denomination in the quarter century following WWII. The third wave came at the turn of the millennium through Minnesota's willingness to translate the message of the gospel into the language of the increasingly diverse and unchurched culture of America.

Enter Executive Minister Truett M. Lawson, California transplant

In the fall of 1989, Stan Droogsma, chairman of the Minnesota executive minister search committee, contacted Truett Lawson in California as the list of suggested candidates shortened. Lawson was the Associate Minister of Missions for the Southwest Baptist Conference. "I realized that there was an openness in my heart for this key position in the Minnesota Baptist Conference. That phone call brought together several streams of joy and meaning to Jill and my lives. One was our love for Minnesota, its land, people and culture. Another was the joy we were finding in district mission work in the Southwest. This work was a newly developed focus of ministry for us after seventeen years in the pastorate. We are here, then, feeling very much led of the Lord, humbled and honored at the same time, ready to be used in whatever way God would choose."[9]

Lawson was 47 years old with three children at home when he began his leadership role in Minnesota. He came out of the culture of church planting in the Baptist General Conference. Many of the existing district executive ministers were nearing retirement. In the years that followed Lawson's election, several districts followed Minnesota's lead and called younger DEMs with a background in starting churches. In many cases, the salaried mission director positions were replaced by practitioners – church planting pastors.

During this 18-year period, from 1990 to 2008, the districts of the national conference thrived. New levels of partnership with national ministries came with TeAMerica, but issues of district vs. national remained complex during this period. In a combined meeting of national and district leaders, church growth expert Ed Spitzer was asked about top-down as opposed to bottom-up denominational models. He answered that any national denominational organization that wanted to see maximum growth would need to support and feed those closest to where the church planting action was done – the districts and the church planting churches.[10]

Lawson had served the Minnesota conference in pastorates in Aurora and Isanti. He had also pastored in Torrance, California. While a pastor at Elim Baptist in Isanti, Lawson had started a new Minnesota Baptist Conference church in Princeton. In Torrance, he had initiated communication with the Baptist General Conference Rengo Association in Japan regarding starting a Japanese language church in the South Bay. This project would become a reality after Lawson's departure for Minnesota. From 1987 to 1990, he led the missions department of the Southwest Baptist Conference, giving leadership to the starting of 25 new churches in California and Arizona. On July 15, 1990, he began his 18-year leadership era in the Minnesota Baptist Conference.

AIDS encounters, caught in the contrasting emotions

Shortly after his move to Minnesota, Lawson received word from Ojai, California, that a collector friend, Bob, had succumbed after a long struggle with AIDS. For eight years, Lawson had collected Rookwood pottery. He had set up for some pottery shows in the L.A. area, often sharing a booth with Bob, an art dealer from Melrose Avenue in Los Angeles. The news came from a mutual friend who added a comment to his call, "Don't wait for my tears. After the deaths of 68 friends and acquaintances, I have none left."

Some of the first cases of AIDS were in Los Angeles. In 1990, the death toll was ramping up until 1992 when it became the leading cause of death for men from ages 25 to 44. Bob and a young man in Truett Lawson's Torrance church both found their way back to Christ during those years. Lawson wrote three articles in *The Standard* in the late 80s. One told the story of that young man. Another challenged the opinion of some that AIDS was the judgment of God on homosexuality. The third was a forum of discussion with an AIDS mom and Dennis Cope, a medical doctor. They interacted on how the church could respond to the suffering of so many in the AIDS crisis.

A month after entering into the ministry in Minnesota, Lawson opened a long, carefully worded letter from a Minnesota pastor who strongly denounced *The Standard* articles. He believed that the compassionate approach of the articles indicated that the new Minnesota executive did not support a biblical view of homosexuality.

Staff changes, smooth transitions

The Anderson era staff was still in place at the MBC – Delmar Dahl, Neal Floberg, Donna Sahlin, Roger Camerer, and Steve Whitehouse/ Will Youngquist. Edna Schultz was encouraged to delay her retirement. Any executive minister in the dissertation stage of his doctorate would have considered carefully how to convince Edna Schultz (an academic herself) to stay at least until the completion of the thesis. But it was not just Edna Schultz who was ready to retire. Delmar Dahl and Neal Floberg, in the next two years, announced their intent to retire. A knowledgeable staff made for a smooth transition for Lawson. But Lawson benefitted also from the almost monthly calls of encouragement that came from Third Baptist Church of St. Louis and his predecessor John F. Anderson. Lawson was in an unusually privileged circle of support as he began his ministry in Minnesota.

In his first annual report, a few months after his arrival, Lawson recorded his vision for the district. "I have arrived as executive minister with a vision: to give leadership to the Minnesota conference so that it will become an outstanding home missions organization, competing in the marketplace of missions. Gone are the days when a denominational office can validate itself only by providing a limited number of services to its constituent churches. These services are critical and will be delivered by the MBC with the highest level of distinction possible. Yet, we must also realize that we have been called to a mission purpose – to do together what we cannot do alone in reaching people for Christ."[11]

Lawson was in a Doctor of Ministries program at Fuller Seminary. D.Min. degree programs were beginning to transition away from the classical research-based dissertations in favor of ministry-based projects. In the 1990 Annual Report, Lawson informed the delegates of his first leadership initiative, "I am committed to a process. I am thankful for the outstanding leaders already provided on the Board of Stewards. Since my arrival, I have been working with the Stewards in the development of an assessment and planning process that will clarify our purpose and secure our vision in the MBC for the next decade. We have entered into a consulting relationship with Nehemiah Ministries to complete a major assessment of the health and vitality of our member churches. We will analyze our ministry and history – its priorities and problems. We intend to do our best to listen and interpret the trends in society, our state, and in our own ministry to understand and respond to the changes that will be coming to us in the next decade. We firmly believe that God is the author of our plans and dreams for his church."[12]

Catching a Second Wind, planning and assessment

This comprehensive planning process was intended to bring insight and direction to the MBC staff and leaders who would be forming five-year plans for all areas of district ministry. It would be completed over the next 18 months. In 1992 the goals and plans were presented to the pastors and churches at the mid-winter Family Get-Togethers (now called Family Gatherings) with the title *Catching a Second Wind*.

The planning began with a growth study of the churches. The process also examined the financial health of the district overall. The MBC staff created lay surveys asking lay people for their feelings about the district and where it should be going in the future. Lawson led focus group gatherings for pastors. The district office sorted the results. Executive Lawson included phone and personal interview information from denominational districts that were regarded as doing "benchmark" ministry.

As the data was received, the Stewards under the leadership of Dan Lindh and Truett Lawson examined several planning themes to clarify mission, and cast a new vision. The facilitators used storyboarding to find agreement. Four essential areas of mission had evolved in the planning process: planting and revitalizing churches, resourcing our churches with new ministry opportunities, providing excellence in camping, and ministry to pastors and their families.

The Steward process identified six critical issues that must be addressed if the future was to unfold according to our plan:

1. The growing tension over ministry styles, contemporary and traditional.
2. Change and decline in many churches, especially in rural areas.
3. The changing ethnic face of the state.
4. The funding crisis related to the shift from general organizational giving to designated project and personality giving.
5. Lack of ownership of our ministry by many people, but particularly the young.
6. Major new camping challenges – more demands on an aging facility.

Additionally, a set of Planning Imperatives were identified in each of the ministry areas. Camping immediately convened staff and committee members around the imperatives. The MBC staff did as well.[13]

Staff out the back door and in the front

New staff configurations were possible due to the retirement of long-term staff people. Neal Floberg offered his last annual report in the fall of 1991. He noted the tremendous changes in methodology he had witnessed in church planting during his era. Church planters were now assessed by a team, representing the entire BGC, before they were deployed to start churches. They raised support independently to bring a flow of funds beyond the denominational grant. They often recruited staff and lay leaders, selectively, before they opened public meetings. And they would seek to start with a "critical mass" before public morning services were launched.[14]

Floberg reported that eight Minnesota churches had been started in cooperation with home missions in the 1980s. But in the last several years, since the initiation of these new strategies, 12 additional churches had been started, five of which were ethnic or urban in nature.[15]

The engines that had been fired up in the Anderson era were moving the train strongly down the track in the 90s. But district church planting was going to see an additional transformation. The leadership role with Floberg's departure was going to be transferred to practitioners – actual practicing church planters in Minnesota, catalyzing their own church planting movement.

Delmar Dahl transitioned to a part-time employee in 1991. He was spending much of each month in his "Camelot" – Sister Bay, Wisconsin. Dahl's working partnership with Donna Sahlin in the retirement retreats built a program that was the envy of every district in the conference.

In the fall of 1992, Lawson announced that a call had been given to Rob Boyd, who had been a vital partner with the Minnesota district in his work at BGC home missions. Lawson envisioned someone who had the skills to assume some of Floberg's work in church revitalization and evangelism. But he needed someone he could trust to work with pastors and their families as well. And ideally this person also could lead the district into significant new opportunities with immigrant Latino and African American partners. "Do you have someone in mind?" the Stewards asked, incredulously, when the position was described. "Well, yes I do as a

Rob Boyd, a friend of the MBC in Home Missions, joins the staff.

matter of fact!" Lawson answered. Rob Boyd brought a large, well-organized box of tools to execute all of the areas under his supervision.

Boyd, however, never liked his title – Director of Church and Pastoral Vitality – although he loved his job. "He asked me what I wanted to do in the Minnesota Baptist Conference, and then he let me do it. But when he told me my title, I said, 'What kind of Lawsonism is that?'"[16]

Most district executive ministers cherish the nickname "pastor to pastors." Lawson questioned his skillset in that area. He and Rob Boyd would share the district's ministry to pastors, occasionally referring to the division of labor as "boxing glove love and kid glove love." Indeed, that "boxing glove love" role of the executive would become painfully apparent in sexual misconduct incidents. Church/pastoral conflict and theological controversies also loomed on the horizon of the MBC. This unique division of roles for Boyd and Lawson proved helpful for the

Can Bishops be a Blessing?

In 1994, an ecumenical gathering of urban churches in Minneapolis invited the heads of Minnesota's church groups to join its participants to promote urban ministry. A lunch was planned following a worship time. The worship band was trying too hard. It was a raucous bunch with suggestive dress. As the bishops in clerical garb entered the room, it was clear that many were traumatized. Most of the guests stayed for the box lunch event, but no facilitator was provided. Halfway through the eating of sandwiches, someone said, "What did you think of that?" To which came the reply from a guy in a long, flowing habit, "What the #*%& was that all about?" Laughter and discussion ensued.

Before the group left, Lawson and two others were asked to design a gathering for bishops and other denominational leaders to regularly pray for the city. During the entire Lawson era, each quarter, the heads of communions met, ate lunch, prayed, read prayers or Scriptures for 30 minutes. Someone would share his or her spiritual journey. A guest would speak about something that mattered to God in the city. This gathering was unique and a huge blessing to all.

district through the mutual trust and collegiality that endured during their tenures. Boyd continued in a ministry relationship with the district well past the Lawson era. Donna Sahlin's and Roger Camerer's long tenures also contributed to the stability and expansion of ministry in the district during the Lawson years.

Once again examining governance and organization

A revised staff and board organizational model sought to adapt the ministry to its changing opportunities. More "members at large" were added to the Stewards in the constitutional revision of 1991. This change contributed to gender balance and ethnic representation that were problems with the all-white, male boards of the earlier periods. Dick Turnwall had created a "house of representatives" kind of election process. There was a nominating committee, but both the harvesting of names from each area and the voting at each area caucus put the election process out of the hands of those who were trying to achieve greater ethnic and gender balance. This was further complicated by the efforts to create balance in clergy and laity. With more "at large" members, the MBC saw more women and minorities on the board.

The executive staff became "directors" of key ministry areas, appointed by the executive minister with one-time ratification by the conference. They were accountable to the executive minister with annual reviews, and could be fired by the executive minister with cause. Constitutional standing committees no longer existed. Directors worked through task groups or committees of their own selection.

Two steps forward and a financial fall on the face

If things appeared to be moving with unusual ease, reality would arrive with the financial director's report at the annual meeting in October 1991. The report revealed an operating fund deficit of $50,000 in the first full year of Lawson's tenure (1991). Behind the numbers was the radically changing financial environment created by the conference's move to designated giving. With much more income flowing into designated accounts, the national conference was also under great stress. Bethel saw a 30% reduction in conference support that same year. Minnesota had always received 50% participation from home missions for church grants. Those funds had dried up. The operating budget was now competing with camping, church planters, Indian ministry personnel, and a host of projects, all trying to raise support out of the same church budgets.

Executive Lawson reduced staff from five executive staff persons to three and three-fourths. The leased cars benefit provided to staff became a car allowance or a high mileage used car. Roger Camerer's salary and benefits had always been paid out of the MBC operating budget. Camp began a three-year plan to enfold the camp director's salary into its own operating budget. Ministries within the district family began strategizing how to raise their own program funds.

Financial numbers turned back the next year, but there were many lessons learned. One lesson was that the MBC could not expect that its member churches' support level would increase in the future. Indeed, income from churches remained constant for the next decade and a half. And the staff would need to work hard to maintain that.

Finding new springs as the old rivers were drying up

It was also clear that this financial environment would require new strategies to promote the expanding mission of the district. Most of the appeal letters that came from the district were directed to churches to raise the conference budget at the end of the year. But now the rules of engagement had changed. Camping started raising scholarship funds. Churches and individuals subscribed to build buildings. A bike-a-thon continued to raise funds for camp.

The MBC began sending regular ministry update letters to individuals with requests for financial support for district ministries. The MBC was realizing that among its constituents were many possible donors. Gary Bawden, a Minnesota pastor with a background in direct mail solicitation, became a partner with the district in these direct mail appeals. Donor lists were developed and expanded. The MBC was finding many new friends. If a new source of funding was imagined, it was investigated.

In the early 90s, church planting had been recognized as a critical link in bringing a spiritual awakening to America. Suddenly church executives were talking about foundations and non-profits that were ready to give money to church planting and new churches. The MBC and other districts set about finding these mysterious funds but without much success. While researching, Executive Lawson found the address of a foundation that liked to help small churches. When the pastor of

Lengby called to see if there was any assistance available to help them install an inside toilet in their old Swedish Baptist church, Lawson gave them the foundation's name. Several months later, to everyone's delight, a nice check came in the mail and after a brief period of construction, the executive minister joined the 20 or so members to dedicate their new facilities-inside-facilities.

The national office declared that it was moving away from large national capital campaigns. They were exhausting for the staff, expensive to organize, and recently performing well below expectations. Instead, they had hired a fundraiser with local church campaign experience to encourage churches to consider the conference when carrying on their local capital campaigns. There were large fees for fundraising organizations – large commissions to guys with Rolex watches and southern accents. But it sounded like a good idea to help the churches with their capital campaigns and assist the conference at the same time.

Lawson contacted Bob Johnson from Sioux Falls, a retired insurance executive with a wonderful history in the conference. In stark contrast to the typical fundraiser, Johnson had a folksy way of raising money in local church campaigns. The MBC dedicated the program to raising money for church planting. For nearly a decade, Johnson did local church campaigns around the state. The MBC paid him a flat fee for his expenses. The church agreed to dedicate 10% of its campaign to church planting in Minnesota. Many churches would sign on to this attractive plan, especially new churches.

Funding challenges stressed the national leadership during the first term of Bob Ricker's presidency. The shift to designated giving had forced the conference to assess a percentage fee for its missionaries to support the Chicago office. But this was a worrisome practice. It could send conference missionaries to other sending organizations.

Ricker hired a development consultant, Bob Screen, to lead a process that would clarify missions and align ministries through a mission-match process. The results would assist the conference in assessing services and ministries that were more attractive to donors and churches. Dennis Smith, a pastor and development officer of the BGC, led the process, but cannot be held responsible for its outcome. It was a productive process until district leaders realized that Screen's process was leading to structural change. The district's leaders at this time were not buying any new management structure that would compromise the district's autonomy. The process blew up in meetings at Rosarito Beach, Mexico. It would take some time to repair the damaged relationships.

Strategic Initiatives energize camp planning

Within Minnesota, the Stewards and the executive minister created a Strategic Initiatives Committee. This group examined existing ministries and proposed projects so that new opportunities would not be missed and core ministries would not be overlooked. It examined funding strategies and promoted fairness. The Strategic Initiatives Committee would provide the framework for a new capital campaign for camping and the MBC in the years ahead.

Camping was faced with unusual burdens while sitting on the edge of some of the greatest opportunities since its founding. The Minnesota strategic planning process had discovered an important demographic trend. Live births in the 80s had steadily increased, meaning that in the 90s, camp would see a steady rise in the pool of potential campers coming from our churches – the pig in the python, so to speak. Additionally, Lawson noted in his annual report that camp would now be serving an MBC family that was 5,000 members larger than eight years before.[17]

There was already a capacity issue at Trout. Trout Lake Camp had begun to see increased numbers after 1987 when it welcomed 1,650 summer youth campers. This number was climbing each year, and Roger Camerer reported an unusual surge in 1992. That year brought 2,145 youth campers to Trout. Estimates placed the capacity of the facility at 2,320.[18] Because total capacity is hard to achieve in a world of age-group camps, Trout was likely at its capacity.

Camp director – "Chief" or CEO?

Roger Camerer had stabilized a camping program that had loosened its stakes somewhat by growth and experimentation. Although stability was a virtue in the 80s, it would not be in the 90s. Trout Lake simply could not report AWOL for one of its greatest periods of opportunity. In 1991, the executive minister revised the job expectations of the director of camping and youth. "Mr. Camping" or "Chief," as lay people often called their beloved camp directors, could no longer be the go-to guy who was always there when you needed him. The new camp director would need to provide critical executive functions to move the camp to the next level. Camerer's job description was rewritten to include planning, marketing, promotion, fund raising, as well as executive staff management.

The planning process had revealed short-term and long-term needs in the camping program and facilities. There had been complaints that Trout was not keeping up with the growing expectations of its constituency in accommodations, food, and programing. These critiques within each department were transformed into *Planning Imperatives*, all of which started with: "We will….." In his 1992 report, Camerer included these imperatives for camping. They included: a marketing study, internal evaluations, the study of other camping models, a site development plan for expansion, creative redesign of traditional programing, a viable winter program, evaluation of the need for a Twin Cities-area facility, improving the fiscal and physical viability of Mink, improving the accessibility of camp for our ethnic churches, seeking full accreditation by the ACA (American Camping Association), reducing the MBC subsidy of camp by 33% per year for three years, creatively using the camp facility to provide rest and spiritual renewal for pastors, and building cash reserves to eliminate the need for credit-line borrowing.[19]

During these days of assessment, Director Camerer hired two experienced staff members to the team. Dan Frank came from the Middle East district. He proved to be an exceptional operations guy with drive and a very high work ethic. He also knew food service and the food at camp took a spike upwards. Scott Brueske came from the Evangelical Free Church camping systems and provided fresh programming to Trout's youth camps.

Camp's imperatives become significant results

There was definitely more to do. Not only were the camps completely full, but Shalom House was seeing record bookings. Its small kitchen was turning out meals on weekends three seasons of the year. Tree House, the promised new facility that could assist in winter camping opportunities, was completed, and together with the Quad cabin provided a nice winter retreat location for up to 60 people. Nine churches booked the first season and three of them were groups from the ethnic churches. Camp had moved beyond the days when the staff would move to the cities for the winter. It must be said, also, that the camping staff were not limitless in energy. In the years to come, camp would deal with staff tension and personal exhaustion, as the pressure of a year-round camping program would affect the staff.

With the numbers up and a strong staff in place, now was the time for camp to make some of the moves it had entertained earlier. Previously, camp had moved from a seven-day camp to six. In 1992, it announced that it would hire 20 full-time counselors. There had been some close calls with volunteer counselors. The threat of some kind of serious accident or sexual misconduct was a horrific scenario. Hiring full-time counselors would provide more training and more supervision for those who were in the closest ministry relationship with the campers.

In 1993, Trout announced that its camps would all be coeducational. To some this move seemed confusing, but it quickly became quite acceptable. Safety and accessibility became a concern in all projects. Trout worked hard to minimize its barriers as adventurous youth with disabilities ventured onto the rooted paths of the camp with assistive devices like motorized wheelchairs.

Mink Lake was always an unusual camp. In the early 90s, it endured as an alternative kind of rustic camp, in a world that was adding luxury and amenities to everything. Numbers regularly disappointed the staff. Facilities were barely adequate. Lack of electricity, tent dwellings, and very old, poorly constructed buildings contributed to the financial losses every year. It was clear that Mink would need a new role in order to endure. Staff sought to enrich the program's attractiveness by stepping up the number of adventure opportunities – rock climbing, portage canoeing, and trekking. Trout was utilizing Mink by shuttling adventure camp participants to Mink Lake for skills training until a van accident reminded the staff of the dangers of such a two-site camping program.

The camp staff pondered various plans to expand the Trout Lake site. Initially they proposed a new camp called "The Village." This project would entail joining two new buildings to Wren cabin. Director Camerer then reported in 1993 that the staff was discussing placing a new camp for younger campers on the 80 acres that the camp had acquired in the 70s. It was now being used for nature and horse trails. The next year this proposed facility was named: The Outpost. The new facility would be a stockade type facility at the base of the ski hill. The Strategic Initiatives Committee and the executive minister began to join this discussion, and assess the capital financing it would require. Future planning was becoming a critical camp function for the first time in more than a decade.

Notes

[1] David T. Olson, *American Church in Crisis*, (review by Roger Ganzel) February, 2008.

[2] Ibid.

[3] John F. MacArthur, *Grace for You*, "Straight Talk about the Seeker Movement," 2004.

[4] George Gallup Jr., *Gallup Online*, "Unchurched on the Rise," March 26, 2002.

[5] George Barna, *The Barna Report 1992-93, America Renews its Search for God*, Regal, 1992.

[6] Rick Warren, *The Purpose Driven Church*, Zondervan, 1995, p. 190.

[7] The author's memory of Schuller's words.

[8] *Religious Congregations and Membership Study – 2000*, Rosemary Research Center, Fairfield, Ohio.

[9] Truett M. Lawson, 132nd Annual Report, Executive Minister's Report, 1990, p. 11.

[10] BGC Leadership Team Meeting, Cozumel, Mexico, 2007.

[11] Truett M. Lawson, 132nd Annual Report, Executive Minister's Report, 1990, p. 12.

[12] Ibid, p. 13.

[13] Truett M. Lawson, *Catching a Second Wind* (MBC publication), 1992.

[14] Neal Floberg, 133rd Annual Report, Mission's Associate Report, 1991, p. 19.

[15] Ibid, p. 21.

[16] Paraphrased from the Boyd retirement event in 2013.

[17] Truett M. Lawson, 134th Annual Report, Executive Minister's Report, 1992, p. 12.

[18] Roger Camerer, 134th Annual Report, Camping Director's Report, 1992, p. 24.

[19] Ibid, pp. 21-22.

— Chapter 13 —

The Lawson Era:
Unsettling Gusts on a
Rapid Journey

The last dollar goes to church planting

With the retirement of Neal Floberg in 1992, Dave Reno, church planting pastor at Grace Fellowship in Champlin was recruited to the position of Minnesota's church planting coordinator. There were now three levels of leadership in the MBC: the executive minister, directors (salaried), and coordinators who received a stipend for their work. Reno understood the principle that local churches were in the best position to start other local churches. He was respected by his colleagues in the district and in the national conference. He had a strong and methodical work ethic. He could light up the room when he brought a challenge to the annual meeting. Reno's position would close the gap between the traditional mission director's function, often occupied by executives who had never started a church themselves, and the church planters, known for their free rein tendencies. From this point, the MBC would hire leaders who were personally part of the church planting movement.

Fewer budget dollars were going to a salaried mission director, so the MBC could offer more assistance to the church planters in the form of start-up grants. They could also assist and support the church planter with fundraising. The finance department set up deputation accounts that receipted the church planters' support contributions. Occasionally these accounts would move into deficit. In one painful situation, the church planter decided to take another job when the church's account was $68,000 in the red. The tiny church felt no obligation to repay these funds. This was a tough lesson for the district but one that led to stronger internal controls of these funds, and greater expectations of integrity in the church planter relationship.

The Minnesota district was not the only district to face these funding issues. Many BGC districts were unable to maintain their staff salaries with operating funds and were forced to look for other capital assets for operations. Always tempting were the assets left to the district by churches that had disbanded. The assets would often be sold and used for district operations. The MBC was able to avoid having to divert funds this way during the Lawson era. All such assets went into the Grant Fund, which made funds available for new churches or existing church projects.

Ministries were helped by the district's extended period of financial health. For most of the Lawson era, the general fund income from churches remained a steady $375k to $400k per year. But the designated part of the operating income (excluding camping) grew to $450 to $550k per year, providing nearly a million dollars annually for MBC ministries plus camping. The finance department was always challenged with this growth and the MBC's multiple accounts. Good reports were always a challenge. Audits were a time for intercessory prayer.

Reno subscribed to the principle that one of the key ingredients in a successful church plant was the support and supervision that could be provided by a mother church. Occasionally "mother" was two churches or even three – a team of mothers. But these links provided financial support and they also enriched the ministries of both the daughter church and the mother. Reno was modeling this at Grace Fellowship when he formed the Minnesota Grace Network. He used the energy of his church planting colleagues to push the movement forward.

Wooddale enters a remarkable period of multiplication

In the late 80s, while in the middle of his church's massive relocation, Leith Anderson led Wooddale to begin planting daughter churches. Anderson understood the risks in church planting and took extraordinary steps to minimize failure. Failure of any kind was not in his vocabulary. In most cases, the church planter joined the Wooddale staff for a year during the first stages of the new church. In several instances, the planter was a staff member at Wooddale, as Joel Johnson was with Westwood. Westwood would grow to more than 3,000 attendees in its first 14 years

Hope, the Passion that Serves the City

In 1996, when Steve and Carol Treichler gathered with 12 other people to discuss starting a church in the heart of Minneapolis (the U of M area initially), some things were clearly seen but many other things remained unrevealed. This was to be a church for the city and a church for the young. What remained unrevealed was how they could find a church home in an area of wall to wall city buildings.

In 2002, Hope established contact with the Central Evangelical Free Church which was closing its ministry. Through the openness of the Evangelical Free Church, Hope found a home in the city in this historic facility. In this new setting, Hope continued to grow to over 1,000 attenders and, by the end of the decade, space was again a problem. Nearby, the Augustana Lutheran Church was declining in their large facility and, in a magnanimous gesture of grace, sold Hope its building for its original 1883 cost, playing forward the gain to this young congregation. It is no secret that the 102-year-old former pastor, William E. Berg, adored Steve's preaching. But Rev. Berg still gave Augustana's final sermon on April 29, 2012, as this amazing building was transferred to Hope Community Church.

of ministry. The church planter was recognized in the congregation and allowed to recruit a core of people from Wooddale for the new work. In the case of Woodcrest of Eagan with Pastor Jerry Schommer, Governor Tim and Mary Pawlenty joined the core group for a time, returning later to Wooddale.

In the years ahead Wooddale started nine churches, and several of these reproduced as well. There was Woodridge in Plymouth, then Woodcrest in Eagan. Timberwood was in Nisswa. Later came Northwood Church in Maple Grove, City Church in Minneapolis, Brookwood Community Church in Shakopee, and Bridgewood in Savage. Wooddale would work with evangelical denominations outside the Baptist General Conference to start churches as well. Anderson would become the head of the National Association of Evangelicals, as Carl Lundquist had a generation before.

Interestingly, a Wooddale church historian found a newspaper article from April 2, 1943, that described the organization of Wooddale as an interdenominational church. Although settled in its affiliation with the Minnesota Baptist Conference, through the years, Wooddale embraced a larger affiliation also. Later in its affiliation statement, Wooddale describes its branding. "Wooddale Church is an evangelical interdenominational church with a constituency from a broad range of denominational and local church backgrounds."[1] Although the original use of the term "interdenominational" is unclear, its use to describe a church in modern times was quite an attractive description of Wooddale. The alternative descriptions, "denominational" or "non-denominational" both had negative content.

Oakwood Community church was a "restart" in Waconia. Over the years, the Scandia Baptist church had declined. After a failed restart, Wooddale assimilated its remaining members within Wooddale and recruited Steve Anderson to be a pastor for them. The group, having grown in size after one year, replanted Scandia Baptist church as the Oakwood Community Church. Oakwood, in spite of a few bumps in the road, remains the longest continuously operating church in the Minnesota Baptist Conference.

Membership and baptism, a serious discussion develops

In 1993, two new churches prepared to join the Minnesota Baptist Conference. Woodland Hills was a church plant led by Greg Boyd and Paul Mitton. Woodcrest was a Wooddale daughter church started by Jerry Schommer. Dave Reno introduced these churches, both of which launched in the fall of 1992. Woodcrest had approached 200 in attendance, and Woodland Hills an extraordinary 600. But the recognition councils who met with the leadership of both churches discovered atypical requirements and processes for membership. These somewhat unusual structures for membership fostered extended discussion at the 135th Annual Meeting, held at Cragun's Resort in Brainerd. The churches were received into the MBC by a vote of 152 to 66 after a one-hour forum. This forum discussion continued and intensified, becoming a national issue in the Baptist General Conference.

Woodland Hills had an unusual membership structure. The church had grown at such a fast pace that it was trying to assimilate its attendees yet carry on its business as a church. It had created membership requirements for its core group that included both a confession of faith and believer baptism by immersion. At the time of admission into the MBC, there were about 75 in the committed group with 600 others attending. An added complexity came when Woodland Hills used the word "membership" to describe the larger group. Everyone who attended was a member, Greg Boyd would declare. But on the books there were only 75 who had accepted the constitutional requirements for being part of the decision-making group at Woodland Hills.

It was actually the two-tiered membership structure of Woodcrest Church, and Wooddale before it, that sparked the most discussion on baptism and membership. In 1991, a future's task force of Wooddale was considering Wooddale's opportunities now that it was ministering from its new Eden Prairie campus. The elders of Wooddale were recommending that Wooddale recognize three membership categories – a *church member*, a *fellowship member* and a *non-resident member*. A *non-resident membership* for students and seasonal participants was not new to BGC churches. The *fellowship membership* status definitely was. A *fellowship member* status did not require baptism, but it allowed most levels of participation in the life of the church. Wooddale had approached the MBC to see if this change would risk their continued affiliation. It was clear Wooddale had not changed their belief or practice of baptism. Wooddale would continue to make baptism a requirement for *church members* and require it for the pastoral staff and elected leaders, but not for *friendship members*. A detailed four-page document explained the history of the recommendations with thoughtful theological and ecclesiastical questions. In early 1993, the congregation of Wooddale approved their new membership procedures.

The baptism/membership issue in the conference was far from over. It was a new issue to the conference but not a new issue to Baptists. The British Baptists were divided over the matter, with some churches requiring baptism for membership and others requiring only a confession of faith to participate.

Open membership (not requiring baptism for believers to join) advocates point to the fact that no historic doctrine is compromised in open membership. Churches still have a regenerate membership. And for many Baptists, denying someone fellowship who is a believer just because they have some confusion over their baptism, is not in the spirit of Christ's church. Open membership advocates see formal membership requirements as more related to Catholic and Lutheran traditions where membership defines the kingdom people. It is implied, in those traditions, that you have to join the church to be assured you are part of the people of God.

On the other side, it was quite clear that our Swedish founders and their successors regarded the requirement of believer baptism by immersion for membership as a very important belief and practice. MBC leaders as recently as Dick Turnwall argued strongly for its importance, rejecting the Evangelical Free Church position that baptism is more related to the Christian's faith journey than to a church's membership requirements.

Executive minister Truett Lawson reported Wooddale's membership changes to Board of Stewards early in 1993. In the May 1993 *Relate* publication, he prepared a lengthy article based on a discussion document he prepared for the Stewards. He took an inclusive position on Wooddale and Woodcrest's membership requirements. Wooddale's membership modifications did not alter their continued commitment to the conference's beliefs and practices of baptism.

Lawson sought the opinions of pastors in a survey on membership procedures. "In the main, our pastors are comfortable with the traditional position of requiring baptism for membership, but they feel that the churches should be permitted to explore these issues, individually, and that our district should not exclude from its membership those churches with differing views of closed and open membership regarding baptism."[2]

The survey revealed that 66% of the pastors were strongly supportive of the conference tradition of requiring baptism for membership. But when asked if a church should be excluded from the conference for not requiring adult baptism by immersion for membership, two-thirds did not favor exclusion. Two-thirds also believed it was a decision that belonged at the local church level, not the denomination.

During this time, Lawson coordinated a forum event with Bethel Seminary and its dean, Fred Prinzing. *Membership and Baptism: A Theological Dialogue* was held on June 6, 1993, with 112 in attendance. The day's program began with introductions given by Lawson and Prinzing. Participants included: Bob Stein on "Baptism in the New Testament," Robert Rakestraw on "Baptism in the Early Church," Jim Mason on "Believer's Baptism in Practice Today," Herb Klem on "Baptism and Missions," Leith Anderson on "Wooddale's Journey in the Membership/Baptism Practice," and Greg Boyd on "The Baptism Decision and the Spirit's Work." BGC president Bob Ricker delivered closing remarks. There was active discussion and questioning throughout the day. There was an amazingly broad variety of views.

Although the focus of this issue was on Woodland Hills and Woodcrest, other non-conforming churches were emerging within and without Minnesota. Minnesota's Emmaus church in Northfield, located in a college town, had practiced open membership for some years. A South Dakota church had as well. Two BGC churches with ethnic constituents were practicing open membership. For these churches, requiring baptism for membership participation would have been a challenging condition. There was a Korean church that welcomed predominantly evangelical Presbyterians, and a Messianic fellowship welcoming Jewish seekers. Both had open membership on the baptism issue.

New church recognition delayed over baptism/membership

The national conference and Ricker requested a one-year delay in welcoming these Minnesota churches. The Stewards reluctantly accepted. The President appointed Victor Winquist to lead a Baptism/ Membership Task Force assigned to lead forums in districts, and then bring a recommendation to the BGC annual meeting in June 1995.

In March 1994, the Stewards adopted a *Statement on Baptism/ Membership* to feed into the ongoing process of discussion in the conference. It recommended a tolerant approach to churches forming new membership strategies. It recommended allowing the unbaptized believer to belong to the church. However the unbaptized should not gain the right to vote on matters of doctrine or affiliation, nor should they serve on the church boards or pastoral staff.

There was a debate as to whether these kinds of conditions were a slap on the wrist to the new non-baptized member. Actually the intent was to prevent a day where the *friendship members* were so predominant that they could vote to change essential doctrines in the church. Wooddale would report just the opposite result was occurring. The choice of becoming a *friendship member* as opposed to a full *church member* seemed to encourage people to go ahead and be baptized for the full membership. This fascinating outcome in two-tiered churches seems to indicate that people are more influenced by being presented with the choice to be baptized, than by being presented with the require-ment to be baptized.

There was clearly a building tension in the conference in 1994. Truett Lawson wrote in the *Relate* publication that the Southern Baptists had reached "conflicting majorities" on issues similar to this. The national body would take a majority position one way but a district body would vote as a majority to hold a different position for their churches.[3]

In June 1995, the Baptism Task Force brought a recommendation to the national conference. Its recommendations were presented as guide-lines. This was helpful as constitutional changes to remove all non-con-forming churches would not have been received well. The guidelines reaffirmed the conference's historical policy of requiring baptism for membership. It recognized "two tier" memberships, but proposed that non-baptized members not be given the name "church member." It also agreed with Wooddale and the MBC that non-baptized church partici-pants should not occupy leadership roles or be given voting privileges in matters of doctrine or affiliation. Woodcrest and Woodland Hills were welcomed into the fellowship of BGC churches.

Growth Resources and Conference on the Family

Growth Resources and Donna Sahlin had never been afraid of a challenge. They had launched an entire curriculum of club materials designed for the smaller church and put it in operation in 70 MBC churches. After the planning cycle of 1991-92 revealed that people and churches were asking for more help in ministries to families, Executive Lawson and Donna Sahlin's department launched the Conference on the Family.

On Saturday, January 30, 1993, 700 adults and 530 children con-verged from across the state to attend 20 workshops at Bethel Seminary. The lead speakers were David and Karen Mains, with Richard K. Allison providing inspiration. For two years, the conference would provide this day of enrichment on the topic of the family and ministry to families.

Ministry to older adults ramped up during the mid-90s. There were nine retirement retreats at Shalom House each fall. Marilyn Starr had stepped away from her role as director of women's athletics at Bethel to lead the BGC Gold – the conference ministry to older adults. The ministry was robust and Minnesota was benefiting. The MBC sponsored a spring older adult event hosted by Fred Tuma at

Ham Lake Church. Most years, MBC Gold sponsored a travel option with Marilyn Starr and the Sahlins.

After the thaw, the women Splash into Spring

Women's ministries in 1989 created plans for a late winter event called Splash into Spring. It was a strong event drawing women from across the state to a Twin Cities hotel location. Christine Kolb's leadership continued to provide strong programming for women through the early 90s. Two of the favorite speakers in the 90s were Luci Swindoll, sister of preacher Charles Swindoll, and Liz Curtis Higgs. Luci had been a corporate executive (Mobil) and opera singer (Dallas opera) and did her own art. She was approachable, devout, and very funny. Liz, however, allowed her audience to confront the struggles of faith and daily living. She would return to speak three times. Numbers swelled when she anchored the Splash conference.

Beth Post replaced Christine Kolb and continued the leadership of Splash and Women's ministries. Daughters and mothers, special church friends, moms ready for refreshment – all came expectantly and received generously from Women's ministries during the Splash years.

In 1997, a well-funded national organization promoted the Women of Faith conference at Northwestern College's campus. They brought a parade of the most popular women's speakers in the country. In the next years, it would be clear that Splash into Spring would find it difficult to compete as both conferences were in the spring of the year. But ministries seem to have a God-intended life cycle. Splash would sponsor its final event in the year 2000.

The Adventure Club, the Conference on the Family, and soon Love Lift for Ukraine revealed certain skills that Donna Sahlin possessed in her department work with Diane Wicklund. Truett Lawson said that Sahlin was a highly skilled prototyper. A prototyper was able to take an idea and build it into a working model. Of course, this applies to widgets and software systems. But it can also be observed in creating programs in an organization. Donna could take a visionary idea and make a working program from it.

This skill was the perfect match for Executive Lawson, who was not short of ideas and also had the persuasiveness to promote the new idea. So for nearly two decades, Lawson and Sahlin worked for the benefit of the MBC. Sahlin would say, "Truett is our visionary!" Lawson would respond, "That may be true, but Donna is the prototyper, who can put ideas into working ministries – and that is a rare and important skill."

Although Love Lift for Ukraine certainly started as a visionary idea, it would move like a fire among the Minnesota churches in the decade of the 90s.

Chernobyl set the fire in Ukraine

A connection between Minnesota and Ukraine would have been unimaginable before 1990. If you had used the word "Ukraine" in a sentence, it would probably have been the object of the topic, "Chernobyl." Everyone knew about Ukraine's nuclear disaster. After several days of tests ordered by the central authorities in Moscow, Reactor 4 exploded and started to burn, sending radioactive clouds around Ukraine, Belarus, and on to Europe. The reactor had repeatedly failed tests to determine whether its back-up diesel engines could continue to cool the reactor in the event of a power failure. The poorly prepared test and its unimaginable consequences reinforced every negative perception of the Soviet state possible.

The problems with the reactor were being ignored or covered up by Moscow's controlling elite. Despite repeated test failures, the problem was bounced around a careless bureaucracy until some incompetents tried a test and put the reactor in distress. The explosion went unreported for two days, and only then was described as a small fire which delayed containment and exposed hundreds of thousands to radiation. Many Ukrainians noticed their elite neighbors suddenly deciding to vacation in Crimea. When local fire crews were called, they were not even aware that there was a radiation risk. Many, and often the most brave, died within days.

But Chernobyl also caused an explosion of a different kind. First it was *Glasnost* – the call for increased openness and transparency that ignited change. Then it was *Perestroika* – a call to reform and restructuring. The population was on fire. Finally, it was obvious that all the king's horses and all the king's men could not put the Soviet empire together again.

A historical door had opened up. At first most of the hundreds of Minnesotans who would travel to Ukraine did not even know how to pronounce the name of the newly formed republic. We are going to "the Ukraine," they would say. That was the old regime when "the Ukraine" was a region of the Soviet Union. Now it was "Ukraine," a sovereign state, exercising its autonomy for the first time in centuries.

But those Minnesota folks, apart from the joy of meeting their new sister church, could recall no greater moment than their visit to the little Chernobyl Museum in Kiev where so many demonstrated with their deaths what was so wrong in their old Soviet life.

A Love Lift across the world

Like the search for the headwaters of the Mississippi River, it is not easy to identify the origins of the powerful Ukraine ministry that would carry so many along for so many years. Key to those origins were Paul and Linda Wicklund, who were generous partners of the MBC in many ministries. The Wicklunds were part of a prayer group in Calvary of Roseville, and had been praying for a new ministry opportunity.

The 1990-91 MBC Strategic Plan had revealed some unexpected outcomes. There was a strong interest in short-term lay missions among both youth and adults. There was a feeling that the organizations that were doing short-term missions were not well-connected theologically and were often poorly organized.

In the middle of 1991, Russia could no longer retain its grip on the states of the Soviet Union. Reforms were not moving fast enough, and in December, after a failed coup, the bankrupt Soviet empire released its grip on the nations it had muscled into its control. During this period, brothers Paul and George Ozerkov visited the MBC office seeking assistance in starting a new church for the stream of Russian-speaking immigrants that was resettling in Minnesota. The staff heard dramatic and troubling stories from these two, who had been deacons in a Baptist church in Alma-Ata, Kazakhstan. During their conversation, the question came up as to how many Baptist churches there were in Kazakhstan. Their answer was 140. This was almost the exact number of MBC churches. "What if we establish sister churches?" Lawson inquired. It was a stunning moment for all, as God had just showed up with an idea.

The Wicklunds and the Lawsons pursued further fellowship with the Russian-speaking immigrants while they investigated ministry options. Lawson wrote to Denton Lotz of the Baptist World Alliance. He had heard that American Baptist churches had aligned with sister churches in Nicaragua during the 80s. The Wicklund family pursued the dream by signing on with Josh McDowell for a mission trip to Russia, visiting the

Born in Ukraine, Growing up in America

Historically, the Swedes and Ukrainians have always had many mutually helpful connections. These days you may find names like Sveta, Marina, Anya, Nadya, Natasha, Yulia, Valia, Zhenya, or Lida spoken in conference homes and churches.

The sister church connection often brought Americans into caring ministries in orphanages near their sister church. Although it was rare, as Ukrainian international adoptions are very restrictive, quite a number of wonderful Ukrainian young people now live among us. To many of these girls, now young women, the MBC's Donna Sahlin was affectionately known as, "Mama Donna."

Girls adopted as children from Ukraine are reaching adulthood in Minnesota.

Baptist headquarters in Moscow. Gregory Kommendant from Ukraine was soon to become president of the Baptists. They brought with them the interests of Calvary and the MBC. But unfortunately, most of the leaders were not in their offices the day of that visit. Visits at that time were impossible to arrange in advance because of poor communications.

In October 1991, Lawson sent a letter to the churches. It was three months before the final dissolution of the USSR. He described the current discussions for "a pioneering mission initiative in the former Soviet Union through a unique partnership of churches." The letter envisioned "sister churches who will explore together ways of mutually assisting each other. You dream the dreams!" It was unclear where this vision might end up. Kazakhstan proved to be a nightmare to reach with even single travelers needing to spend one or two nights at the Moscow airport. Through the persistence of the Wicklunds, the MBC learned that the Slavic Gospel Association had a trip planned to Ukraine in the spring of 1992. They could also arrange a meeting with Baptists in Cherkasy, Ukraine, one of the regions of the Baptist Union of Ukraine.

In the spring of 1992, Paul and Linda Wicklund and Jill and Truett Lawson departed for Ukraine. The country was still using Russian rubles for currency. The darkness of Communism still overshadowed most of the public settings. After riding down the Dnepro River on board a marine taxi, the travelers were greeted in Cherkasy, Ukraine, with American flags, spiritual blessings and, occasionally, unexpected kisses on the lips.

Vladimir Belous, the senior presbyter for the region, served as a guide as the two couples traveled to churches, schools, orphanages, hospitals, and political offices. Belous continued to serve as a guide of another sort. He wisely maneuvered between the cultures of the Americans and the Ukrainians, to reveal their common heart for the gospel. The Lawsons and the Wicklunds were introduced to the desperation of the strangled remains of Soviet promises. But with this sadness was an insatiable sweetness in spiritual fellowship. The Baptist believers told stories that sounded like Jews in the holocaust. And doors everywhere were opened up to help with the spiritual hunger and human suffering that was apparent.

The travelers returned to the U.S. profoundly changed and extremely motivated. The Minnesota Baptist Conference had its first sister church link. Calvary of Roseville would partner in ministry with Zolotenosha's House of Prayer. The visitors met with the church in a home that had been left to the Zolotenosha believers by a Christian widow. About 30 people, mostly older and mostly women, formed what would be not only the first but also one of the strongest sister church links in Minnesota. Through the link with Calvary, this house church with its shoemaker pastor would build a lovely building and become a strong church in the region. Zolotonosha and Pastor Victor Deev would also partner in the sistering experiment with other churches. Calvary of Roseville and Zolotonosha set the pace for sistering in Ukraine.

Over the next two years, the visits continued and a handful of sister church relationships developed. It was not easy. Risk takers, and those who could not say no to friends, were the first to travel to Ukraine. It was expensive, and staying in homes was not anyone's idea of a vacation. Paul Wicklund, an orthopedic surgeon, opened doors for doctors to partner with doctors when he demonstrated an arthroscopic knee surgery before an amazed group of Ukrainian doctors. It was the first such procedure done in that region and perhaps the country. What they were shown, the Ukrainian doctors would continue. When Paul returned, the doctors proudly paraded their first school of knee surgery patients walking with good results.

The Wicklunds and the Lawsons visited orphanages. They learned that the communists featured a showcase orphanage in each region, perfect in every respect and available to visitors. But when pastors in local communities took the visitors to see the orphanages in most major towns, the tours were heartrending. Linda, an educator, began to look for partnership opportunities in the public schools. She began to talk to churches about children's work. Christian teaching of children was forbidden in the church, under the communists, so the majority of churches had almost no children's ministries.

In the fall of 1992, Donna and John Sahlin joined the growing group of interested Minnesotans. John and Jan Carlson travelled with the Wicklunds, and the team began to percolate with ideas. Orphanages were the broken heart of the nation and would become the passion of many women, including Donna Sahlin and Linda Wicklund. Both sensed the great opportunity that might exist for ministry to children. They were both passionate about children's ministries after their amazing collaboration in Adventure Club. The Carlsons found home-based agriculture to be an area of opportunity to assist Christian families in establishing sustainable mini-farms.

Executive Lawson recognized the Sahlins' passion and ask Donna to assist him with what would become the Love Lift for Ukraine, a sister church movement between Minnesota churches and the Ukrainian Baptist churches. By the fall of 1993, there were 19 sister church relationships.

A division of labor as Sistering moves on

Brochure to introduce sistering in Ukraine to Minnesota churches.

At this early stage, the Ukraine ministry would face its first quiet crisis. Paul and Linda Wicklund invested their lives, their resources, and their passions in this emerging ministry. Linda's Adventure Club became the basis for adventure camps for children in Ukraine. Paul's medical contacts led to amazing partnerships with doctors. Many early travelers were from Calvary, encouraged by the generosity of the Wicklunds.

Truett Lawson and Donna Sahlin became the voice for the recruitment of other churches. The MBC office began to set an enormous pace of support for churches willing to sign on to the sister church adventure. Small churches raised funds and goods in their towns like international charities. The office began to arrange trips and produce Adventure Camp materials. Pavil Grigas became the coordinator on site in Ukraine for the teams. Arlo Auch had a special interest in the ethnic German areas of Ukraine, but became a key leader in arranging travel. Bethel Church in Mankato under Pastor Dave Banfield and Ham Lake under Fred Tuma became successful examples of churches setting up sister church relationships.

Eventually the Wicklunds/Calvary and Lawsons/Sahlins/MBC realized that there were two centers developing in the ministry. Tension began to inflict pain to dear friends in the process. It was not easy, but in 1994 the Wicklunds decided to continue their partnering ministry under the non-profit name Shepherd's Foundation. The MBC, with Truett and Donna, would continue linking new churches under the title of Love Lift for Ukraine. Looking back at the results of this first real crisis in the ministry, one cannot help but discern the will of God at work here. God clearly was preparing both leadership structures for the opportunities ahead.

After the first two years of creating sister churches with Ukraine, executive Lawson and the Wicklunds asked for time in the BGC World Missions board. Love Lift for Ukraine was linking sister churches in Minnesota, but other BGC churches had signed on as well. District organizations had traditionally not become involved in world missions before this. The board was gracious and listened to the presentation. It did lead to some lively discussions outside the board meeting. Some career missionary strategists warned that the direct linking of churches across cultures was either unwise or unnecessary. There was always a fascination with this new Minnesota explosion in missions.

Lawson's re-election – the MBC more like a parachurch organization?

In mid-year 1995, the Board of Stewards initiated an evaluation of Truett Lawson. A comprehensive evaluation survey was mailed to senior pastors, church staff, lay leaders, Stewards, and former Stewards. Lawson's performance was in the 4s and 5s on a Likert scale of 5. Two areas were lower – camping and financial development. There were some negative comments, citing his active role in the Baptism/membership debate. At the Alexandria annual meeting in October 1995, the delegates voted to reappoint Lawson for a second term by a percentage of more than 90%. Newly re-elected Lawson wrote in *Relate* under the title "I Hear You! Negative evaluations are the most growth-stimulating input for me."[4]

Lawson reported in his 1996 Annual Report that one comment in his performance evaluation that year especially caught his attention. "Truett has made the Minnesota Baptist Conference more like a para-church organization." Lawson reflected that the comment both disturbed and pleased him. "If the evaluator meant that under my leadership, the Minnesota Baptist Conference no longer provides the services to its churches it once did, then we have failed." Parachurch organizations suck energy and finances from churches, but do little to serve them in return. "But if the evaluator saw, in the MBC, a strongly focused mission-orientation, the critique feels like a compliment."[5]

Lawson and Boyd at work

Rob Boyd's presence on the staff was a key ingredient in strengthening ministry to pastors. Boyd became active in pastoral placement. He was perceptive and supportive. He would say to prospects for Minnesota pastorates, "I will take 29 minutes in this interview, because after 30 minutes I tend to fall in love with people and lose my objectivity." The Lawson-Boyd team reconfigured the traditional Minnesota role of the executive minister. It offered to pastors two different people in the district office – two skill sets. Boyd would demonstrate his unique skills in support and mentoring. Lawson could bring perceptiveness, analysis, and recommendations that were needed in placement and in difficult circumstances.[6]

Church/pastor conflicts usually saw Lawson taking the active role when the conflict involved the pastor. But because the potential losses and risks were so great in a conflict of this nature, the staff often joined Lawson by conducting every member phone interviews. Lawson would say that a church could lose 10 years of church growth in one badly handled year of conflict. Clearly, every member phone calling required hours of staff time. Families and individuals would sign up for phone appointments. MBC staff would schedule their calls and ask the church attendee to be ready to answer these questions. What has been your association with the church? What attracted you to the church? What difficult things do you observe happening in the church now? Is there anything you believe the MBC ought to know about this situation?

The interviews revealed the pattern of the conflict. The fact the every member had received a call would assist with the congregation's buy-in on a recommended solution. After the interviews, Lawson would write a report and form recommendations, first with the church staff, then with the Board, and finally with a report to the full church. Several independent evangelical churches came to the conference for help after experiencing destructive internal conflicts.

Together in the wasteland, clergy sexual misconduct

In the early 90s there was an increasing public awareness of clergy sexual misconduct. First there was the outrageous conduct of television evangelists, then came the almost weekly unfolding of inappropriate conduct of Catholic priests. And almost always, as the stories were told, there were reports and records of church officials making efforts to minimize, deny, or hide the damage done in these situations. Church organizations were not just being held accountable for their clergy's behavior; they were being scrutinized for any attitudes that might lead them to give their guilty pastors a pass.

The Minnesota Baptist Conference began to deal with clergy sexual misconduct allegations from the past. Victims were realizing that they were not to blame. Although they were complicit in the moral failure of a pastor, they had placed their trust in a person with great spiritual power over their lives. And they had been betrayed. In 1991, Lawson was asked to assist with 15 clergy misconduct situations in Minnesota churches. Over half of these came from victims of past misconduct who from fear or guilt had never come forward with their stories. Now, either confidentially or openly, they were ready to confront the pastors who had hurt them.

When Rob Boyd joined the staff in 1992, the MBC was able to provide a greater level of assistance in these situations. An accusation of clergy sexual misconduct demanded immediate attention for the protection of everyone involved, but the emotional content tended to exhaust the staff. Participating as a team brought perspective. Nils Friberg was becoming a recognized authority in misconduct and its impact on the church, and also made himself available to the staff and the churches.

Accusations of misconduct needed to be investigated. Pastors needed to be confronted. The MBC pastoral staff talked about the anger, disenchantment, and even cynicism they felt after being lied to so much and petitioned so often for cheap grace. Yes, there were pastors who were filled with shame for their sins – for following a hunger in their hearts or not setting careful boundaries in their relationships. Boyd carried on an effective ministry to the pastor involved and to his family. But there was also persistent lying by other pastors, a frightening indicator of years of denial of some unwholesome darkness. The staff always invited other victims to come forward in a confidential environment. Sometimes there were more victims.

Many victims experienced shame, fear, embarrassment, and regret as they tried to put their lives or marriages back together. Some, who were younger at the time, were now struggling with wounds that persisted, leading them to therapists and affecting their marriages. For others, this crisis was simply greater disaster to be added to an already painful life. They had been vulnerable, unable to turn away the attention or affection offered them by a pastor. Victims were always spoken to with an advocate of their choice present. There was always an offer of professional help.

Churches, too, were deeply affected by a moral failure of a pastor. If there was only an accusation, the church could easily divide over the truth of the accusation, although during the Lawson era there was never an accusation from a victim investigated that proved to be false. If a pastor persisted in minimizing or denying his role, the church was in serious difficulty. People sometimes turned against each other, and many would simply flee the unpleasantness. Even when misconduct was handled in the best way possible, churches often experienced the stages of grief: denial, anger, and depression.

During this era, a sexual misconduct policy for churches was made available. It was not always an easy sell as congregational pride could easily say "It will never happen here." But together with the *Guidelines for the Restoration of Ministers,* the staff believed it had the tools to provide for pastors a biblical process of restoration to wholeness. They also believed they had learned how to provide a safe and healing environment for victims. Churches needed wise counsel from the MBC, and never more than during a crisis of clergy sexual misconduct.

Lawson was asked to speak in other districts about the issues involved in clergy sexual misconduct, such as the causes of the misconduct, power and vulnerability issues, legal reporting requirements, proper procedures in investigation, and victim consideration.

During the 18 years of Lawson's tenure, two churches were sued by victims. One case was dropped and the other was settled with the church's insurer paying. However, that church was ordered to pay an additional judgment. The district was named in one suit but, after multiple depositions, the judge removed the case against the MBC as having insufficient evidence of any responsibility.

Pastors provided with a Staff of a different kind

Boyd and Lawson collaborated on another entrepreneurial ministry that would have a positive extended impact on many pastors. Lawson was convinced that certain core ministries in the conference, if presented as a giving option, could find their own financial supporters within and without the constituency. Boyd had a passion for helping pastors through their various personal and financial challenges. These two passions contributed to the creation of Staff of the Pastor, a totally confidential ministry to pastors and their families.

In 1994, a 501c3 non-profit corporation was formed to receive gifts for this unique ministry. A small board provided oversight. There were substantial gifts made by people who wanted to do more for pastors. A Minnesota couple who knew Boyd when he was a pastor, and who were looking for a ministry to make an impact, became major benefactors. Pastors with medical bills, needs for educational assistance, personal or family psychological issues, now had a place to seek confidential assistance. Each year, 30 to 40 pastoral families received assistance.

Boyd continued the tradition of the Minnesota Baptist Conference Pastors Council. During the Lawson era, the council provided churches with a periodic salary survey. This survey was extremely helpful for pastors who were underpaid. The Pastor's Council realized in the 90s that the salary survey was also an opportunity to ask pastors questions about personal feelings about ministry. The result was a wellness inventory intended to alert the district of the spiritual and emotional health of its pastors, not just financial needs. Pastors and their families were being served in new ways for a new day.

Our immigrant story becomes immigrant ministry

The 1980s brought satisfying progress in starting ethnic churches in the Minnesota conference. Neal Floberg in the Anderson era had laid the groundwork for a flagship Filipino church, and during the Lawson era this church was started in cooperation with Bethany of Roseville. Filipinos adapted easily to American culture. There was a growing number of FilAm churches in other districts, forming a critical mass for growth and empowerment in the conference. Minnesota called Gonzolo and Anita Olojan from Cebu to start a church. Immigration of pastors was always a touchy issue with conference world missionaries who talked about a talent drain of immigrating pastors to the United States. However, the Olojans were near retirement age, but still were energetic and respected. In the next decade, Minnesota would see two strong Filipino churches develop from this initial commitment.

In the Fleming era, a Spanish-speaking church was started in Minneapolis. Latinos were the fastest growing ethnicity in Minnesota after 1970. They were a force both in the city and in the rural areas. Both St. Paul and Minneapolis had strong Latino populations. But greater Minnesota also saw a strong influx of Spanish speakers, initially as seasonal agricultural workers but then as year around residents. All across western Minnesota, from Worthington to the Red River Valley, towns had established Latino populations.

The First Evangelical Baptist Church (Primera Iglesia Evang Bautista) of Minneapolis had been organized from a group of Latinos who were welcomed by the Olivet church in the early 1970s as a gathering but not a church. Antonio De Paris, an Argentine layman, was in charge of the group. When De Paris wished to organize the group as a church, Olivet's leaders felt that its agreement with the group had been violated. The group moved to Bethlehem where, under De Paris, the church was officially organized on May 4, 1972.

The early years were rocky. Antonio De Paris moved to Florida. A split saw more than half the church leave to organize another Latino church. Missionary Bob Swanson assisted the church for a period. In 1977, missionary Delmar IntVeld began a 23-year term of leadership in the church, followed by Rev. Ephrain Contreras. In the early 90s IntVeld assisted MBC churches who had a vision for reaching local populations of Hispanics. Outreaches were tried in Blomkest, Willmar, Montevideo, and Alvarado, Minnesota. Retiring from the church in 2000, IntVeld developed training materials for the Spanish-speaking churches in Minnesota.

A blessing for Minnesota came in 1994 when Chuck and Betty Selander returned from the mission field, due to family concerns, and appealed to world missions to allow them to serve the Minnesota Hispanic population. The Selanders entered into the ministry with gusto. Juan Jose Filipe was recruited out of the Hispanic seminary in Chicago to lead the ministry in the Red River Valley.

With a growing team of leaders, the Hispanic movement organized HiMAC, the Hispanic Ministries Advisory Council. HiMAC included Minnesota representatives from the majority culture to strengthen the cross-cultural ties. At the end of the Lawson era, there were eight Hispanic congregations in the Minnesota district.

Slavic immigration, a new Minnesota opportunity

The Russia Baptist church, started by Paul and George Ozerkov, became a strong multi-national Russian-speaking church. After outgrowing several rented church sanctuaries, the church acquired a building site in Lino Lakes and designed a lovely structure for a first unit. Paul Ozerkov had been the founding pastor, but leadership was a challenge for this Slavic immigrant church. A high number of immigrants were pastors as immigration law permitted persecuted groups a special status. Most pastors in the Soviet Union were regularly persecuted. And of course the pastors all wanted to shepherd this strong congregation of 500 worshippers.

In the late 90s, the Russian church appealed to the Lino Lakes City Council for a variance to build on its property. They asked Executive Lawson to say a word on their behalf at the city council meeting. Arriving at the meeting, Lawson unexpectedly met John Bergeson (from Bethel) who happened to be the Lino Lakes mayor at the time. Bergeson would be chairing the council. Lawson introduced Mayor Bergeson to the nervous Russians, who nearly dropped to their knees that such a miraculous provision of God was being handed them. Their project was approved.

The building project was a painful process for the church as a construction accident nearly took the life of one of its volunteers. Church families took out personal loans to provide funds to finish the building. Music is a centerpiece of worship in Slavic churches. Yet, with the completion of the building, there were not enough remaining funds to buy a piano. At this time, Edgewater church had decided to cease ministry and, with some remaining assets, provided a lovely Yamaha grand piano to the church in time for its dedication. Two other Russian-speaking Slavic churches came from this mother church. A Latvian church also sought affiliation with the MBC.

Shepherd's Foundation, digging deeper

During the mid-1990s when the MBC was expanding the sister church movement in Ukraine, Shepherd's Foundation demonstrated how deeply an American/Ukrainian partnership could go. Both Shepherds Foundation and the MBC filled and shipped between 30 and 40 humanitarian containers when goods of any kind were scarce in Ukraine.

In a very pragmatic way, Shepherd's Foundation began as a partnership of Calvary of Roseville and Zolotonosha. In its early development, American doctors partnered with Ukrainian doctors. They visited, staying in their homes and seeking to assist them with their work, providing advanced equipment and techniques, and expressing their faith in their lives. These home-stays were not only the source of deep friendships, but also spiritual conversations.

Keith and Brenda Johnson led an amazing team of dentists who worked among the orphans, and most needy people. They raised funds for portable dental equipment that would allow them to visit orphanages and homes. Shepherd's Foundation connected with teachers, sister schools, social workers, business people, athletes, youth specialists, computer trainers, and language instructors. In each case, the foundation arranged links and programs for them with their Ukrainian counterparts.

Shepherd's Foundation helped develop programs to promote foster families for orphans among Ukrainian Christian families. They sought to assist seniors and then youth by a creating a center for them in Zolotonosha. In later years, they partnered with Baptist Christians in the Poltava region, who were helping youth with addictions and HIV/AIDS. Shepherd's Foundation also helped other organizations to come alongside their Ukrainian counterparts, such as Minnehaha Academy and School No. 2 in Zolotonosha.

Katrina Kare

In the mid-90s, Scottye Holloway came from the church planting assessment center to start a suburban African-American church in Richfield. Ambassadors Baptist Church thrived for a time but failed to reach the critical mass to endure. Holloway was thoroughly enjoyed in the MBC. The son of Rev. Joe Holloway, he personified grace and approachability. One often wonders what God is up to when a church fails. In Holloway's situation, there was unexpected consolation. While Scottye Holloway found a new ministry opportunity in another state, the Holloway connection opened a great future ministry opportunity for the MBC during a major disaster.

In 2005, Katrina, the sixth strongest hurricane recorded in the Atlantic, slammed into New Orleans and the gulf coast. Joe Holloway, Scotty's dad, was pastoring an African-American church in Laurel, Mississippi. Laurel was inland, but directly in the path of Katrina. It was devastated. With the chaos in New Orleans, smaller communities like Laurel were given minimal assistance.

The MBC, rather than just giving offerings, mobilized construction teams of lay people and pastors under the banner Katrina Kare. The Holloways had watched the Federal Emergency Management Administration (FEMA) move through their area. The Holloways' church knew who was the most neglected. Churches like Journey North, Mark Bjorlo's church in Brainerd, made multiple trips to replace FEMA's blue tarps with solid roofs. Greg White, a local contractor from Bethel in Mankato, made himself available to many church groups that would build roofs in Laurel. Significant funds were raised and distributed to displaced people who were found by Rev. Holloway. It was still more evidence of what makes Minnesota conference churches special.

Diversity in new church planting reveals Minnesota's new face

There were six African-American churches started in the Lawson era. Additionally, we welcomed Liberian, Vietnamese, Hmong, and Laotian churches. Twenty-nine ethnic churches were included in the fellowship of the state conference between 1980 and 2008. With its Swedish immigrant story in the back of its mind, the closing quarter-century allowed the Minnesota churches to live out their own history in the immigrant stories of others. God multiplied the spiritual harvest.

Diane Wicklund was the administrative assistant in what was later called the Short Term Mission Department. She was excited about her work and began to exercise more leadership in programs like Kids in Country. In February 2004, as part of a degree program at Bethel, Wicklund organized an ethnically diverse group of 20 women in the district who talked about their leadership roles as women. African American, Caucasian, Filipino, Latina, Native American, and Russian, Wicklund found they all had one a spiritual link. They all had dreams about what God could do through them. After a leadership exercise for Wicklund's project, the women decided to meet together regularly to pray for each other and their dreams. They gathered to pray for the next year at the MBC office.

In 1998, Dave Reno stepped back from his active role as coordinator of the MBC's church planting. The demands of an active reproducing 1,000-member church were taking their toll. Noteworthy in Reno's 1997 annual report was the announcement that the MBC was working with Dan Maxton of the national staff to provide a new system of coaching for pastors in new churches. Galilee in Lino Lakes was preparing to start a new church. Joel Nelson, Galilee's associate, would join the team. Clearly pleased, Reno also added that Steve and Carol Treichler launched an urban church targeting university students and the millennium generation. The office saw new faces: Verna Christianson, Cheryl Voss, Mary Pearson, and Judy Jones in finance.

Victor Winquist, another transplant from the national office

With a change of leadership, Lawson was configuring the organizational structure of the next generation of church planting. He gathered church planters together to consider new leadership structures. Ahead would be the adoption and completion of a goal to start 50 new churches between 2000 and 2005. The church planters asked the MBC for more staff time for church planting. As various plans for staff support were considered, the group became aware that Vic Winquist was retiring to the Twin Cities area and was available. Winquist was an excellent manager and one of the architects of TeAMerica in the national home mission's office.

When Winquist joined the staff of the MBC, the church planting ministry structure was being revised. Two teams of practitioner church planters were created. A TeAMerica representative often joined the team. A Resource Team worked with the various support systems so critical for a new church. A Launch Team worked in planning, demographics, and recruitment.

Winquist also gave leadership to the Prayer Commission. The 90s saw strong prayer movements develop in the U.S. President Robert Ricker had created initiatives in his administration for evangelism. He later created a prayer initiative. Dana Olson joined the national staff to catalyze prayer in the districts and local churches.

There was an annual MBC Concert of Prayer in the Minnesota district. Winquist and his wife Marilyn initiated prayer walks, prayer weekends, and 24-hour prayer vigils. The Winquists gave leadership to the prayer initiatives in Minnesota. A prayer resource manual for the churches was developed by the Minnesota prayer commission. Marilyn Winquist would lead women's prayer retreats at Shalom House.

One cannot study this period without being deeply impressed with the extent of God's blessing on the churches. But one must also be impressed with the intentionality of praying in so many ways and in so many places. Clearly this was a spiritual inhaling for a time when the district was breathing out so much new ministry.

Notes

[1] Wooddale Church website, "Who Are We? Our History."

[2] Truett M. Lawson, Relate, May/June 1993.

[3] Truett M. Lawson, Relate, "Conflicting Majorities," January/February 1993.

[4] Truett M. Lawson, Relate, December 1995.

[5] Truett M. Lawson, 138th Annual Report, Executive Minister's Report, 1996, p. 8.

[6] Based on Boyd interview, 2013.

— Chapter 14 —

The Lawson Era:
When Seeds Bloom,
the Hard Work Begins

Receiving megachurch blessing

Three new sources of church growth were fueling this unprecedented growth period in the MBC from 1995 to 2007. There was the multiplication of newly started churches, the growth of turnaround churches, and then there was the astonishing expansion of the megachurches. Church attendance averages in the conference increased some years in this period at the normally untouchable rate of doubling in a decade.

The megachurch became a phenomenon in evangelical America and in Minnesota. By definition, a megachurch is a church of 2,000 worshipers or more. Megachurches are almost entirely evangelical protestant churches, some with and some without denominational affiliation. From a theological perspective, they are all moderate to conservative. It has been suggested that most megachurches are able to sustain growth only through a single pastoral tenure. The noteworthy example was Robert Schuller and the Crystal Cathedral.

Megachurches create community through the design of their facility, through small group programming, and through ministry interest areas. "Some researchers suggest that this church form is a unique collective response to distinctive cultural shifts and changes in societal patterns throughout the industrialized, urban and suburban areas of the world."[1] If they are a passing fancy, they do not appear to be passing yet. There are four times as many of them in the U.S. in 2014, as there were in 1990.

A large church in the Minnesota conference historically has been about 500 worshipers. In 1995, Executive Lawson observed that there were 10 churches with more than 1,000 in Sunday services, including several with more than 2,000 and two with more than 3,000. These large numbers would only increase.

Megachurches have been described as denominations unto themselves. Indeed to maintain and build this level of sustainable energy, these churches simply must be constantly regenerating. They are known for their independence. If they are affiliated with denominations or aligned with missionary agencies, these alignments will not figure prominently in their church life.

North Heights and the second campus forum

A new model of expansion captured the imagination of Minnesota's large churches. In 2002, Doyle Van Gelder, pastor of Friendship Church in Prior Lake, started a second campus in Shakopee. Lawson and Van Gelder met to discuss second campus church multiplication. This model was uniquely pioneered by North Heights Lutheran Church. North Heights was a fast growing charismatic Lutheran church that, somewhat by its circumstances, fell into its multi-campus philosophy. The church was outgrowing its building in Roseville and was building a new campus in Shoreview. Trying to weigh the challenges of making the shift to the new campus, an idea came in through the back door. Why don't we continue to minister on both campuses as we fully prepare the new campus? But eventually the church would continue ministry on both campuses as one church. That was a defining moment for a new church model in America.

North Heights' pastor, Morris Vaagenes, agreed to tell his story to an interested group at the MBC office. A significant delegation from large conference churches listened to Vaagenes and talked about their own thoughts and dreams. Several would establish second campus ministries. Multi-site ministry was attractive to large churches because it maintained their brand on the new site, increasing the chances of success. Actually the churches that would be most successful in this type of multiplication were churches that had a unique brand, a distinctive ministry. For these churches, church planting posed many risks. If a daughter church veered from their template, they could do little to intervene. But a second campus church was still under their control.

The Military Families Care Initiative

In 2003, Governor Tim Pawlenty began the first of two terms as Minnesota's chief executive. Governor and First Lady Mary Pawlenty were part of Wooddale Church. Mary was a district judge and served on Bethel's Board of Trustees. In March 2003, First Lady Mary saw an opportunity to reach out to families of Minnesota's military who were being called up and deployed to the Iraq war. She founded the Minnesota Military Families Care Initiative. The initiative was an online opportunity for charities, businesses and faith-based organizations to link with military families who were trying to cope during the absence of one of their military family members who had been deployed.

The First Lady called the Minnesota Conference offices, as she did other church leaders, and explained the program to Truett Lawson who, in turn, put out the word to the churches. Several pastors reported that they were able to assist a family through this care initiative. After the Pawlentys' tenure, the Minnesota National Guard continued the program.

The definition of multi-site churches is one church in two or more places, with one governing board and one checkbook. Calvary of Roseville would create a second campus. Bethlehem would see strong acceleration in its growth, when it went to two campuses in 2002 and three campuses in 2009. But Eagle Brook, more than any other church, built its megachurch strategy around multi-site ministry. By 2007, Eagle Brook was ministering on three campuses to 8,500 people. In the following years, that number would increase to five campuses and 18,500 people.

The church world would love to understand the secret ingredients that have led Eagle Brook from being a megachurch to a multi-site megachurch phenomenon. Certainly the church has had an outstanding communicator in Bob Merritt. Yet, like Bill Hybels, Merritt has brought in equally gifted speakers and pastors. From the early years, there has been a strong leadership core guiding the decision making. Eagle Brook chose the multi-site model and demonstrated how effective it can be in avoiding the logistics issues with massive one-site megachurches. There is little doubt that Eagle Brook has also been able to create an exciting and inviting place for typical unchurched people in Minnesota – and there are many.

TCCH, partners in senior housing

In 1996, Twin Cities Christian Homes (TCCH) blossomed again. The failure of Brightondale in 1990 had left the organization tentative at a time when senior housing opportunities in Minnesota were ramping up. The two premium assets that the organization still possessed were Castle Ridge Care Center, a nursing home, and Kristi Olson, a very effective marketing staff member. Castle Ridge was a strong financial asset. It had one of the finest ratings of any facility of this kind in the state. But the State of Minnesota was re-engineering senior care. It would reduce reimbursements to discourage nursing home development and encourage assisted living facilities. Eventually Castle Ridge would be sold to Presbyterian Homes.

TCCH promoted Kristi Olson to president and the organization began planning its resurgence. During this time, TCCH moved into the MBC's north office suite. Camping was moving into four season ministry, so the staff no longer returned to the MBC office – except for one Mink Lake Camp director who decided to make the office his winter bedroom.

TCCH secured an option on a piece of property in Shoreview, but with the size of the project, the organization did not have adequate reserves to provide a cash down payment to launch the project. In 1994-1995, the TCCH board approached the MBC about becoming a financial partner in the project, sharing a 45% position and providing 45% of the down payment. Because the MBC was not directly in the housing business, it was agreed that TCCH's Scandia Shore's corporation would hold title to the property. TCCH Services would manage it. The MBC's financial interest would be secured by a secondary legal agreement. MBC would only benefit on its investment in the case of cash distributions or an eventual sale.

The same plan was put in place for WestRidge in Minnetonka (25%) and Main Street Village in Richfield (15%). Attorney Wade Anderson, who served as the chair of the Board of Stewards for a time, offered valued legal guidance. These facilities provided an outstanding lifestyle for hundreds of retired Minnesota Baptist Conference older adults, as well as an outstanding ministry opportunity in the community. Nancy Starr later assumed Kristi's role later in the Lawson era. During this period the TCCH board distanced itself somewhat from the conference by removing the requirement that half the board members receive the affirmation of the MBC Stewards.

The Next Step, the best step

In 1994, camping laid new plans for another capital campaign. Trout was turning away almost 400 campers a year. A few red flags went up at the thought of a capital campaign. The 40 More campaign had been a major disappointment. The Stewards agreed that the greatest capital needs were in camping, but they also believed that a stronger response would come with a combined MBC/camping effort. Both the MBC and camping would give the campaign a 100% effort, but the proceeds would be divided 25% to MBC (Ukraine, church planting, office) and 75% to camping for capital projects.

Camping suggested a financial development firm for the campaign. With the consultant, the MBC began to assess its giving potential. A case statement was written describing the vision. Based on the advanced interviews, a goal of $1.5 million was established. The campaign would be named The Next Step.

It must have been a good choice because Bethel College and Seminary and various churches would borrow the name for their campaigns. The staff was excited, but somewhat overwhelmed, with the challenge. Lawson and Camerer trained campaign volunteers. As the campaign proceeded it would be the personal visits of those two executive staff members that would encourage major donors.

Launched in 1997, the campaign exceeded its goal, with $1.6 million committed and more than $1.5 million received. The good will of the people visited was tremendous. An unforgettable moment for this campaign came in the early stages, when a businessman from Calvary of Roseville contributed stock in the company he had just sold. The gift would contribute more than $160k to the campaign, the largest capital gift the MBC had ever received.

On the MBC side, the campaign allowed the update of office computers and phones. It provided a new van for the regional office in

Ukraine so teams would have safer transportation. It paid for dozens of humanitarian containers to Ukraine and resupplied grant funds for new churches.

For Trout, it allowed the camp to purchase a nearby private residence and 40 acres of adjacent property from retiring Hez and Loretta Miller. The Millers had provided great service for Trout for more than a decade. Trout was able to build a long overdue central kitchen. It created a 12-unit RV park that would have multiple functions in the maintenance and programs of the camp. But more than that, it allowed us to begin building cabins for Timber Ridge. In 2001, Trout set another record attendance with 2,900 youth campers. The future plans were weighing in just in time.

Five years later, Lawson and Roger Camerer would hop on the fundraising train again. Timber Ridge was the great Minnesota project for this campaign. The Extreme Steps campaign was initiated by a cooperative effort between national BGC and the districts. Each would receive half of the proceeds. National was designating its portion to church planting in the U.S. and worldwide. The MBC designated all of its portion to Trout Lake. A retired Herb Skoglund, and a wonderfully committed businessman, Tim Doten, made the difference in this campaign.

The Timber Ridge project would keep MBC camping building for a decade. Trout had on staff Mark Grindahl, a remarkably talented building contractor, but even with these skills and volunteer labor, the future costs were in the millions. Karin Larson and many others contributed legacy gifts for the first major expansion of Trout Lake since it beginning.

The Timber Ridge miracle story

The story of Timber Ridge is a lesson in God's providence. The hill property acquired in the Emmett Johnson era had been purchased for recreational use. It was not on the lake, although it stacked up nicely behind the existing Trout property. It was an unusual plot of land with an abandoned warming house on a vintage ski hill that descended rapidly to a hollow below. A young Bob and Karl Smith had experimented with a homemade rope tow on the hill for a couple years. But for 20 years the hill was viewed as a nice open space for horses and hikers.

In the 90s when Trout's capacity was reached, the camp staff had decided to build The Outpost – a counselor-centered camp for the youngest campers. Primary camps were a growing edge for camp at that time. With resources coming in, Camerer and Lawson began to walk the land. The Strategic Initiatives committee received their assessments.

In 1998 camp leaders moved away from a primary camp at the base of the hill to a stunning plan for a year-round facility, initially targeting junior highers, on the top of the hill. Because of the unique hill and view of Trout Lake at the top, the camp was renamed Timber Ridge. The peak of Timber Ridge was the highest point in Ideal Township. Soon, in the building process, the hill was provided with a tubing rope tow. It was clear, that this site better suited the adventurers of junior high, rather than primaries and juniors envisioned for The Outpost.

Camerer was networking with log home builders in the Brainerd Lakes area. The camp borrowed a logging band saw called a Wood Mizer. Camerer's volunteers began to produce thousands of board feet of oak flooring and hundreds of thousands of linear feet of building logs, both square logs and D canted logs. In the next years Camerer's guys literally built a village of buildings out of logs they acquired and milled. John Dekkenga, as well as Jim and Arlene Ledin, were tireless laypeople and highly effective in recruiting a constant team of volunteers. At this busy time in the Camerers' life, Jean Camerer was struggling with a serious cancer. But it almost seemed to those involved that as Roger Camerer and his guys built Timber Ridge, God was rebuilding Jean's health.

Camerer also found skilled log scribers, who built real log cabins. Some of them were looking for extra work in their down time. John Hurst, a retired log builder, was instrumental to the process. The Next Step campaign launched a perpetual building program for the next decade and beyond. Hez Miller and Kenny Elg ran a D8 Caterpillar over the intimidating hills to create the terraces and paths of our unique camp. The commitment of volunteers launched one of the most exciting junior high camping programs on one of the most unique settings in the country.

Mink Lake was not neglected. In 2002, the loggers completed the first log structures to replace the army tents. Designed to accommodate either youth campers or two families in privacy, the new Mink Lake was on its way to a new and useful future, without mice running over the sleeping bags at night.

The Ukraine explosion, "Come and help us!"

From 1995 to 2000, Love Lift for Ukraine exploded in the Minnesota Baptist Conference. Several Scripture verses emerged as spiritual callings for the hundreds of participants. Executive Lawson pointed to the dream of Paul in Acts 16. A Macedonian man calls out from another country

Love Lift logo as seen on humanitarian containers sent to Ukraine.

and another culture, "Come and help us!" Two church groups have found each other, although they are separated by cultures and geography. Because of their spiritual connection, the one who was blessed materially hears these words: *At the present time, your plenty will supply what they need, so that in turn their plenty can supply what you need.* II Corinthians 8:14 (NIV)

An illuminating mutual history

Students of Love Lift for Ukraine discovered fascinating and previously unknown history linking the origins of the Swedish and Ukrainian Baptist movements. It has long been known that the spiritual force that seeded the pietist movement in Sweden was the return of the Swedish soldiers from Siberia where they had been sent after Sweden's Charles the XII was defeated by Peter the Great in Poltava, Ukraine, in 1709.

The Swedish king was a great military leader before this defeat. He was concerned about the spiritual condition of his men. He had allowed dedicated German pietists to serve as chaplains to the troops. Charles' army of Swedes and Ukrainians was defeated by Peter an hour away from Zolotonosha, where the MBC sistering movement was begun. Most of the defeated who survived (20,000 some say) were send to Siberia.

There were great revivals in spite of imprisonment. Five thousand of the soldiers were allowed to return to Sweden. They ignited the pietist movement that would catalyze the Swedish Baptist movement there and in America. There are threads that indicate that the remaining soldiers formed a pietist diaspora throughout Russia. These pietist-like movements would resurface as Baptist movements in the middle of the 19th century in Russia and Ukraine.[2]

Love Lift's training to serve

In March of each year, the summer's Ukraine travelers would gather for a full day of training. There was a keynote speaker. The day would be stretched across 20 training seminars. The teams would split up to glean all they could from the idea-rich seminars. Seminar leaders were practitioners who were passionate about the ministries they saw God doing in the churches. Dawn Marcus, Annette Benson, and Naomi Ludeman Smith gave unique perspectives. Smith had done an interesting study of Ukrainian Baptist theological distinctives. Pat Dutton, an educator, had perspectives on ministry in schools. Joanie and Larry Wiken, Marilyn Winquist, and Mike Snyder presented on ministry to men and women, prayer, and team building. Beth Post gave insights into children's camps. And Ruslana Westerlund, a Ukrainian from the Cherkasy region, covered the important cultural traditions, so very unusual for Americans.

Lawson reviewed the history and philosophy of the ministry and its unique and fragile nature. Sistering had the long-term results of career missions, but the energy of short term missions. It had awakened the sleeping giant – the laity – like no other form of missions. Sistering developed its own financial resources rather than begging for funds from the already pressured church mission's budget. It could transform missions in the small church, which became one of the dominant participants.

Sistering was very pragmatic. It allowed the two churches to define their ministry agendas together. Love Lift for Ukraine avoided the concept of *equipping,* as it had a paternalistic side to it. Love Lift was all about *partnering* in ministry with one's sister church. People shared their Ukraine stories, and always their faces shone with the knowledge that God was using them.

Adventure camps were the beginning

The Adventure camps for children were a launch point for the church partnerships. In 1993, Linda Wicklund and a group of hardy ladies from Calvary of Roseville piloted a day camp for orphan kids in the most difficult of conditions. In the summer of 1994, 75 Minnesotans came with Love Lift to do Adventure camps in their sister churches. The camps were so well received and appreciated that they made a wonderful first step into ministry partnering.

The number of camps would increase dramatically. For most of the late 90s, 10,000 to 12,000 Ukrainian children attended camps. The MBC's Love Lift department produced new curriculum each year using the talents of Sandy McMaken, Ruslana and Rob Westerlund, and others.

In the late 90s, the Ukrainian and American leaders realized that the excitement created in their sister church villages could become an outreach to other villages who had no evangelical church voice of any kind. A new strategy was adopted by Ukrainian and American leaders to bring children's camps to these *Shadowed Villages*. A significant number of camps were led by Ukrainian young people who began as helpers to the Americans in early Adventure camps. In many cases, the camps created Sunday schools and perhaps even a church.

A majority of the American churches first brought their sister church a financial gift to assist in the building, expansion, or renovation of their sister's church meeting facilities. In many cases they helped purchase existing buildings that were available. Then there were men's outreaches, women's events, and camps targeting youth. Ministries were established in local orphanages, prisons, and sanatoriums. "American dinners" were put on for local government and school officials. Contacts in the orphanages led to a number of adoptions in Minnesota.

In the spring of 1994, a Women's Ministries team from Minnesota met with Nadia Kommendant, wife of the Baptist president and the national head of women's ministries. Teams of women traveled each spring doing Christian women's conferences. This pattern thrilled Kommendant. It gave her a strong program platform to bring women together under her leadership. Americans like Marilyn Wallberg, Barb Holmberg, and Janie Pearson joined the teams.

Ukrainian Baptist leaders, Ukrainian friends

Love Lift for Ukraine had found a great friend in Dr. Gregory Kommendant and his wife, Nadia. Educated in Germany, Kommendant was elected president of the Baptists in the Soviet Union in the early 90s. After the separation of the Soviet states, the Baptist union was also separated. The Kommendants returned to their home country where Kommendant became president of the Union of Evangelical Christians, Baptists. The awkward title was an indication that the Baptist Union was an inclusive covering for many evangelicals, not just Baptists.

In later years, Kommendant chided the Minnesota delegation as rule breakers for going first to Cherkasy's local churches instead of his Kiev office. In reality, the Kommendants and the leaders of Love Lift found a deep love and respect for each other during the Love Lift years.

Ukrainian Style

After 15 years and 60 trips to Ukraine for the Shepherd's Foundation, Linda Wicklund acted on a personal dream of her own. She began to research and write about the homes, decorations and applied arts of the land she had served and loved so much.

Linda Wicklund published book with a unique view of Ukrainian life and arts.

Published in 2011 in both English and Ukrainian, *Ukrainian Style* tells a story of both the simplicity and the beauty of the Ukrainian home, bursting forth with stunning pictures of the people and their customs. Wicklund relates her visits to simple communist-era apartments only to be welcomed by the warmth of their interiors with richly colored hand-made textiles, ceramics and utilitarian objects. We are taken to many villages with their thatch and white plaster cottages to see the colorfully embroidered traditional clothing and other handwork, which is beautifully photographed throughout the volume.

When this book was released in Ukraine, it was noticed by the cultural institutions and museums, and was nominated for an award with the national department of culture. Linda Wicklund received their annual award for contributing to the culture of Ukraine. (Linda Wicklund, *Ukrainian Style,* Sunflower Press, 2011)

It was the regional senior presbyter who could open doors of opportunity for local ministry at orphanages, schools, or government offices. Vladimir Belous welcomed the first visitors, but was replaced by the impossible-not-to-like Vasily Olenik. This spiritual leader's winsome ways opened many doors for the teams.

The possibilities rest with you and God

The intelligence, energy, and spiritual hunger of the youth mesmerized many of the Americans. The MBC partnered with the senior presbyter to bring the youth together for annual youth gatherings, a first for the Cherkasy region. Love Lift was hiring more than 100 interpreters each summer, many of whom were unusually talented university students, mostly non-believers. Interpreters were coming to Christ both at the youth conferences and at the Adventure camps.

In 1995, the MBC created an Interpreter's Conference to initiate the camp season. The camp oriented the interpreters to the curriculum of the camps, but also offered language help with Christian terminology and English idioms. Tutorials were designed to assist with the interpreting of sermons or testimonies. Gifted educators like Keith Meyer, Naomi Ludeman Smith, and Bob and Paul Harer were there when the doors opened. It was becoming clear that the conversion of interpreters (some of the best and brightest in the land) was a major impact of the ministry.

Dr. Scott Larson, founder of Straight Ahead Ministries, visited Ukraine with Love Lift. Staff member John Kinsley continued the organization's presence, reaching deep into Ukrainian juvenile prisons and ministering in the name of Christ. Straight Ahead organized a Christian rock band called Sounds of Boston. Between 1995 and 2000, Love Lift organized huge Christian rock concerts with raucous youth, and a direct word for Christ at the close.

The MBC hosted professional groups and events to elevate the reputation of the local church in its community. Classical music is deeply loved in Ukraine. The MBC helped Roger and Michelle Frisch, violinist and flutist from Minnesota's Orchestra and Opera Company, to do clinics and then large concerts with faith messages. Bethel's Herb Johnson and Carolyn Nordquist provided accompaniment.

Dennis Port formed Evangelium in 1995. It became an extraordinary professional choir that would tour for a decade, first sponsored by the MBC, and then by Shepherd's Foundation. Together with Bethel's Jonathan Veenker and Lowell Becker, Port demonstrated that Christian music alone could be the voice of God in the hearts of many.

Dale Rott, theater arts professor from Bethel, used his retirement to energize the medium of drama for the international church, especially in Ukraine. Rott traveled with Love Lift and Shepherd's Foundation assisting churches in the use of drama in their local settings. He also established relationships with Ukrainian theater arts professionals collaborating on the production of Barabbas in cities across Ukraine.

A home-grown, AG (agricultural) team led by Neal and Jolene Anderson, seeded economic projects with startup funding. Seed money raised by the team helped start many businesses, with the repaid interest supporting local churches. Sid and Char Veenstra led pastors and wives retreats that allowed a strongly felt blessing of God to fall on many tired ministry couples. John and Jan Carlson and David and Claudia Arp brought insights into marriage and family.

It misses the point to view Love Lift as a mission enterprise or even a missionary movement. It was really a vessel that individuals received and filled with whatever passions and gifts God had given them. Olivia Bradley was a successful businesswoman in the north suburbs. Olivia realized that her business acumen could allow Ukrainian women to use their traditional skills in textile design to have a small business, as Olivia would market their things in the U.S. Tim Herman was a financial consultant and joined his sister church team. It would change his life, and cause him such a passion for Ukraine and for ministry, that he would move his life work into ministry. Love Lift for Ukraine was also transformational in the way it linked the district with its lay people. Those who had been to Ukraine were the first to sign up for Family Gatherings or special MBC events.

When Love Lift for Ukraine celebrated its 10-year anniversary, Gregory and Nadia Kommendant, head of the Ukrainian Baptists, were invited to speak. "You are the silent ministry," Kommendant announced. "Most ministries who want to work with us want recognition. You just go to the churches and do amazing things. May God bless you."[3]

Kids in Country and more ministry

Beth Post took over the leadership of women's ministries in the late 1990s. It was an exciting time. Pamela Heim, the national women's ministries director, developed an extremely rigorous training program for women who wanted to be better equipped to provide local church leadership in women's ministries. The first School of Women's Ministries was held in Minnesota. There would be four Minnesota cohort groups that would complete this training in the next several years.

In 2001, Executive Lawson heard of a reformed denomination that was encouraging farm families to host an inner-city child on their family farms in the summer. The idea for Kids in Country (KIC)

was born. Its mission was to bring kids from the worst neighborhoods in the city and allow them to spend a week on a MBC family farm with all its unique and new experiences.

Diane Wicklund had been working with families of immigrant and urban people in the MBC as part of her course work at Bethel University. Wicklund embraced this ministry with passion. She sought out models from across the country. Funding was investigated. City representatives from urban churches coordinated the selection of children who might benefit. Marlene Johnson, niece of Herb and Jesse Nyquist, had worked with inner-city children for 20 years. Now, together with Jill Anderson and other urban workers, children who could benefit were located. Pastor Efrain Contreras was a wonderful link with urban Latino families. Pastor's wife Jessica Forman and Shawna Horn represented churches in the city.

Diane Wicklund and John Sahlin worked with the farms and eventually the lake homes that would host children. It is rare to find a program that makes a genuine impact on at-risk children. KIC had a tremendous impact on all participants and became a passion for the MBC staff. Each summer 50 children participated as farms were enlisted.

The summer's experience for the children was culminated by a week at Mink Lake camp, hosted by Courtney and Rob Eastlund and volunteers from North Isanti Baptist Church. A memorable moment was when a "homeless person" (Truett Lawson) wandered into camp. He asked whether he could stay and eat. The leaders differed as to whether this was a good thing and put the question to the somewhat frightened children who debated the issue from their fears and their compassion. It was an unforgettable moment for all when the truth came out.

Over the years, a maturing group of urban alumni developed from Kids in Country. Many mainstreamed into Trout's camping program. The urban leaders could point to young adults who looked back to their Kids in Country experience and report that this was where God redirected their lives.

In 2007, KIC sponsored a celebration at the new theater at Bethel University. JoJo Spencer, a youth minister at New Life in Cambridge, had spoken to the kids at a summer KIC camp. His life story mirrored the lives of many of the KIC kids. Truett Lawson wrote a booklet called *JoJo's Story* with urban comic illustrations, and made it available to the families. Diane Wicklund organized the program, as a room full of KIC alumni and parents heard JoJo tell his story. It was an amazing moment.

Telling the story on Open Theism

In 1997, a pastor shared with some pastoral colleagues, including John Piper, his concern about a phrase written in Greg Boyd's Gold Medallion award winning book, *Letters from a Skeptic.* Boyd wrote to his father, an atheist: "…God can't foreknow the good and bad decisions of the people he creates until he creates these people and they, in turn, create their decisions."[4]

Piper brought his concerns to President George Brushaber at Bethel where Boyd was on the faculty. Brushaber convened a Committee for Theological Clarification and Assessment and met with Boyd. The committee report was read by the Bethel Trustees who agreed that Boyd's views were "not outside the acceptable spectrum of evangelical thought." Piper and several pastors organized the Concerned Pastors who, with time, would decide to challenge Boyd's presence at Bethel, and his position as a pastor in the conference. Unsatisfied with Bethel's response, the group decided to pursue the issue through the resolution process in the national and district annual meetings.

On June 25, 1999, in St. Petersburg, Florida, the Baptist General Conference delegates voted to reject a resolution brought by the Concerned Pastors. The proposed resolution was a provisional amendment to the Affirmation of Faith, the belief statement of the conference. It would have added language to the Affirmation regarding the nature of the future and God's foreknowledge. After a day of tense debate, the resolution was defeated 275 to 251.

The next year at the 123rd Annual Meeting, the Concerned Pastors, renamed the Edgren Fellowship, brought another resolution to the annual meeting at Bethel. It simply stated that the delegates, by their vote, were affirming God's exhaustive knowledge of all events – past, present, and future, and that the "openness of God" view was contrary to our fellowship's historical understanding of God. The motion passed overwhelmingly.

However, a second motion came from the leaders of another group that called itself the Committed Pastors. It proposed that by also passing their resolution, the conference was stating that the historical Affirmation of Faith was sufficiently stated in regard to open theism. And further that by voting on their resolution, they would be affirming the Bethel Trustees' position paper on the issue. That position paper had stated that Greg Boyd's views did not warrant his termination from Bethel, and further, that his views fell in the "acceptable bounds of the evangelical spectrum."

The vote of the BGC delegates affirmed this resolution by a strong majority (423 to 363). In the following October, both Sam Crabtree and Ron Saari brought resolutions seeking opposing affirmations from the Minnesota annual meeting. Both resolutions were defeated or declared out of order. The Minnesota fellowship was tired of this and wanted to be done with this controversy.

Behind the scenes in the foreknowledge debate

The Committed Pastors (for Boyd) were organized when the Concerned Pastors (for Piper) rejected an appeal by President Bob Ricker, the district executive ministers (1 dissention) and the BGC Leadership team. Their appeal to the Concerned Pastors (for Piper) was to agree to a moratorium on actions and resolutions regarding open theism in favor of a two-year period to debate the issue. Before that, on March 15, the Minnesota Stewards made a similar appeal to Rev. Carey Olson, who had become a leader of the group. Truett Lawson had maintained during the period that organizing resolutions only politicized the issue before debate. The MBC had sponsored a Piper/ Boyd debate on open theism, the year before.

During the period of debate and resolutions, it was clear that the two sides saw the issue from very different points of view. Those who agreed with Piper saw Boyd's open view of the future as limiting God in the area of foreknowledge, and thereby questioning the omniscience of God. It was a view that would de-God God. Their view was that no human freedom is beyond God's sovereignty, therefore the future must be settled and therefore known in its entirety by God.

Boyd's view was that all of the future is not settled, nor could it be. Human free will had yet to determine some of the content of that future. He would argue that his view was not an attack on any of God's attributes. It was rather a view of the future which respects human free will as created by God and taught in Scripture. God's knows the future, but He knows the facts that are determined, not those that are open because of human free will.

The rest of the foreknowledge story

Although the theological debate revolved around the writings and responses of John Piper and Greg Boyd, the public resolution debate was different. The Committed Pastors (for Boyd) were not advocating open theism. They simply did not believe Boyd's views were heresy, or disqualifying. Rather, they saw Piper's group as ultimately attacking the identity of the conference, which had always been a loose coalition of Armenian and Calvinist views. They believed that certain key values in the conference were being swept away by this uncharacteristic behavior in our fellowship. This was an attack on our Baptist fragile freedoms – freedom to debate, to strike the balance of unity and liberty. In fairness, the Piper group was not composed only of predestinarian Calvinists. It was a coalition of conference people who were unsure of Boyd's thinking. Boyd's openness theology was new thinking to the conference, and although it was not widely held, it was viewed as a threat by many.

The foreknowledge debate became a perfect storm for the Minnesota conference. It involved two of the brightest and most actively ministering large church pastors. Truett Lawson strongly supported the Committed Pastors (for Boyd), though other conference leaders joined the opposition. Words and typifications were made by many in the heat of debate. Lawson heard that Piper had made some apologies to his church for things he had said about Boyd. In hearing that, Lawson messaged Piper confessing he felt he had been unfair with Piper. "I referenced you where I did not need to. You were an easy target and I took aim….I did it as a call to arms of sorts….I do want to apologize for that. I do not expect a response except that you would know that I have thought about it and believe I was wrong."[5]

As the Millennium turned…

In the years after 2000, it was clear that the MBC staff was getting a bit long in the tooth. Rob Boyd had already had the first of his several retirements, all of which led to new arrangements that allowed the conference to pay him less and get the same 60 hours a week. Similarly, Donna Sahlin reached retirement and the MBC rehired Donna and John. Fred Tuma joined the paid staff in older adult ministries after making a tremendous impact on that ministry as a volunteer.

In 2003, Vic Winquist was ready for a reduction in his responsibilities when Joel Nelson walked in the door of the MBC. Nelson was an appreciated member of the church planting Launch Team. He had decided to pass the leadership in his church plant over to the other lead pastor on his team. Nelson joined the MBC team as Church Planting

Director, and Winquist remained part time, organizing the prayer ministry. Gary Bauer, Shirley Erickson, Joy Pearson, Janet Boyd, and Cheryl Voss were supporting the staff leaders of the conference.

Notes

[1] Hartford Institute for Religious Research, http://hirr.hartsem.edu/megachurch/definition.html.

[2] Truett M. Lawson, from a monograph prepared for the students and faculty of Odessa Theological Seminary, 2001.

[3] Gregory Kommendant, recollections of Truett Lawson.

[4] Greg Boyd, *Letters from a Skeptic*, Victor Books, April 14, 1993, p. 30.

[5] Truett M. Lawson, email archive, 2000.

CE and Short Term Missions

1. Lee Kingsley assisted the MBC's growth in the 50s with Sunday School and age group resources.
2. An early Christian Education Committee meeting.
3. "Chief's" tenure of 20 years was celebrated in 1972 with the Kingsley family.
4. Delmar Dahl joined the Emmett Johnson team in 1976 at a time when Emmett really needed him.

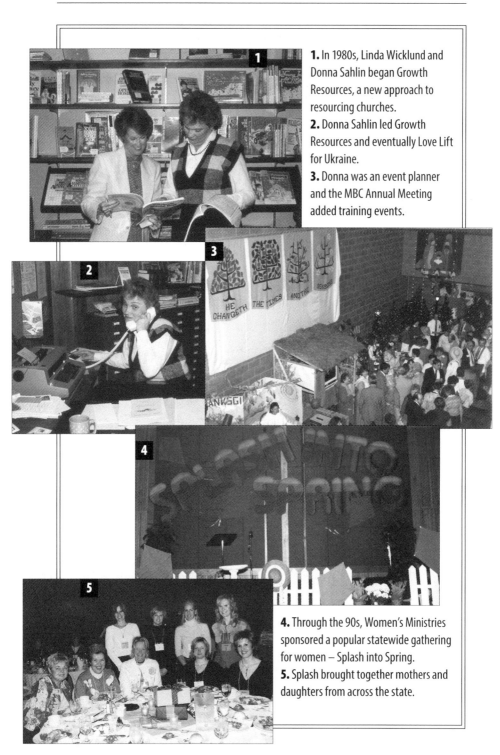

1. In 1980s, Linda Wicklund and Donna Sahlin began Growth Resources, a new approach to resourcing churches.

2. Donna Sahlin led Growth Resources and eventually Love Lift for Ukraine.

3. Donna was an event planner and the MBC Annual Meeting added training events.

4. Through the 90s, Women's Ministries sponsored a popular statewide gathering for women – Splash into Spring.

5. Splash brought together mothers and daughters from across the state.

1. For two years Conference on the Family attracted over 700 in a gathering to strengthen families.
2. With the breakup of the Soviet Union, Ukrainian Baptists had unusual opportunities for ministry.
3. The Lawsons and Wicklunds journeyed to Ukraine to meet Baptist leaders in Cherkasy.

4. The captain of the river boat welcomes his American passenger.
5. At the pier of Cherkasy, an unbelievable welcome from the Ukrainian hosts.

1. The Wicklunds, representing Calvary of Roseville, meet the believers in Zolotenosha.
2. Children and youth were electrified by American visitors and listened intently to the Good News.

3. The pastor to pastor relationship often strengthened the sister church relationship.
4. With the value of the dollar, MBC churches could see much for little in the building of their sister's church.
5. Lawson joins senior presbyter Vladimir Belous in praying to prepare candidates for baptism.

1. Living in the homes of believers and enjoying Ukrainian food helped create bonds between people in Love Lift experience.
2. In the first five years, the MBC and Shepherd's Foundation filled dozens of humanitarian containers.

3. Loading containers was exciting but unloading in Ukraine must have been amazing.

4. Children's Adventure Camps were the first partnered ministry in the sister relations.
5. Pavil Grigas and Vassili Olenik, leaders of the Cherkasy Baptists, coordinated Love Lift in Ukraine.

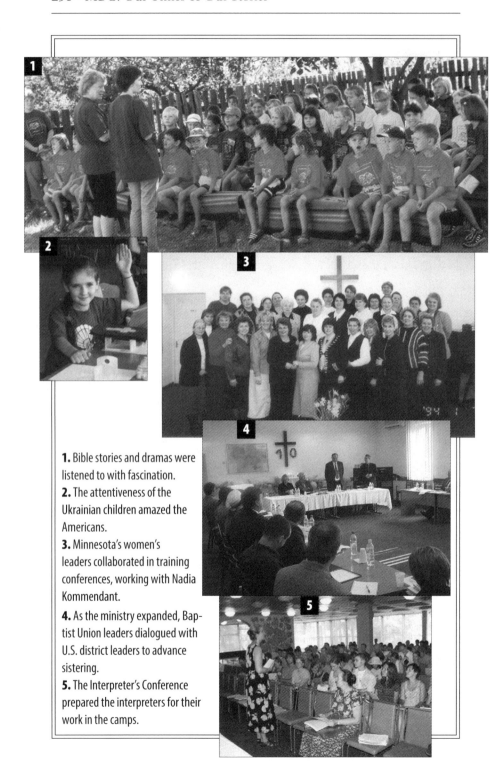

1. Bible stories and dramas were listened to with fascination.
2. The attentiveness of the Ukrainian children amazed the Americans.
3. Minnesota's women's leaders collaborated in training conferences, working with Nadia Kommendant.
4. As the ministry expanded, Baptist Union leaders dialogued with U.S. district leaders to advance sistering.
5. The Interpreter's Conference prepared the interpreters for their work in the camps.

1. A talented crew of experienced lead interpreters worked with Minnesota volunteers.

2. Memorable moment – the first Christian rock concert in Ukraine sponsored by Love Lift.

3. The Sounds of Boston joined Love Lift for area concerts and evangelism outreach in Ukraine.

4. Kairos, a Minnesota classical ensemble, traveled with Love Lift and filled auditoriums, leaving a strong testimony.

5. Ten percent of Ukraine is Romanian speaking and the MBC visited those regions.

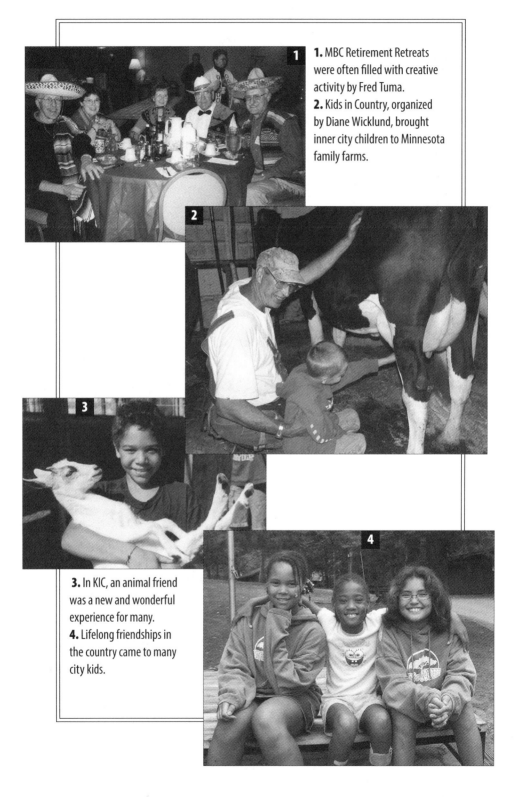

1. MBC Retirement Retreats were often filled with creative activity by Fred Tuma.
2. Kids in Country, organized by Diane Wicklund, brought inner city children to Minnesota family farms.

3. In KIC, an animal friend was a new and wonderful experience for many.
4. Lifelong friendships in the country came to many city kids.

— Chapter 15 —

The Lawson Era:
Coming in for a Landing

A millennium with something to celebrate

As the geeks fretted over Y2K and the impending world computer disaster, the Minnesota conference looked both backward and forward with thanksgiving.

The 142nd Annual Meeting in 2000 was held at Trout Lake. It was the turn of the millennium and Truett Lawson led a presentation to define the leadership goals of the Minnesota conference for the next five years. The vision included the debt-free completion of Timber Ridge Camp, 50 new churches, expanding Love Lift for Ukraine to other districts in the conference, and investigating and initiating other short term missions opportunities. And finally, it was proposed to seek new ways of replanting the church in rural and urban Minnesota. He expressed sadness for the joy that had been taken from our fellowship after the foreknowledge controversy. He vowed to actively seek healing in the fellowship.

Based on a motion of the Stewards, the delegates re-elected Lawson for another five-year term. John F. Anderson, previous executive minister, preached. He spoke from Ephesians 4, to "bear with one another in love" and to "maintain the unity of the Spirit in the bond of peace." He reminded the delegates that our Baptist history is a story of dissenters – a spirit that tolerates disagreement but embraces unity for service.[1]

Two years later Lawson wrote in his 2003 annual report that the growth of the MBC was actually accelerating after 2000. In 2000, the conference achieved a decadal growth rate of 45.8%. In 2005, that rate had increased to 64.4%. But he was careful to note that the credit belonged to the churches. He told of a Bethel executive who had relocated to St. Paul and was church hunting. After the executive had visited six or seven area churches, he sent a note to Lawson expressing his excitement at the rich diversity of ministry styles among Twin Cities churches.[2]

Beyond Minnesota, beyond Ukraine

In the peak years of Love Lift for Ukraine and Shepherd's Foundation (1995 to 2005), there were more than 600 travelers to Ukraine annually. Nearly 80 Minnesota churches would partner with a Ukrainian church. A number of churches outside Minnesota joined the movement. The Mideast district would create its own highly effective parallel program with leadership people like Dan Peterson, Lois Mooney, and Bill Heaton. John Cowan brought churches from the Great Lakes district, as did Larry Odle from the Heartland district. Bob Barnes, a layman in the Northwest, joined the group as well.

In 1999, profoundly moved by the sister church ministry at Calvary in St. Cloud, Bill Arvan raised support so he could join Love Lift's MBC staff. Over the years, Pastor Rich Schoenert of Calvary in Roseville developed a mini-seminary curriculum that he offered annually at a pastors conference in the region. George Johnson, publisher from Cambridge, used his printing background to make Christian literature available. Eventually Johnson and Paul Sanders would found Read Ministries to make Christian materials available for church libraries, with Read-trained librarians. Bill Arvan would join the Read Ministries staff. "You dream the dreams!" Executive Lawson had stated in one of the earliest publications for the ministry.

The Love Lift for Ukraine's partnership across cultures caught the attention of others. The Baptist General Conference had a strong, autonomous group of Filipino churches. In 2002, the Filipino group held a forum on futuring and invited Truett Lawson to talk about the sistering model. Out of this, Bayanihan was born – sister churches in the Philippines. Several MBC churches joined the movement. In 2007, the MBC partnered with North Haven church in St. Paul to expand its sistering relationship with Mexican Baptist churches in Culiacan. Several other Minnesota churches joined this movement as well.

Growth Resources had gone through nearly two decades of ministry metamorphosis. Its passion for Christian education and adult ministries did not keep it from recognizing the transformational power of short-term missions and the Love Lift for Ukraine. By 2005, the number of Love Lift participants had dropped off some. Many churches were continuing their own sistering ministries in Ukraine without the MBC's assistance. But the size of the Ukraine ministry, all partners considered, was breathtaking.

"Someone calling from Brazil, Jerry."

In 2010, BGC/Converge president Jerry Sheveland received a request from the Assemblies of God in Brazil asking if a representative of the fellowship (formerly called the Swedish Baptists of America) might bring a greeting at their 100th anniversary celebration. They wanted to honor two Swedish Baptist men, Gunnar Vingren and Daniel Berg, who had traveled from the United States to Brazil where they founded a church which became the mother church for the modern-day Assemblies of God movement in Brazil. And might there be some historically important materials available as the 100th celebration would feature the faith of Vingren and Berg in their origins? In the next days, the story of Vingren and Berg's mission emerged. To add to his excitement, when Sheveland checked with the History Center archives, Vingren's hand-written thesis was located and permission was given for it to be hand-carried by the BGC/Converge delegation, including Sheveland and newly elected MBC executive Dan Carlson, to enrich the Brazilian celebration.

When Jerry told this story to Truett Lawson, he realized that he and Jill would be host and hostess for the King and Queen of Sweden at the American Swedish Institute. Her majesty Queen Silvia is Brazilian. In dinner conversation, Lawson told the story of the two Swedes founding the AG in Brazil. Astounded, the queen responded, "They go to poorest and most helpless people and preach and help, do you have this story in print?" The next day the queen had the story in hand.

Succession planning for a good handoff

Anticipating his own imminent retirement and that of some of his colleagues, Lawson presented a succession planning model to the Stewards in 2003. In 2002, the Stewards had re-examined the arcane language in the description of the executive minister's duties. The next year, the conference acted on a revised mission statement and a new position description of the executive minister, who was now regarded as the Chief Operating Officer of the Minnesota Baptist Conference.

In 2004, Roger Camerer announced his retirement after 23 years. He had led Trout with responsible financial care and excellence during some of its most demanding years. He was a master of volunteerism which had allowed the camp to do so much with so little. Timber Ridge, too, was bursting with many of Camerer's projects. Shalom House, originally built in response to the Shalom movement had become an integral part of the ministry of Trout and the MBC. Prior to Emmett Johnson's death in 2002, Camerer had presented a plaque to Johnson honoring his vision for Shalom House. Roger announced his desire to continue serving Trout as a volunteer worker. He hoped he and his wife Jean could occupy one of the new RV spots in the summer. With Camerer's announcement, the Stewards appointed a search committee for a new director of camping.

Excellent resumes were received, but after interviews with Jon Wicklund and Lisa Olson, it was clear that the committee had an extraordinarily difficult decision to make. Olson and her husband had built a benchmark camp in Michigan with an extremely creative approach to camping. She was a high capacity manager and a passionate Christian. Wicklund was a natural born leader and had ideal credentials for leadership of camp with an MBA in business. He knew the camp and he knew its people, but he was untested. The committee decided to hire Wicklund, but Lawson approached Olson with an offer to join the staff for a period as a part-time consultant. The partnership between Executive Director Wicklund and Strategic Consultant Olson poised Trout to chart the course that would drive camping for the next generation.

The end is a beginning of a new camping era

Jon and Aleeta Wicklund entered into their new camping lifestyle with energy and focus. James Rock had joined the camping staff in program development. Rock was becoming a guru in the world of camp programming. He was creative and he was publishing. The Wicklunds joined the Rocks in raising their families in the chaotic but wonderful environment that was Christian camping. Rock became a vital creative force, and Wicklund a true visionary leader.

A professionally developed site plan provided a solution for the integration of the camp with the new Timber Ridge site. An entirely new approach to programming and site development was announced. "Imagine a camp where, in the same week, you could drop off your three children at primary camp, junior camp, and junior high camp

Jon Wicklund (center) welcomed every camper to Trout.

and then…take a little vacation yourself knowing that each child was in a camp geared to their age, with staff selected and trained for that age, doing that camp over and over all summer with excellence. That is where we are headed!"[3]

By 2008, Trout was completing the construction of its central building in Timber Ridge. Soon visitors to Timber Ridge Lodge would step into one of the finest Christian camp lodges in the country, look over the valley at Trout Lake, and enjoy a meal from a world class kitchen. Howard Deardorff demonstrated his gift by producing an amazing new site plan for Trout. Marty Walker built the enormous foundation for the lodge. Doug Carlson, a master mason, created one of the largest stone fireplace structures in the state at Timber Ridge. Any visitor would comment, "This is not masonry, this is art." Director Wicklund launched a "365 Project" that would allow camp supporters to contribute $365 per year for the upgrading of the existing camp facilities.

In that same year, camp took to the road with a VW minivan partnering with local churches to provide day camps to replace tired, under-staffed Vacation Bible School programs. Every day new visions in camping were introduced.

New challenges and new ministry plans

Women's Ministries and Men's Ministries had always enjoyed a strong partnership with camping through their retreats. The Lawson era saw challenges for both. For the men, there was the competition for several years in the mid-90s with Promise Keepers events. Attendance at Men's Retreat was affected. But Promise Keepers did not have Jerry Healy! Nor did they have Russell Johnson to lead God's world nature hikes. After 2000, attendance bounced back. Will Healy tells the story of convincing his dad to join him on a trip to Atlanta for Promise Keepers. That's what dads and lads did in the 90s. Halfway there, Jer said, "Not going to do it. Let's turn back." And they did. Jerry was Trout Lake Men's Retreat and Men's Retreat was Jerry.

Historically, Minnesota women have been at the forefront of service to Trout's ministries. Great leaders have led the women. After Beth Post came Barb Holmberg, then Sue Rima, and finally Mandy Johnson. Like the men, the women were also struggled with filling the camp twice in fall retreats. Retreats had always been profitable enough to support the rest of camping, so adjustments were being made. But this is the nature of ministry – adapting to a new setting.

In 2003, Joel Nelson assumed leadership in MBC church planting just as Jerry Sheveland and his mobilization team were unifying church planting systems at the national level. Nelson surveyed the new MBC churches that had been started since 2000 and found that they averaged 227 in attendance with a median of 140. They had been baptizing an average of 14 people each year per church. There were challenges spiritually and physically. Nelson communicated his plans. We would continue to support the outstanding BGC assessment center for church planter recruitment. And we would organize pastors and lay people into prospect-generating Lead Teams in accordance with the national model.

A blessed goodbye to a white man and an Indian

On January 2, 2008, Wally Olson passed away in his bed, his family gathered around him. Olson had become a legend in the district. His ministry spanned 50 years of this Minnesota story. In the final months of his life, God gave him the same special grace that often had been witnessed in his ministry. With his listening spirit, Olson blessed his visitors with the presence of Christ. On September 26, 2007, he was made an honorary member of the Bois Forte Band of the Chippewa – no small honor.

Kevin and Kathy Lasley had come to Nett Lake to take over the Olsons' work. The Kevin Lands would follow. The Mark Salmelas had provided leadership at Nett through the 90s. The MBC and the Salmelas had helped the Nett Lake church to build a new building in 2002. Phil and Carol Ratzlaff were serving in Grand Portage. Phil's physical condition deteriorated until, in 2006, he and Carol retired and moved east to be with family. But he had designed an extraordinary structure for the church, and though he was not present to see it completed, his mark will always remain on the tribe there. For years, the Indian ministries committee had viewed the Northwest Angle of Minnesota near Warroad as being a special opportunity. In 2007, at the end of the Lawson era, the Ken Danielsons joined the IMAC team to begin ministry in the Northwest Angle.

Les Connor, a Native leader from Nett Lake, was elected to the Stewards in 2002. He brought joy with his intelligence and quiet Native American spirit, not to mention his humor. The first gathering of the board was always a dinner meeting at the Lawsons' bed and breakfast in Stillwater. Connor drove down from Nett Lake arriving early. While waiting for the board's start time, he lost his keys somewhere inside his car. After the meeting he realized that he was in deep trouble and returned to the group embarrassed with his dilemma and asking about a locksmith. Lawson and a couple of board members found a pry bar and a coat hanger and, after 15 minutes, had retrieved the keys. A grateful Connor then dropped this unforgettable line: "I stood there wondering if a policeman might come by…he would have to report that there were three white guys trying to break into an Indian's car."

Connor passed away a couple years later. Many in the conference would grieve his loss. Some realized that in so doing, they were entering into the deep grief of Native people in America. The Connor legacy at Nett Lake Baptist church would be continued by his siblings: Mike, Vern, Marty, and Jan.

Notes

[1] 142nd Annual Meeting agenda, 2000, and Lawson's recollections.

[2] Truett M. Lawson, 145th Annual Report, Executive Ministers Report, 2003, p. 11.

[3] Author's paraphrase of statement by Jon Wicklund.

Churches Started or Welcomed: 1990-2007

1990

Christ Community Church
(Shoreview)

First Baptist Church (LeRoy)

Immanuel Baptist Church
(Minneapolis)

Hmong Faith Baptist Church
(St. Paul)

1995

Ambassadors Baptist Church
(Richfield)

Valleybrook Community Church
(St. Paul/Woodbury)

Westwood Community Church
(Chanhassen)

1996

Hope Community Church
(Minneapolis)

Crista La Roca

Riverwood Community Church
(Cannon Falls)

1998

Hope Fellowship (Ramsey)

Northbridge Station (Circle Pines)

1999

Cedar Creek Community Church
(Hayfield)

Vietnamese Church Plant Trinity
(St. Paul)

Crosswinds Community Church
(Stillwater)

Waterbrooke Fellowship (Victoria)

2000

Cornerstone Community Center
(Oakdale)

Northridge Fellowship (Rogers)

Oakwood Community Church
(Waconia)

Willowbrook Church (Forest Lake)

2001

Quarry Community Church
(Monticello)

The River (Bloomington)

Woodland Fellowship (Elk River)

2002

Living Waters Baptist Church
(Lakeviille)

Crista La Repuesta (Jordan)

St. Paul Fellowship (St. Paul)

Lounge Divine (St. Paul)

2003

2:42 Community Church
 (St. Cloud)

Countryside Church (Henderson)

Northbrook Community Church
 (North Branch)

Grace Baptist Church (Alexandria)

Iglesia Evangelica Bautista de
 Willmar (Willmar)

The Journey at Rush Creek
 (Maple Grove)

Amazing Grace Ministries
 (Brooklyn Park)

Jasper Community Church (Jasper)

Iglesia Bautista de St. Paul
 (St. Paul/Maplewood- Trinity)

2004

Journey Church (Rochester)

The Journey North (Brainerd)

Timberwood Church (Nisswa)

Missio-Dei (Minneapolis)

Adoration Church (Savage)

New Hope Church (Cambridge)

The Crossing (Elk River)

2005

EnCompass Church
 (Vadnais Heights)

City Church (Minneapolis)

2006

All Nations Christian Fellowship
 (Minneapolis, Brooklyn Center)

Evergreen Community Church
 (Pine City)

The Gathering (Bemidji)

Agape Fellowship (St. Cloud)

Hiawatha Church (Minneapolis)

2007

Glory of Christ Baptist Church
 (Elk River)

Providence Church (Crosslake)

Nueva Iglesia Cristiana

— Chapter 16 —

150 Years and a Great Celebration

In early 2007, Truett Lawson received a call from retired Executive Minister Richard Turnwall suggesting to him that in 2008 the Minnesota Baptist Conference would be having a birthday, and it was a big one. Lawson appointed a 150th Anniversary Committee chaired by Jonathan Larson, who began to make preparations. G.W. Carlson from Bethel joined in, along with John F. Anderson and others. The giant in the room was Dr. Virgil Olson, who not only knew the beginning from the end, but in so many ways personally represented what was special about the conference movement.

The same year, 2008, would also be the 150th anniversary of the State of Minnesota. The Minnesota Historical Society created a historical exhibition at the Minnesota History Center. In 2007, the American Swedish Institute sponsored an exhibit of liturgical Swedish textiles and art. They also featured religious groups with immigrant roots in Sweden. The Augustana Lutherans were included, the Covenant and Free Churches, and the Minnesota Swedish Baptist Conference. Truett Lawson wrote the 52-page exhibition script and the staff gathered the art, photos, and objects that would accompany it. It would draw the largest audience the ASI had ever welcomed for an exhibition.

Midway through this year of historical preparation, Rev. Dan H. Carlson was called to become the new executive minister of the Minnesota Baptist Conference. Carlson was pastoring Faith Baptist Fellowship in Sioux Falls, South Dakota. He did not need to be introduced to Truett Lawson, with whom he would spend much time over the next several months. Carlson's family and the Lawson family shared many roots and connections of ministry. During the transition, Carlson was introduced

Prepared for the Mantle of Leadership

Although a couple months of leadership transition helped to prepare Dan Carlson for his new role as executive minister of the MBC, his real preparation was his life journey. Dan grew up watching ministry-gifted parents. His father, Howard Carlson, was a pastor in Chicago and in Sioux Falls, S.D. He was serving a highly effective term as executive minister for the Southwest conference when he passed away during Dan's final year at Bethel. Dan's mother, Carol, was an active pastor's wife and also entered into the life of the BGC by chairing the Board of World Missions and serving on a presidential call committee. Carol married Ray Lindskog, who had also lost a spouse. The conference church in Whittier was started in the Lindskog home.

Having such a heritage of ministry, Dan attended Bethel to prepare for ministry himself. He met his wife Sarah at Bethel, and they began their own ministry on the staff of Wooddale Church in Eden Prairie, Minn. Then they served at the Lincoln Avenue Church of Escondido, Calif., and Faith Baptist Fellowship in Sioux Falls, S.D. Dan and Sarah have four children: Hannah, Peter, Rebekah and Rachel, whom they enjoy very much. It is clear to those who know them that Dan and Sarah also thoroughly enjoy ministry to individuals, to churches and to the district, which is now known as the Minnesota-Iowa Baptist Conference.

Dan and Sarah Carlson
with Jill and Truett Lawson
at the Lawson farewell.

to the MBC staff and pastors. He also traveled to Ukraine to meet with the Ukrainian leaders who had been partnering with the MBC for 16 years.

After his retirement in 2008, Lawson was asked to continue to lead the 150th anniversary preparations, learning first to spell and pronounce *sesquicentennial*. A reflective newspaper would be written by Lawson and published by George Johnson in Cambridge. It featured a panoramic view of the history of our movement, which we knew as the Minnesota Swedish Baptist Conference.

On September 14, 2008, in Bethel University's Great Hall, 800 partygoers of every generation gathered for the grand celebration. It was the 150th birthday party of the Minnesota Baptist Conference. Avis Soderstom had prepared lovely dishes that were served on party trays to the delighted and surprised guests.

After the amazing resurrection of some Swedish ancestors who welcomed the audience, Virgil Olson upstaged the scheduled comedian with his anecdotes. Governor Tim and First Lady Mary Pawlenty rose to greet the guests. Governor Pawlenty brought a heartfelt greeting and salute to the conference, spoken as someone who knew us and was part of us. The media technician cued up a video presentation of our fascinating and devout pietist founders who more than anything in life wished to serve Christ with all their hearts. Now well fed, the delighted guests listened to Bob Stromberg, Christ follower and comedian par excellence, who made us laugh until we cried. It was a night to remember.

Which brings us all to that late night hour, 150 years after our founding, with only a few minutes left to ask the *one unanswered question* – a most important question. The Minnesota Baptist Conference is the largest district in size. Yes! Are we not the most colorfully decorated with fascinating historical leaders? Yes! We lived through the greatest period of growth and change in the history of our exceptional movement. Yes! But one question remains in debate: Is the Minnesota Baptist Conference the oldest organizational entity in the Baptist General Conference/Converge Worldwide? To this question, for our definitive closing argument, we turn to the March 2008 edition of *Trail Markers* from the History Center:

Which was the first BGC district to officially organize? Minnesota celebrates its 150th anniversary this year and has claimed the title, but Illinois disputes that claim.

There was a district meeting in Rock Island, Ill., in 1856, two years before the Minnesota churches had their first meeting. At the Rock Island meeting, delegates of seven churches from Illinois, Iowa, and Minnesota met June 20-25 to discuss theology, the nature of church membership, and issues related to how to spread the gospel among Swedes across the United States. Calling themselves "the Swedish Baptist Conference" (Konferensen), the seven churches included Rock Island and Chicago (Ill.); Village Creek and New Sweden (Iowa); and Houston, Scandia, and Chisago Lake (Minn.). Representatives from the Swedish Baptist church in St. Paul and from the Swedish Baptist church in New York City, which were not yet fully organized, also attended.

Two years later, in 1858, Minnesota churches met in the little church in Scandia, Minn., to organize as an independent state or regional conference. During this period, Illinois churches were meeting with delegates from Iowa in an Illinois-Iowa conference until 1883, when the Iowa delegates dropped out to form their own separate district. The Illinois churches then became the Illinois Conference.

Carl Lagergren, later the dean of Bethel Seminary, argued that since the churches in the Illinois-Iowa Conference eventually evolved into the Illinois Conference, the "oldest state conference" was Illinois. The argument continued in the Nya Wecko-Posten *(the weekly paper of the Swedish Baptists). Finally, Adolf Olson, who wrote the history of the first 100 years of the Baptist General Conference, concluded in 1952 "that the origin of an independent Illinois state conference cannot be traced farther back than 1883, leaving the Minnesota conference as the oldest state conference"* (Centenary History, *1952).*

Trailmarkers *congratulates the Minnesota Baptist Conference on 150 years of historic ministry. Today, the Minnesota Baptist Conference, with 165 churches, is the largest and strongest district of the BGC. The MBC supports church planting, camping, ethnic ministries, and extensive missionary work in Ukraine and Mexico. In 2007, the* Minneapolis Star Tribune *stated that the Minnesota Baptist Conference was the fastest-growing religious organization in Minnesota. Congratulations go to outgoing District Executive Minister Truett Lawson for the progress over the last [17] years in the MBC. We also take this opportunity to welcome Dan Carlson, newly designated Minnesota district executive minister.*[1]

With this salute we end our narrative on the Minnesota Baptist Conference. It is history, richly defining who we are. It is whimsy, allowing us to laugh at our colorful selves. But it is devotion, re-enlisting us in the pursuit of Christ and the service of His world.

Notes

[1] BGC History Center, *Trail Markers*, Vol. 7, No. 3, March 2008, p. 3.

A Third Story is Told

The story of the Minnesota Baptist Conference has been told three times during its history.

In 1918 the Historical Committee, preparing for the 60th Jubilee celebration at Cambridge, enlisted P. Ryden to write a history of the conference from 1850 to 1918.

The first two stories.

The committee was chaired by the venerable Frank Peterson who had pastored First Swedish Baptist, adding 100 members a year for nine years. This robust 275-page pictorial history focused on pioneer leaders, Minnesota churches and other ministries such as Bethel Academy and Mounds Park Sanitarium. It was written in Swedish.

The Centenary Committee of 1958 also produced an 80-page pocket history called *Pioneering with God's Promises*. Although Virgil Olson is often credited with the volume, he actually created the outline and seminary student Florence Jacobson researched and wrote the first draft. It has many similarities to Ryden's history.

This volume, *Our Times & Our Stories* by Truett Lawson, is more of the author's interpreted history. It focuses on the changes in culture affecting the ministries of the conference over 150 years, and the district's responses to new ministry opportunities.

Resources

Alexis, Gerhard T., "Sweden to Minnesota: Moberg's Fictional Reconstruction," *American Quarterly*, Spring, 1966, pp. 81-94.

Anderson, John F., "Happenings," MBC, May, 1985 – Midwinter, 1990.

Anderson, John F., "Of One Mind," MBC, June, 1985 – January, 1990.

Annual Meeting Minutes, Minnesota Baptist Conference, September 12, 1940 – October 25, 2007.

Annual Reports, Minnesota Baptist Conference, September 12, 1940 – October 25, 2007.

Asplund, Charles, "Olaus Okerson," *Pioneering*, pp. 24-26.

Backlund, J.O., *The Pioneer Trio*, Conference Press, pp. 5-11.

Backlund, J.O., *The Standard*, Swedish Baptist Conference, July 28, 1944 – July 8, 1945.

Baptist General Conference, "Centennial Program 1852-1952."

Bengtsson, Jesper, *Granatlockaorna i Myitkyina: En berättelse om Burma* (The Bells of Myitkina: A Tale of Burma), Norstedts, 2006.

Bergeson, John H., *Churches Everywhere*, Columbia Baptist Conference.

Bergeson, John H., "Minnesota Ministry Memories," uncopyrighted memoirs.

Bilynsky, Stephen S., "Doing Philosophy as a Pietist," copyright 1989.

Brokaw, Tom, *The Greatest Generation*, Random House Paperbacks, May 1, 2001.

Brown, Dale W., *Understanding Pietism*, Revised Edition, Nappanee, Indiana: Evangel Publishing House, 1978.

Dahl, Delmar, and Johnson, Emmett V., *Let's Celebrate*, MBC, 1972.

Erikson, Martin, *Centenary Glimpses – 1852-1952*, Chicago, Illinois: Baptist Conference Press, 1952.

Erikson, Martin, and Ericson, C. Geo., *Advance 1951*, Chicago, Illinois: Baptist Conference Press, 1951.

Fleming, S. Bruce, "Contact," MBC, January 1966 – October 1969.

Griffin, Emilie, and Erb, Peter C., *The Pietists*, Selected Writings, San Francisco: Harper San Francisco, 2006.

Hedman, Jorgen, *Gammalsvenskby, the True Story of the Swedish Settlement in the Ukraine*, copyright 2007.

"History Center Friends to Celebrate 150th Anniversary of the Scandia Church," *Trail Markers*, May, 2007.

Hoffbeck, Steven R., *The Haymakers*, St. Paul, Minnesota: Minnesota Historical Press, 2000.

Holmes, Arthur H., *The Grieving Indian*, Winnipeg, Manitoba, Intertribal Christian Communications, 1991.

Jennings, Peter, and Brewster, Todd, *The Century*, New York, New York: Doubleday, 1998.

Johnson, Emmett V., "Contact," MBC, June, 1970 – January, 1978.

Johnson, Emmett V., "It's Happening," MBC, January, 1972 – November, 1975.

Jorgensen, Ruth J., *Herb Nyquist, White Man Indian*, privately published.

Lawson, Truett M., editor, "Minnesota Churches Today – 150th Anniversary Historical Newspaper," 2008.

Lawson, Truett M., "Exchanging Tears for Smiles," *The Standard*, January/February, 1995, pp. 18-22.

Lawson, Truett M., "Finding Satisfaction in All this Toil, Life and Times of Andrew Peterson," Presentation to Friends of the BGC History Center, 2008.

Lawson, Truett M., "Pietism Rocks," unpublished document. 2007.

Lawson, Truett M., "Relate – A Leadership Letter to Pastors," May, 1990 – November, 1997.

Lawson, Truett M., "Script for American Swedish Institute Exhibition," unpublished document, 2007.

Lindberg, Carter, *The Pietist Theologians*, Cornwall, England: Blackwell Publishing, 2005.

Magnuson, Norris, "How We Grew," Arlington Heights, Illinois: Baptist General Conference.

McCallum, Dennis H., "Philip Jacob Spener's Contribution to the Protest Doctrine of the Church," *A Research Project 1987*, unpublished.

McKnight, Roger, *Moberg's Emigrant Novels and the Journals of Andrew Peterson*, New York: Arno Press, 1979.

Mihelich, Josephine, *Andrew Peterson and the Scandia Story*, Minneapolis, Minnesota: Ford Johnson Graphics, 1984.

Minnesota Baptist Conference, "Centennial Program 1858-1958."

Minnesota Baptist Conference, "Missions in Minnesota," May/June 1951 – October, 1965.

Moberg, Vilhelm, *A History of the Swedish People*, New York: Pantheon Books, 1973.

Moberg, Vilhelm, *The Unknown Swedes*, Carbondale, Illinois: Southern University Press, 1978.

Nelson, Joel, "The Three Waves," MBC, unpublished manuscript, 2007.

Olson, Adolf, *A Centenary History*, Chicago, Illinois: Baptist Conference Press, 1952.

Olson, Robert W., "Birth Pangs of a Camp," unpublished document.

Olson, Shirley, "The History of Indian Ministries," unpublished document.

Olson, Virgil, with Jacobson, Florence, *Pioneering with God's Promises*, St. Paul, Minnesota: Minnesota Baptist Conference, 1958.

Premack, Laura, "The Holy Rollers Are Invading Our Territory: Southern Baptist Missionaries and the Early Years of Pentecostalism in Brazil," University of North Carolina at Chapel Hill, 2008.

Qualey, Carlton C., "Diary of a Swedish Immigrant Horticulturist, 1855-1898," MHS Collections, Minnesota Historical Society, Summer, 1972.

Rendahl, Stan, "The Scandia Church Building," unpublished document.

Ryden, P., *Svenska Baptisternas i Minnesota Historia,* Minneapolis, Minnesota: Nygren Printing Company, 1918.

Sisell, A., *A Missionary's Notes and Experiences on the Red River Valley Field*, Chicago, Illinois: Fridhem, January, 1940.

Spickelmier, James and Carole, *Five Decades of Growth and Change*, St. Paul, Minnesota: The History Center, May, 2010.

Stephenson, George, "Background of the Beginnings of Swedish Immigration," *American Historical Review*, July, 1926.

Sweeney, Douglas A., *The American Evangelical Story*, Grand Rapids, Michigan: Baker Academic, 2005.

Swenson, Wayne, *Houston Baptist Church, the First 125 Years*, privately published.

Sword, Gustaf A., *Light of the Jungle, the Life Story of Ola Hanson of Burma*, Baptist Conference Press.

Turnwall, Richard, "F.O. Nilsson, a Baptist Heretic," *The Baptist Pietist Clarion*, July, 2003.

Turnwall, Richard, "Take Five," MBC, January 11, 1980 – January 11, 1984.

Westman, Tama, "Swedish Homesteader a Celebrity in Homeland," unknown source and date.

Picture credits:

The History Center: Archives of the Baptist General Conference and Bethel University, St. Paul, Minnesota.

The Minnesota-Iowa Baptist Conference, St. Paul, Minnesota.

Billy Graham photos are from Wikipedia Commons and news4themasses. wordpress.com.

About the Author

Truett Lawson was born in 1943 to Maurice and Muriel Lawson, who had Swedish Baptist immigrant roots. Andrew Peterson, the patriarch on his mother's side, followed Christ in Sweden through the influence of Anders Wiberg, and farmsteaded in 1868 near Trade Lake, Wis. "My mother was raised on sunfish and fresh vegetables on the Pine Lake farm, but she always said that my father rescued her from the farm for a life of adventure." Indeed, Truett grew up while the Lawsons taught at Bethel, and pastored in Illinois, Minnesota, and California.

Truett graduated from Whittier College, and earned a Master of Divinity degree from Bethel Seminary and a Doctor of Ministry degree from Fuller Seminary. He served pastorates in Minnesota and California, and entered district leadership in California in 1987. He served as the District Executive Minister in Minnesota from 1990 to 2008.

Truett and his wife, Jill (McKenna) Lawson, have three children and four grandchildren. They have operated the James Mulvey Inn Bed and Breakfast in Stillwater, Minn., for over 20 years. They also enjoy collecting Swedish and American art pottery and Minnesota impressionist paintings. Truett has restored vintage Lotus cars since his college years.

In 2007, Truett worked with the staff of the American Swedish Institute to curate an exhibition that included Swedish Baptist immigrant origins. He joined the Board of ASI, becoming its chairman from 2012 to 2014. Truett and Jill were hosts to their majesties, King Carl XVI Gustaf and Queen Silvia during their royal visit to Minnesota in 2013. Truett wrote and delivered two monographs to the Friends of the History Center and directed the events and publications of the Minnesota Baptist Conference 150th Anniversary Gala.

Index